The Art
of
Shapeshifting

Other Ted Andrews Titles

The Art of Shapeshifting

by

Ted Andrews

Dragonhawk Publishing   Jackson, Tennessee

A Dragonhawk Publishing Book

The Art of Shapeshifting

Text Copyright (c) 2005 by Ted Andrews
Cover Copyright (c) by Ted Andrews

First Edition

Book design by Ted Andrews

ISBN 1-888767-32-4

Library of Congress Catalog Card Number: 2004115576

This book was designed and produced by
Dragonhawk Publishing
Jackson, TN
USA

- For Sir Nigel Witherspoon -
Thank you very much.

Table of Contents

Shapeshifting Exercises

Part I

Sacred Metamorphosis

In Nature, most insects go through an amazing metamorphosis and thus, they can often teach us how to adapt and change in the most creative and productive ways possible. And change is essential to life. It ensures growth and helps us to shed the old so that we can express the new. Helping us shift the shapes and patterns of our life, shapeshifting is a magical key to both dynamic creativity and powerful manifestation.

The Master and the Pupil

Once there was a poor boy that was looking for work. In his travels, he heard of a great wizard, a teacher who needed a servant. The boy sought out this man. He came to a large castle and banged loudly upon its door.

Before long, a man appeared at a window and called down to the boy, "What do you want?"

The boy replied, "I am looking for work, kind sir, and I have heard you are in need of a servant."

"Do you know how to read?" asked the wizard.

The boy hesitated. He was not sure how to answer, as the question sounded a bit like a test.

"No," he lied, "but I am a quick learner if you are worried about being able to teach me."

The wizard replied, "I do not want anyone who can read, so I will hire you."

The boy entered the castle. The man greeted him at a tall stairwell and motioned for the boy to follow him up. They ascended the stairs in silence. At the top they entered a room that appeared to be a mix between a laboratory and a library. In the center of the room was a pedestal upon which sat a very large book.

"While I travel, I expect you to dust this room and to protect its belongings, particularly this one book," he said.

The boy nodded and looked at the book with curiosity.

Before long the Master left on an extended trip. He was no sooner out the door when the boy opened the large volume on the pedestal. He immediately began reading. It was a book of magic and wonders throughout the universe. And the boy began to study.

Every time the Master left on a trip, the boy would read and study voraciously from this book. And he was always careful never to let the Master know what he was doing while he was gone on his trips. After three years, the boy learned the entire book by heart.

When the Master returned from his next trip, the boy told him it was time to be on his way. He packed his things and left the Master's castle. The boy returned home to his poor parents, anxious to try out his new knowledge.

On the eve of the village fair, the boy spoke to his father. "Tomorrow, you will find a magnificent steer in the stable. Take it to the fair and sell it, but make sure you return with the rope."

The next morning, the father did indeed find a magnificent steer in his stable. he took it to the fair and was able to sell it for a good price. On his way home, he heard footsteps behind him. He turned and saw his son. Seeing the puzzled look on his father's face, he explained that he had turned himself into the steer and when he had been sold, at his first opportunity, he turned himself back.

Both he and his father were delighted with the deal. Each time money ran low, the boy would transform himself into a steer or horse or whatever else could be sold. After the sale, at the first opportune time, he would transform himself back.

What the boy did not know was that to a true wizard, a true master of magic, any display of magic within the land would be recognized. Thus it was only a matter of time before the Master for whom the boy worked discerned that something was truly amiss in the land, and it did not take him long to discover that his young servant was the reason. Now it was just a matter of waiting for his own opportunity.

The next time the father brought his transformed son into the village to sell, the Master recognized him and bought the boy in the form of a horse from the boy's father. He then took the father to a pub and made him drink so much that the father soon forgot the rope by which he led the animal and which enabled the boy to return to his normal form.

While the father was passed out from too much drink, the Master took the horse to the blacksmith.

"Give my horse a good shoeing," he said and left the horse in the hands of the smithy. As he left, he smiled at how the young boy would certainly learn his lesson now.

Before the blacksmith got a chance to begin shoeing the horse, a young child came along and the horse whispered to her.

"Untie me," he ordered in a hoarse whisper.

The child was so startled by this that she did as she was told. No sooner was the horse untied when he transformed himself into a rabbit and ran off.

The Master saw this and transformed himself into a hunting dog, giving chase. The rabbit came to a lake and turned himself into a fish. The Master bought the lake and ordered that all the fish within it be caught and cleaned. As the fish that was the boy was just about to be cleaned, it turned into a lark and flew away. The master transformed himself into a hawk and gave chase.

Weary from the chase, the lark dived down a chimney and turned itself into a grain of wheat which rolled under a table. The hawk followed and saw the change. He immediately turned into a rooster and began pecking at the loose grains upon the floor. The boy waited until he was just about eaten and then transformed himself once more. This time, he became a fox, and before the Master, in the form of the rooster, could respond, he was eaten by the fox.

And the boy and his parents lived out the rest of their days in wealth and prosperity in the castle of the old Master.

Chapter One

The Truth About Shapeshifting

Of all the magickal arts in lore and in practice, none capture the imagination more than the ancient art of shapeshifting. Shapeshifting is the ability to effect a change in oneself, in others or in the substance of the environment. This change can be physical or spiritual.

In more ancient times, there were certain individuals capable of living between the physical and the spiritual. They could adapt themselves and change their energies according to their life circumstances. They could shape and mold the environment, creating whatever they desired and becoming whatever they dreamed. These were the shapeshifters. They lived the dreamtime while awake or asleep. There were few limits to where they could go or who they could be. These were the alchemists, shamans, magicians and wise ones of our myths, tales and legends.

Folktales and myths around the world reveal heroes and villains alike with this most fantastic ability - the ability to transform themselves or others according to need or desire. In Greek mythology, Circe changed Odysseus' men into swine. In the Nigerian tale "Nana Miriam", Nana Miriam transforms herself to fight a giant hippo and save the village. In Eastern Europe, Rumplestiltskin transforms straw into gold. For most people, tales such as these are the stuff of fiction, but there is more to them than mere fictional entertainment. They reflect a hidden ability within every human being. They are the outer reminders of what our own dreams hint.

Shapeshifting has been called many things throughout the ages. It has been called transformation, metamorphosis and even transmogrification. It has also been aligned with alchemy and linked to the transforming or shapeshifting of lead into gold. Although many types and variations of shapeshifting are described in literature and in magic, they can all be synthesized down to one of five primary forms. The first is familiar to most people and it is a pure form of shapeshifting, called *zoomorphism* - the change from human to animal form. Of its many variations, aleuranthropy and lycanthropy are the two most familiar. Aeluranthropy is the human transformation into a cat. This was depicted in recent times in the remake of the movie *CAT PEOPLE*, starring Malcolm McDowell. Lycanthropy is the transformation of humans into wolves, and there are few who have not seen on screen or read in books tales of the wolf-man. It is by no means confined only to these forms as we will explore throughout this book.

Many of the stories and tales of complete physical transformation are merely symbolic, or they reflect a time in the evolution of humanity when we were not so solidly locked within the human form. In those earlier times, we may have been able to mold our shapes more easily. When the human body was less dense, we may have been able to metamorphose into other forms. It may still be possible, as all things are within the realm of possibility, but as yet, it is beyond my scope of demonstrating. Over the years, I have heard of individuals capable of performing this kind of physical transformation, but I have never seen a legitimate demonstration of it – although I have seen more than a few fakes.

The second form and very advanced technique is what I call *joining*. In this form of shapeshifting, we join or merge our spirit with the spirit of an animal . Many of the tales of shapeshifting that have come down to us were more likely this form rather than an actual zoomorphic change. Most commonly, the joining is with an animal spirit, but the joining with tree spirits or some other element of the natural world can also done. The animal is usually a totem or familiar - an animal that we have developed a trusting relationship with. Our spirit is able to travel within this animal and see with its eyes, hear with its ears and experience through its senses. It is more than just a powerful creative visualization. There is an actual merging of spirits, which can have life-changing effects upon us. It is similar to astral projection or conscious out-of-body experiences, but more complicated, and requiring much greater control. This can be developed for remote viewing, for more dynamic clairvoyance, for powerful spirit and animal communication and much more. Joining can even be developed for amazing forms of healing. We must understand that some animals never experience certain kinds of diseases. Thus a merge with them has the potential to shift our body's ability to fend off specific imbalances and diseases. We will not be exploring this advanced form of shapeshifting in this book, but we will explore the following three forms - and they lay the necessary groundwork for making joining possible.

The third type of shapeshifting is *auric shapeshifting*. Our auras (the energy field surrounding us) can be changed to take the form of an animal or creature. In such changes, it becomes easier to express the qualities of the animal or creature. Thus if we need to be more bearlike in a situation, we make our aura more bearlike. And sometimes this auric change can become visible, manifesting like a mask over the person. Have you ever seen someone take on a birdlike appearance or see their face shift briefly to that of a cat or some other animal? Many have experienced this auric shift when calling upon the medicine and energies of a particular animal. We will explore this more fully later in Part I and also in Part III.

The fourth type is *dream shifting*. We can learn to move in and out of dreams in the forms of different animals. Many find it easier to initiate a conscious out-of-body experience in the form of an animal. It is not unusual to have people dream of being an animal or becoming part human and part beast. In the dream state, it is always easier to shapeshift – not only ourselves but also our dreams. We will examine this more closely and teach some techniques for shapeshifting ourselves in our dreams in Part II. These techniques will make your dreams more colorful and more lucid. And they empower your waking magical efforts toward shapeshifting, stimulating tremendous magical flexibility within you. It is also important to learn this if you ever wish to develop the joining techinique more effectively.

The last form of shapeshifting is *personification*. We can perform simple and even ecstatic dances and rituals that create such a powerful change in consciousness that we feel as if we are actually changing and personify the essence of the animal or creature. In such cases, even though we may not physically change to observers, internally we may have a profound transformation that can be accompanied by dramatic physical responses and releases. These kinds of experiences awaken hidden abilities and are empowering. They can be used for powerful protection, weaving glamour and unlocking hidden potentials. And we will explore this in Part III.

The focus of this book will be upon the latter three forms - auric shapeshifting, dream shifting and personification. They are the foundation upon which more advanced techniques are enabled. They elicit power inner transformations that will stimulate tremendous healing, higher consciousness, out-of-body experiences, spiritual and creative illumination, heightened spirit contact - along with many other benefits. They should not be treated casually or lightly dismissed simply because no physical change is observed - *for these activities ARE techniques of shapeshifting.* And they are, in fact, part of what you will learn to do through this book.

If you change your imaginings, you can change the world!

Practical Aspects of Shapeshifting

- Relating to people and adjusting behaviors to work and live as conditions warrant.

- Being gentle according to need and yet capable of expressing great strength.

- Disciplining self to achieve a goal.

- Adapting to any change that presents itself, pleasant or otherwise, and gain benefit.

- Turning a foul mood into a pleasant one.

- Taking and using limitations as part of the growth process.

- Finding the creative possibilities within limitations and thus overcome them.

- Putting aside hurt and/or fear to accomplish a task or goal effectively.

- Transforming the pains & hindrances of life (past and present).

- Developing discipline that can be applied to all aspects of life.

- Strengthening observation skills.

Mystical Aspects
of
Shapeshifting

- Strengthening and adapting the aura in all situations

- Facilitating lucid dreaming.

- Invisibility.

- Healing.

- Greater spirit contact.

- Enhances traveling within the spirit world.

- Assists out-of body experiences.

- Connecting to Nature.

- Physical and Psychic Protection.

- Aligning with one's spirit animal/totem.

- Creating greater flexibility and adaptability to life - physical and spiritual.

- Creating inspiration and intuition.

- Traveling through time.

Shapeshifting in Everyday Life

Shapeshifting is natural and instinctual within humans, but it also involves more than just transforming oneself into a beast. Everyday we shift our energies to meet daily trials, responsibilities and obligations more effectively. We learn early in life the use of camouflage, merely one tangent within the art of shapeshifting. We learn early in life when and how to smile to cover what we are feeling or to express open friendliness. We learn when to be serious and how to be apologetic. We learn how to seem studious. I know of no one who didn't learn how to appear innocently studying during their early years of school. All of us express a wide variety of personas according to our needs.

Each of us is many things, and rarely will any two people ever see us exactly the same way. I am a teacher, a writer, a storyteller, and much more. To many though, I am "the hawk man" because of my work with animals and birds of prey. I am all of these things and more. I have many parts to me, and the same is true for all of us. We play many roles in life. Those who are truly successful in life learn to draw upon all of their aspects as they are needed. This ability to shift to those aspects of ourselves that can handle the circumstances surrounding us more successfully is part of being a shapeshifter.

It is said that Merlin practiced shapeshifting continually throughout his life. When kings summoned him, he disguised himself as a poor shepherd, a woodcutter, or as a peasant. He could present himself to others in any way he desired and people would believe he was just as he appeared. Because of this, he was able to accomplish much more within his life.

We are the shapeshifters of our life. We will all wear different masks at different times. The masks and forms we put on though should be ones that reflect the magic within us. They should reflect our inner power. When we learn to do this, we can re-create our life and change how people respond to us. We can weave our life into anything we hope, wish or dream.

Our body language reflects much of our instinctual potentials for shapeshifting. We have all learned and practice behaviors and postures that make us more or less vulnerable. We fold our arms in front of us if intimidated. We look down or away if lying. Many of our behaviors and shiftings are so natural, that we do not even think of them consciously.

A shapeshifter is one who can relate to and adjust behaviors and energies to work and live more effectively - as the conditions warrant. A shapeshifter is one who can adjust, control and shift his/her own energies to fit the needs of the moment - to facilitate drawing upon whatever qualities or energies are necessary. It is a matter of controlling and utilizing one's highest energies and potentials to meet whatever situation life requires. This has both practical and mystical applications and benefits, as you can see from the previous pages.

Shapeshifting is a process of becoming active in life, of controlling what manifests rather than being passive and allowing to manifest whatever may come. Today, it involves a concentrated and effective use of the faculty of creative imagination, and it is this kind of shapeshifting which we can develop to a tremendous degree. It is something we can all accomplish. It is the spiritual lessons behind all dreams, regardless of message or content. All of us have taken physical form to learn to shift energies and consciousness of the past into new and more creative expressions.

Anyone who can discipline himself or herself to achieve a goal is a shapeshifter. If you can adapt to change, pleasant or otherwise, you are a shapeshifter. If you can turn a foul mood into a pleasant one, then you are a shapeshifter. If you can adjust your behaviors, speech, attitudes and/or actions to relate to a wide variety of people and life conditions, then you are a shapeshifter. It is this kind of shapeshifting that we can all develop to a high degree.

Although today most magic takes place within the mind at a different level of perception, it isn't any less real or useful to our outer lives. When we can accept that, then we have taken the first step to becoming a true shapeshifter - the true modern magician. With practice, you can strengthen the imaginative faculty and learn to consciously control and shapeshift it along any lines you desire. *When we change our imaginings, we change our world*.

This is what this book will help teach you. It is only the beginning, and it won't make you a master shapeshifter. It will help you to stretch and strengthen your imaginative faculty. It will assist you in attuning to and manifesting the energies you desire to mold and shape within your life. It will give you the tools necessary to empower your life. It will help you to shift your dreams to reality and to walk the thread of life between worlds. It will help you to live the dreamtime whether awake or asleep.

Commitment to shapeshifting is a commitment to becoming the modern spiritual disciple - the spiritual seer and sage - the Merlin or Morgan le Fay of your own life. Through the ancient art of shapeshifting, we learn to transmute our energies to create a new being. Through it, we align with our greatest dreams and visions. We can re-create and re-manifest what has been relegated to fiction. Our life becomes like those of all sages throughout history. We can walk in all environs, visible and invisible. We can bridge the physical with the spiritual. We can even weave a tapestry of life that becomes a carpet of continually shifting fibers of light and radiance, a carpet upon which we can fly through all doorways, all times and all dreams. The possible becomes probable.

Why Shapeshifting?

A multitude of methods, tools and techniques exist for awakening our innermost energies and potentials. Most of these though do little more than simply awaken. For many, this is comparable to stirring up a hornet's nest. Energy awakened inappropriately (especially when ill-prepared) results in chaos. Energy unused or misused once awakened becomes disruptive.

Although there are lessons we can learn from chaos and disruption, there are much easier ways of learning. Martyrdom is highly overrated. We do not have to suffer in order to grow and develop. I am a firm believer that suffering is only good for the soul if it teaches us how not to suffer again. The key is to know how to absorb and integrate the energy that is awakened.

Most methods for awakening our potentials and for accessing the universal and magical/spiritual energies of life fall into one of two categories: **meditative** and **ceremonial.** One is neither better nor worse than the other. Both include the use of symbology, visualization, creative imagination, pathworking, mantras, yantras, and many other tools to awaken the universal energies. The primary difference is that ceremonial methods often involve more intricately ritualized physical activities.

Shapeshifting employs aspects of both methods on a much simpler level so that we can achieve success more easily. It is not a shortcut and it does not mean there is no time or effort involved, but we have to change our perception that spiritual growth is complicated, difficult and/or traumatic. Traditional meditative and ceremonial techniques can be adapted to simpler and more powerful methods – one of which is shapeshifting.

The techniques throughout this work are created to elicit very specific results. *And their effects are accumulative.* They build and add to each other. (Refer to the information on page 26.) This will allow you to experience the power of the shapeshifting and to use it more effectively. They will enable you to increasingly manifest the universal and magical forces more tangibly into your daily life, without being overwhelmed by them. The shifting will become a bridge to the Divine world. At the very least, it energizes your entire life, increases your creativity and enhances your expression of life while in the physical.

Our magical beliefs must have a strong foundation. We must strengthen their possibility. Through study, practice and the right kind of exercises, we make our beliefs increasingly more probable. The progression of exercises throughout this book assists in this. If we believe we will win an Oscar but never study acting or do nothing more than local theater performances, we are not laying the foundation for our beliefs to be fulfilled. We must put practical effort into our magical and spiritual activities. And that includes shapeshifting.

Imbalances and Precautions

Shapeshifting is simply one tool for opening and expanding awareness. It is a magical technique that incorporates very specific guided imagery (sometimes archetypal), creative visualization and imagination with specific dance and movement to open new dimensions and realities. It creates shifts in the body, mind and spirit. Shapeshifting is sometimes viewed as the means to manifesting our most wonderful innate gifts - as the epitome of magical unfoldment. It is seen as the pot of gold at the end of the rainbow, but this is somewhat misleading. It is a technique that merely opens a pathway to the pot of gold. That pathway must still be traveled. We must also remember throughout the journey of life that all true magical arts will show us our greatest potentials while also revealing our greatest weaknesses. They will manifest our greatest rewards and our greatest tests.

Many enter into metaphysical, magical and occult practices as a means of escaping their daily lives. They look for mystical practices to solve their problems. Many see the spiritual path as leading up into some blinding light into which all of their troubles and problems will be dissolved. In reality, metaphysical and mystical practices are paths to find the light within so that we can shine it out into our lives. If an individual has difficulty handling the situations of daily life, invoking spiritual and magical energies will not necessarily make things easier.

More likely, the energies will serve to intensify the daily, mundane circumstances of life - forcing a reconciliation or resolution of daily troubles and problems. Our own fears, doubts, limitations and perspectives - whether self created or imposed upon us by society - create barriers to accessing and expressing all of our highest capacities. The art of shapeshifting helps us realize our barriers. It helps bring them to the surface so that we can do something about them. This forces a shifting in our self and our life that ultimately makes us more responsible and stronger. At the same time, it manifests wonderful rewards for us.

When we start our spiritual journeys, everything may be goodness and light - which is as it should be. This is the strengthening process, preparing us for mysteries to be undertaken. When we use shapeshifting, we are proclaiming to the universe: *"I am ready for the change. I am ready to take on greater work and responsibility, and I am taking it on in full awareness of what that entails!'*

There is no fast and easy way in working with shapeshifting though - or any of the magical and spiritual disciplines for that matter. Having done so in a past life does not override the training necessary in this life and those who teach or profess such are living an illusion. We may have learned to read in a previous life or even ten life times, but we still had to relearn it in this life. We had to learn the alphabet, the phonics, develop a vocabulary and so on. We must be cautious of our assumptions drawn from misinformation, half-truths and incomplete knowledge.

Today, the spiritual path demands a *fully* conscious union with the spiritually creative worlds. This cannot be accomplished by mere clairvoyance or psychism of any kind. Today's path to manifesting a higher destiny requires a genuine search and use of knowledge and truth. Unfortunately, we live in a fast food society. People like to pull up to the drive through window, get their food and drive on. They look for the quick and the easy, even with the spiritual. Many spiritual students want to pull up to the drive through window, get their psychic stuff and then drive on as well. No effort, no work, no problems.

Unfortunately, many spiritual and magical aspirants attempt to *be* before they have learned to *become*. It always trips them up through a variety of imbalances. So often people tell me, "You know, I had this great vision and I acted on it, and things started out wonderfully. Then it all changed and everything went wrong." There is an old Qabalistic adage: *A vision of God is not the same as seeing God face to face.* In other words, a vision is not a promise of what will be. It is a reflection of what can be if there is the proper preparation, knowledge and application of focus, energy and persistence. This is part of what shapeshifting develops and it is why the exercises throughout this book build upon each other.

When working with shapeshifting, we are trying to bridge our magical and spiritual essence to our physical being, so that we can express it consciously at any time we desire - for any purpose we desire. By working with shapeshifting techniques, we are learning to consciously stimulate the release of energy and to direct its flow and expression into our daily lives. When we work with shapeshifting, there will *always* be an increased flow of creative forces that will manifest in our lives - with the potential of affecting all levels of our being and all areas of our life. This energy, once released, must find expression. The expression can be beneficial or detrimental. Remember that energy is neutral - neither good nor evil. Only our own individual expression and use of it will determine that.

That expression of energy released through shapeshifting exercises has the potential to become disruptive and destructive, finding inappropriate outlets within our daily life. It can overstimulate us in a variety of ways, affecting our physical, emotional and mental health and balance. If not aware or prepared for it, shapeshifting can often find outlet through your own weaknesses, augmenting them and bringing them out into the open.

It is also easy to misuse energies awakened through the techniques provided within this book – even with all of the safety precautions built into them. It is easy to express them in an unbalanced fashion. We are not trying to dominate the universe. We are trying to learn how to work within its rhythms. Those who "dabble" with a little bit of knowledge and experience are the ones most likely to find themselves in difficulty.

The following are some of the more common problems that can occur when working with shapeshifting. If these begin to manifest, cease all of the shapeshifting activities for a time – at least a month. Work on simple meditation and concentration techniques.

Possible Shapeshifting Imbalances

1. You become more self-centered. Other things and people within your life seem to be increasing intrusive.

2. You are motivated increasingly by greed, lust and a desire for knowledge and power.

3. You find yourself wanting to always be out in front of people. This includes wanting to make sure everyone knows how knowledgeable you are. It also includes feelings of knowing better than anyone else.

4. You may find yourself working with speedier and less troublesome methods of developing psychic faculties. This includes focusing solely on psychic phenomena, and even psychic thrill seeking.

5. You express the new energies and abilities in a misplaced manner – such as through manipulation of others, sexual gratification, power over others, etc. This may even involve ancient, inappropriate methods to attain effects or taking shortcuts through the use of drugs or alcohol to achieve results.

6. You may develop premature trance, premature in that you do not have the development of accurate intuition, clairvoyance and a solid knowledge base to discriminate what and who works through you.

7. You display increasing hypersensitivity in many areas of your life. The increased sensitivity alone can render you suspicious and quarrelsome. It often results in a loss of discrimination.

8. You are unable to distinguish and verify real spiritual experiences from your own illusions. You develop uncontrolled fancy. With shapeshifting, this can be one of the more common difficulties.

Shapeshifting or Uncontrolled Fancy?

Shapeshifting dusts off deep levels of the mind and opens up our perceptions of other dimensions. We can perform simple and even ecstatic shapeshiftings that create such a powerful change in consciousness that we feel as if we are actually changing and becoming the animal or creature. In such cases, even though we may not physically change to observers, internally we may have a profound transformation that can be accompanied by dramatic physical and psychic responses and releases. These kinds of experiences awaken hidden abilities and are empowering. They can be used for powerful protection, weaving glamour and unlocking hidden potentials. They can also create hypersensitivity and escapist delusions.

Experiences with non-physical and subtle states of existence have a powerful effect upon us. It tends to draw the living from the plane of objective, physical life - which is where we are supposed to be focused. This occurs even when higher energies are contacted - even more so. This is why slow, careful integration with the physical is so important. It is why we must also work to maintain the health and balance of the physical body. It is essential to staying grounded. It is also another reason why the physical aspects of the exercises are important. It enables us to maintain some grounding. And as long as we take some relative precautions and follow the guidelines in this book with some degree of moderation, the most that you will have to contend with is uncontrolled fancy.

Work with the spiritual and magical should never imply neglect of the physical. If the physical is unbalanced, then the expression of the spiritual and magical through us will be also. This is why – especially when shapeshifting and magic are concerned – uncontrolled fancy is one of the most common problems that can arise. *Uncontrolled fancy* is the inability to discern the maya and illusions that affect us when we begin to open to deeper levels of consciousness and the more ethereal realms of life. Visions, channelings, insights can be nothing more than uncontrolled fancy, a manifestation of our own imaginings to stroke the ego. What may come through as spiritual insight or a magical epiphany may be little more than a fanciful manufacturing to verify what we already know or to justify our viewpoint.

Imagination is important to shapeshifting and to unfolding our higher potential, but it must be controlled. Sometimes the difference between spiritual/magical illumination and uncontrolled fancy is difficult to detect, which is why continual self-observation is essential in all of the spiritual practices - including shapeshifting. Not delving deeply enough, accepting blindly and failing to be objective can all lead to uncontrolled fancy.

Today more than ever, there is a much greater need to test and validate all of our experiences. The difficulty for most people is figuring out how. There are not always clear signals. Sometimes, the determining is trial and error, but that helps us to learn and grow. This is why I recommend a journal of some kind to keep track of responses to exercises, insights and energies stimulated in you, along with keeping track of events that unfold or change in your life in the month following major shapeshifting practices. Within a month's time – and usually within a week – we will see effects within our outer daily life. Opportunities may manifest. People, family and friends may treat us differently. Issues may come to the forefront and more.

The Seven Basic

Because shapeshifting can be such a convoluted subjecct, I have worked throughout this book to make the process both understandable and progressively developmental. The exercises build from simple to more intricate and they incorporate body, mind and spirit. Overall, the process can be broken down into seven basic stages that are necessary to develop the basic skills of shapeshifting.

1. Developing Magical Fexibility (Chapters 1 and 2)

It is easy to become rigid in our perceptions and our imaginative abilities. Even those who have been involved in magical activites for years need to stretch and loosen their magical faculties when it comes to shapeshfiting. There must be flexibility in body, mind and spirit. We must stretch our magical and spiritual "muscles" so that we can begin to perceive and experience on a much wider scale than in the past - opening to new realms more consciously. Yes, everyone is at a different level of perception, awareness, knowledge and experience, but the more flexibile we are, the more successfully we can adapt, adjust and shapeshift to life's everchanging circumstances.

2. Learning to Direct and Control Energy (Chapter 3)

With shapeshfting, we are learning to recognize, control and direct the energies of the body, mind and spirit. Control of the environment begins with control of ourselves. Learning to work with energy is critical to this process. Since everything is energy in some form, the better we can focus it, the more success we will have in shifting it for our own purposes.

3. Awakening and Developing the Magical Body (Chapter 4)

The first step to actual shapeshifting is the development and use of the magical body, our innermost creative essence. This is where our efforts in flexibility and focusing of our energies and our imaginative faculties begins to take shape for us.

4. Shifting Veils and Weaving Glamour (Chapter 5)

In order to shapeshift efectively, we must learn to perceive in new ways. We must be able to recognize and then shift the veils between the physical and the spiritual - between the dreaming and the waking. True shamans and

Stages of Shapeshifting

shapeshifters can walk between worlds and can see many dimensions. Developing this ability helps us realize more tangibly that we can control the environment and ourselves on both very real and very subtle ways.

5. Developing Lucid Dreaming (Chapters 6 & 7)

Every tradition taught that the dream world was just as real and just as important as the waking world. Part of learning to shift veils is opening to the dream realm more consciously. Lucid dreaming is where we become conscious - while we are dreaming - that we are dreaming. When we become aware or lucid, then we can change what is going on in the dream. Learning to stimulate and control the dreamtime is important to the development of good shapeshifting abilities. Dreams are constantly shifting and changing, so if we learn to be conscious in them, they will provide an environment for practicing, applying and strengthening the flexibility and adaptability of our magical essence.

6. Becoming a Dreamwalker (Chapters 7 & 8)

What we do on one level, always affects us on other levels, so what we do in our waking life, affects our dream life. And what we do in our dream life, affects our waking life. If we can create changes in the dreamtime, it will shifts things in the waking time, making it easier for us to create changes that are desired or necessary. If we take on the form of an animal in our dreams, its qualities become stronger within us while awake. If we can shapeshift ourselves into new forms in our dreams, then we can shapeshift ourselves in our waking world more easily and effectively. We begin to become our true magical self.

7. Awakening Animal Medicine Within You (Chapters 9-12)

Shamanism is an experiential growth process. It involves becoming the master of your own initiation. In shamanism, the individual ultimately answers to no human or totem and is alone with the supernatural. Yes, he or she maintains a true sense of belonging and connectedness to all life, but the individual is able to move through veils to visit the heavens and the underworld. To reach this point, the individual must be able to learn from all life forms. Developing powerful techniques for awakening the animal's medicine within you is critical to this initiation.

An Important Word about the Exercises

All of the exercises in this book are essential for developing effective shapeshifting skills and for creating a truly magical life. Some are developmental, helping you to develop imaginative, intuitive and magical skills. They will stretch your magical muscles. They are like the warm-up exercises before sporting endeavors – especially those exercises in Parts I and II of this book. Failure to stretch and warm the muscles properly will eventually result in problems. *To attempt complicated shapeshifting activities - no matter how enticing - before you are truly ready, will result in imbalances that will affect your everyday life.* These potential imbalances can be emotional, mental, mundane and/or spiritual and we will discuss more aspects of them throughout the book.

The exercises incorporate all aspects of your being. They will stretch the imagination. They will stimulate emotions and they will also encompass physical elements that must be employed as well. So often the physical aspects are the most neglected in the magical teachings of the modern world. And yet, it is one of the most powerful and critical elements of magic. We are a microcosm of the universe and we must learn to employ all aspects of our energies – including the physical to truly succeed in spiritual and magical initiations. The physical elements are what grounds the magical energy into our outer life.

The human body is a magnificent mechanism. It is an energy system. The human body gives off light, sound, and thermal energies. It radiates both electrical and magnetic frequencies. And every time there is a muscular movement within the body, an electrical stimulus is also elicited. Understanding this and working with this is critical to successful shapeshifting. For example, if we need to be more bearlike in a situation, we should move and posture like a bear. This creates an electrical change in our body, shifting it to a pattern that is similar to and resonates with a bear. This shifting will enable us to express those bearlike qualities more easily and effectively. This is why the physical elements are more critical to the success of shapeshifting than in other magical and spiritual arts.

Being human though, I realize that we also need confirmation of our magical endeavors, and thus many of the exercises are experiential – as well as developmental. I have always been very result-oriented. I like to know - and to teach others - that if we do such and such, we can expect certain definable results. I have designed most of the shapeshifting exercises to be experiential. These are designed to elicit tangible results. These experiential exercises will play themselves out somewhere in your physical life, so that you get confirmation of and reinforcement for your efforts. It is very important that we know when we do certain things that we can expect and will achieve certain results. You will feel, see and experience the effects of these exercises. The exercises will enable you to achieve some success and thus motivate you to pursue your shapeshifting work further.

There is a mixture of the developmental and experiential throughout Parts I and II. They lay the foundation for the more intricate exercises of Part III. They are also exercises that you can easily use and adapt to other magical and spiritual practices in your life. As you will discover, they have benefits beyond just shapeshifting work.

Some of the exercises will also be synthesizing. In many ways, these are the most important because they help you to put your experiences into proper perspective. They help you to gain insight into your magical and spiritual experiences, helping you to realize what works and what doesn't work for you as an individual. They help you to realize to what degree and within what time frame the magic is unfolding for you. And that is where the shapeshifting journal comes into play.

The effects of the exercises in this book are accumulative. They build upon and add dimensions to each other. Think of the art of shapeshifting as developing new magical muscles or greater magical flexibility. We don't want to pull a muscle or strain anything, so we start simple. We build a foundation from the ground up. Because of the ground work laid, by the time we get to the exercises toward the end of the book, the effects are more powerful and even more amazing than if you skipped to them at the beginning. And once we've reached the end of the book and then go back and repeat earlier exercises, the effects of those earlier exercises become even more intense.

Shapeshifting
Exercise
(synthesizing)

The Shapeshifting Journal

Skills & Benefits:
- **helps recognition of success in your endeavors**
- **improves communication between the conscious and subconscious**
- **heightens the imagination**

One of the best things you can do to assist yourself in becoming a shapeshifter is to become more conscious of your shapeshifting development. In life, change usually occurs continually and in subtle ways. Even the more dramatic/traumatic changes we experience in life are usually preceded and forecasted by signs and indications that the average individual either ignores or does not recognize. One of the many advantages of working with the ancient art of shapeshifting is that it puts you more in the flow of Nature's transformative forces. When we are within that flow, we can control and direct its effects upon us and our lives more advantageously.

We are always within the flow and forces of transformation, but we are often so wrapped up in the day-to-day activities of life that we do not realize it. *If we cannot see the patterns, we cannot work with them or change them.* Journaling is one of the most effective ways of becoming and staying conscious of the changes and patterns within our life. It can crystallize the forces at play and substantiate your own growth and development. It makes you more conscious of the subtleties at play within your life.

There are a number of good books on journaling, but our focus here will be on creating and using a shapeshifting journal. Maintaining a record of our shapeshifting experiences is one of the most effective tools for the development of the ability. It is a way of being conscious of the changes (subtle and obvious) we are enacting. It is a way of telling the subconscious mind (which controls over 90% of the body's energies and activities) that we are serious about learning to shapeshift and transform ourselves . When we record our practices and experiences regularly, we acknowledge the growth and we become more conscious of the subtle changes. It is a also means of thanking ourselves for the sacred journey we have begun.

Record all that you experience or don't experience from the exercises - whether you feel they are imagined or not.Remember that the imagination is not the same as the unreal. The imagination is the image making faculty of the mind. All that is imagined has threads to something real within our life, or we could not have imagined it. The journal recordings take the ethereal experiences of shapeshifting and make them more concrete for us. Since humans in modern society tend to disbelieve, even when seeing and experiencing, this is a crucial tool.

Record your dreams, your experiences and any change that occurs in every area of your life. It takes no more than a month of consistent journaling before you are able to recognize the subtle changes occurring. You will see them reflected in outer, everyday occurrences. The changes you see in your everyday life, in other people around you and in yourself are simply outer reflections of the inner transformations. They acknowledge and confirm your efforts - affirming your movement into the transformative rhythms of Nature. Within a month, you will see changes! It helps us to draw out and manifest even more strongly our natural shapeshifting abilities. Most important we develop the ability to recognize, create and more effectively align with the flowing patterns of change around us.

There are many ways of setting up and using a shapeshifting journal. Use your own creativity. Keep in mind that the more care you take in your journal work the more crystallized the actual shapeshifting work. The following pages contain seven basic guidelines for setting up your shapeshifting journal. They are guidelines only. Do not be afraid to *adapt and change* them according to your own wants and wishes.

1. In the front of your journal, write a dedication to this sacred process.

2. List the goals you hope to be able to accomplish through shapeshifting. (Leave space to add to them. Our goals change, as does everything.)
Give a description of everything you hope to be able to accomplish on every level by developing the ability to shapeshift. They do not have to be grandiose, but by listing even those that are for your own entertainment and pleasure is a way of preparing the proper mindset. Although some may not seem "spiritual", they are part of our potential, and later we will explore proper use and misuse of shapeshifting. For now, list as many possible uses you feel you can derive from shapeshifting. Remember there are no limits.

3. Describe the magical you - the magical body or essence that you intend to create through the art of shapeshifting.
This is an important step. It crystallizes your desires and helps align both the conscious and subconscious mind toward this accomplishment. Chapter four will help you in defining the magical you.

4. Decide on a regular time to perform your exercises and your journaling.
Setting aside an hour per day for this may be difficult in your busy lives, but if there is to be minimal success, you should commit to at least 3 times per week for the exercises and follow-up journaling. To be a true shapeshifter, you must develop flexibility and you must be able to focus solely upon yourself. This requires re-training. We live in a society of great distractions. People and events take our time and attention. It is amazing how many people complain about having no time for themselves. If we have no time for ourselves, what is the quality of time are we giving to others? Shapeshifting is sacred, and everyone deserves some sacred time and space throughout the week – if not the day. It is absolutely essential to our overall health - spiritual and physical. This is a simple way of showing reverence and respect for the essence of whom we are and who we are becoming.

If it is important to you, you will find the time. Keep in mind that this time investment will pay great dividends later. It will save you time by making you more effective at everything you do. The hour investment need not be all at once. Splitting it into two, half hour can be very effective. Take a half hour for the exercise of the day (although most will only require 20 minutes), and schedule another half hour for the journaling. Commit to this for one month, and the success will encourage you to continue.

5. Have a place in your journal to record the day and date of the exercises, particularly those recommended for the first month.
The is especially important for the first month's activities . A sample calendar guideline is found at the end of this chapter. Remember that everyone is different. Some may see results sooner than a month - some longer. Regardless, everyone will get some results within the first month by following this timeline. After that, do not be afraid to repeat the month or to incorporate and substitute other exercises in the place of those listed.

6. Begin your journaling.
Many times, people don't know how to start, but once it is started, the flow begins. One of the easiest ways to start that flow is by describing the exercise you performed for the day. Write a brief description of your preparation for the exercise. This sets the tone, and opens the doorway between the conscious and subconscious mind.

The subconscious is very much aware of everything you experience on every level of your being through the exercise. The journaling helps to tap that awareness, drawing it out into the conscious mind. The description of the exercise, serves to ring the doorbell and tell the subconscious what information and insight you wish to tap specifically. Describe the major feeling or emotion generated in the experience. Was it more visual? Tactile? Auditory? What sense seemed the more strongly stimulated? As you write, ask yourself questions. Does the exercise seem to apply and/or relate to any situation or experience in your present life more than another?

Write down everything you feel or experience, no matter how trivial it may seem or no matter how extraordinary. In the beginning this is most essential as it helps you to recognize where the new energies are beginning to emerge within your life.

In essence, you are logging a shapeshifting report that will help you identify your new parameters and potentials as they begin to unfold. Most of the exercises in this book have titles and functions. List them at the top of the page. Then simply describe the effects that the exercise seemed to have upon you. What is the major emotion? What were you feeling while in the midst of it? What were your feelings upon completion of the exercise? Was there elation? Success? Was there fear? Do you feel excited? Empowered? Drained? What questions are strongest upon your mind?

7. Leave a space in your journal, after each session for a periodic review. Occasionally go back and review the record of your exercises, especially when you repeat them, after that first month. List the major events in your life between the last time you performed the exercise and the most recent. Is there any correlation? Did the exercises precede any of the major events? Do these events in your life in any way reflect the images and purposes of the various exercises?

For some people a review after a three to four day period is sufficient. It allows enough time to pass to see what unfolds in the outer life as a result. Others find it more effective to do it weekly. Some do this daily. Others do no reviews until the first months work is accomplished. Find what works best for you, but remember that the review is most important for recognizing the shapeshifting rhythms awakening within your life. The exercises are designed to elicit transformations in your personal physical and spiritual energies, helping you to recognize, manifest and enhance your natural shapeshifting abilities. Events in the circumstances of our normal lives are where these changes will first reveal themselves. These confirm and reflect the more subtle changes occurring within you.

I still use my shapeshifting journal periodically - not as frequently as when I first started working with it years ago. Now I use it mostly when I need to loosen my "shapeshifting muscles" a bit. Once you have unfolded your ability to shapeshift, the schedule of exercises does not have to be adhered to as strictly or conscientiously. They are still very beneficial though to re-stimulate those rhythms. Think of the exercises as getting yourself in shape. If we have neglected ourselves for a time, it may require greater effort on our part to get into good physical condition. Once we are in good condition, it requires less effort to maintain that condition than it did to get into it. The journaling and the exercises help keep your shapeshifting muscles limber and ready.

30 Day Quick Start to Shapeshifting

1 Begin journal Phoenix Rising	2 Activate Microcosm Phoenix Rising	3 Activate Microcosm Phoenix Rising	4 Activate Microcosm Sun & Moon	5 Sun & Moon 2 week enhancer	6 Sun & Moon 2 week enhancer	7 2 week enhancer dancer's pose
8 2 week enhancer dancer's pose	9 2 week enhancer dancer pose Magical body	10 2 week enhancer dancer pose Magical body	11 2 week enhancer dancer pose Magical body	12 2 week enhancer	13 2 week enhancer	14 2 week enhancer Spirit cloth
15 2 week enhancer dancer's pose Tibetan Walk	16 2 week enhancer dancer's pose Tibetan Walk	17 2 week enhancer dancer's pose Tibetan Walk	18 2 week enhancer	19 Tibetan Walk Balance postures	20 Tibetan Walk Balance posture	21 Dream tantra Rite of Dream Passage
22 Dream tantra Mythic Dreamwork "Master & Pupil"	23 Dream tantra Mythic Dreamwork "Master & Pupil"	24 Dream tantra Mythic Dreamwork "Master & Pupil"	25 Dream tantra Spirit Contact	26 Dream tantra Owl mask making	27 Dream tantra Owl mask making	28 Dream tantra Becoming the Owl
29 Dream tantra Becoming the Owl	30 Dream tantra Becoming the Owl					

Chapter Two

The Basic Principles

All of the magic that we read about in tales and myths is real…in a way. But the laws of magic – including those of shapeshifting – are not always what we believe. The magical arts are never fully understood by anyone – no matter what they say. You see, there will always be as much that magic can't fix as there is that it can. Unfortunately, many believe that the magical arts – of which shapeshifting is but one – are developed so that we can get what we want. Contrary to this misconception though, they are for revealing and unfolding our greater potentials. And that especially applies to the magical art of shapeshifting.

There will always be elements of life that we cannot control as long as we are in the physical – even with magic. This play of "free variables" in life is what keeps nudging us to become ever more creative and productive. It creates a shifting in our life parameters. Through techniques such as shapeshifting though, we become more active within our life, and we unfold our own power and magic. Through shapeshifting, we are able to take a more creative and active role in our life circumstances and we are able to handle those free variables more effectively.

Shapeshifting is the process of using Nature's elements, symbols and images in an imaginative (and sometimes mythologized) manner - in conjunction with directed physical movements - to elicit specific changes and effects within our body, mind and spirit. It enables us to open the psychic and spiritual planes more consciously. Shapeshifting can be developed for astral travel, scrying in the spirit, past life exploration, healing, communication with animals and more. It traverses the mind and the various planes of existence. Through shapeshifting, we awaken dormant and untapped resources within us.

This has been accomplished through a variety of meditative and ceremonial techniques throughout the ages. But it is the application of movement and dance that awakens and releases this ability within us more dynamically. It is what triggers the actual shapeshifting of energies on all levels of our being. And that is why sacred dance and movement will be a major focus of this book. It is a crucial element of magical and spiritual unfoldment and yet it is so often neglected by seekers. One of the reasons yoga has remained a very old, very powerful and very successful spiritual tool is that it combines visualization, breathing and especially movement. As we will explore later, movement is a critical element for metamorphosis on any level within our world.

It is very easy in our modern times to think we know all about the world, its various realms and its energies. After all, explorers have touched the four corners of the Earth. We have ventured into space, into the ocean depths and into new levels of the mind. Many people are now beginning to explore the more subtle realms and dimensions of life, realms that have served as the inspiration to most of our ancient myths, legends and archetypes.

Reading about these realms and experiencing them are two entirely different things. We cannot truly know something until we have experienced it. Theory and knowledge without application is limited, if not impotent. To most people our legends, myths and ancient teachings are merely words, but there are ways to discover the truths and realities upon which they are based. One of the most powerful means of discovering their truths is through the art of shapeshifting.

*"...in your own Bosom you bear your Heaven
And Earth and all you behold;
tho' it appears Without it is Within,
In your Imagination of which this
World of Mortality is but a Shadow."*
- William Blake

The Three Principles of Shapeshifting

Life is a process of change, and everything within the natural world is in a continual cycle of transformation. This is part of the magic reflected within the sacred seasons. Each season has its own magic, spirit, energy, feel and rhythm to it. The winter rhythm is one of slowing down and going within. In Nature, it is a time in which seeds stay within the earth and there is internal activity and germination. The spring brings a rhythm of re-emergence. Seeds begin to sprout and grow, working their way out of the earth. Summer is the time of fertility and coming into fruition, as the seeds bear fruit. Autumn brings the time of harvesting and the planting of seeds for the next year.

In our modern society, we have distanced ourselves from Nature. We have convinced ourselves that the laws that apply to the natural world do not apply to us as humans. And yet everything that impacts upon the natural world also impacts upon us - whether we choose to recognize and acknowledge it or not.

Several of the natural laws are essential to understand if we are to develop and apply our natural shapeshifting abilities. These laws and principles are found within the myths, religion and philosophy of every society. Whether we speak of the Hermetic Principles, The Twelve Natural Laws of Christian Gnosticism, The Shadow World Teachings of the Northwest Natives or even quantum physics, every society expressed these basic principles in a manner understandable to those within the society. When examined, common threads are found to run through them all. When there are such common teachings - especially in societies that had no contact with each other - it should make bells go off. It tells us that there is something very universal and wonderful at play.

A few of these natural laws and principles apply directly to the art of shapeshifting. They are what make it possible.

 Shapeshifting is possible because creation and change are constant throughout the world in every expression of life.

Life is constant change. Change ensures growth. It helps us to shed the old so that we can express the new. If we resist change and the natural flow, our life becomes stagnant like water that is trapped. Change is essential to life, and shapeshifting teaches us how to flow with the changes more effectively. Like water, which will adapt its flow to the environment, shapeshifting teaches us how to adapt and change in the most creative and productive ways possible.

Change in the form of birth, death and rebirth are repeated literally and symbolically in all growing things throughout the natural world. The old is laid down for the new. Nowhere is it more evident than within Nature. A plant may die, but its seeds struggle forth to take root, work its way through soil and sprout – extending itself. Acorns transform themselves into mighty oaks. Flowers and leaves die off, disappear and then are reborn again with cyclic rhythms. Seeds germinate, grow, flower, release a new seed and die often in one growing season

In the insect world, there are distinct stages for most forms of metamorphosis. There is the egg stage where we birth. From the egg, there is a larva stage, a stage of feeding and strengthening to develop a solid foundation. Then there is usually a cocoon or even chrysalis stage. These are stages of reorganization. There are cellular changes – a reminder that in the creative process we do what we must and can do, and then let the creative project take its own natural course. And then from this stage comes a new life, a new expression of life. In the insect kingdom that new life usually has wings with all of its symbolic associations.

In humans, we are born, develop, and go through puberty and adolescence. We move into maturity of body and mind and on to old age, death and rebirth. And each stage has its own physiological, emotional, mental and spiritual changes. And throughout each stage we are confronted by changing conditions around us at all times. Nothing ever stays exactly the same. Change is constant. The mysteries of life, death and rebirth play themselves out in a multitude of ways throughout our lives. And the more we develop abilities to adapt, adjust and work with those changes, the more effective we become in life.

 Shapeshifting is possible because all things are related.

Humans are a microcosm of the universe. This does not mean that we merely reflect the energies of the universe. It means that we have within us all of the energies of the universe. We are thus connected and a part of all life and all expressions of life. We exist in everything and everything exists within us on some level. This is sometimes called the Principle of the All. One of things I stress when I teach workshops on animals and Nature is that we are part of Nature. No matter how much we cloak ourselves in civilization, we are always going to be a part of Nature on at least a primal level.

In quantum physics and in the study of holograms and holographic paradigms, some amazing things have been discovered. Studies at Stanford University by Dr. Karl Pribram showed that if we take a holographic photo of a horse and cut the head off, something amazing happens. When that piece is enlarged, we do not get a large image of the head. Instead, we get a picture of the whole horse in a condensed form.[1] The part contains the whole and the whole is in each part. This can be extended to humans potentials. We are part of the whole, and each part is contained the whole.

Though we often see ourselves as separate, everything is connected to everything else. Every person is connected to every other person. Every person is connected to every plant, animal and mineral. Every event is linked to those of the past and to those of the future. Everything relates to everything else. *As above, so below. As below, so above*. There is no such thing as coincidence. Every action has a reaction. Everything we do and think sets energy in motion and shapes what will unfold somewhere within our life. If we do one thing, something else will result from it.

The difficulty though is figuring out how things relate. True divination comes from recognizing what the connections are or will be. Sometimes the connections will be obvious. Other times though, it takes a great deal of effort before we figure out these connections or why things happen the way they do. An encounter with a skunk may be alerting us to be careful of our boundaries. On the other hand, it may also indicate that we may need to take a bath. The appearance overnight of a group of toadstools and mushrooms may just reflect that the excessive rain has created an extremely moist and fertile environment for them. But because mushrooms act in almost the reverse manner of normal plants, their appearance might indicate that it is time to recycle ideas and activities and take an entirely different perspective in some situation around us.

All things are related. What we think, do and believe on one level always affects us on other levels – physically, emotionally, mentally and spiritually. All elements and aspects of our life are connected. Magical shapeshifting reveals these connections and helps us to use them make our lives more effective and creative. A shaman who sprinkles a plant with water isn't just "watering the plant". He is also inviting the rains to come. A healer not only works with the body but also the emotional, mental and spiritual aspects of the person that helped create the problem. A shaman who dances the movements of an animal isn't just honoring the animal. He or she is creating a change in his/her own system (body, mind and spirit) enabling him/her to become an expression of that animal. Shapeshifting helps us to see the connections and use them to make our lives more productive.

---

1 Wilbur, Ken, ED. *THE HOLOGRAPHIC PARADIGM*. New Science Library; Boulder, CO. 1982, p.2.

Shapeshifting is possible because we are energy and what we do with our energy on one level always affects us on other levels as well.

To understand how shapeshifting can create magical changes in us and our lives, we need to see ourselves as an energy system. The ancients and modern scientists agree that everything in life is formed of vibration. That vibration is the result of the movement of the electrons and protons of every atom in every molecule of substance. Vibration exists in objects, animals, people, and in the atmosphere around us. The vibrational frequencies of animate life are more active, vibrant, and variant than inanimate matter, but vibration does exist in all. Every atom of every molecule of every cell has vibration.

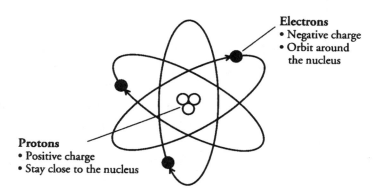

Electrons
• Negative charge
• Orbit around the nucleus

Protons
• Positive charge
• Stay close to the nucleus

The Energy Vibrations of Atoms

The human body is comprised of many energy fields. These energy fields surround, emanate from, and interact with the physical body and mind. The task of the modern metaphysical student and scientist is to determine which energies, intensities, and combinations are most effective for different processes - physical and spiritual.

When we run, the activity of the atoms increases, and there are corresponding physiological changes. The heart beats faster, the lungs work harder, circulation increases, and there are other changes. Some affect emotional and mental states. It is recognized that long distant runners experience a kind of euphoria. This is due partly to the release of endorphins by the brain during this sustained activity.

Through the use of specific shapeshifting techniques, we induce energy changes along definable avenues. We learn to direct very subtle, yet very real changes within our energy system. We will change the shape of our thoughts and the shape of our aura and we will shift our world of possibilities.

Because the human body is an energy system, we can use different energy expressions to interact with our system. We can employ color, sound, fragrance, and especially dance and movement to elicit specific changes. This can increase intuition, stimulate creativity, induce deeper altered states of consciousness, expand perception of the spiritual realm of life, and heal. Through this book, you will learn to employ a number of these in combination with spirit masks, sacred costumes and much more to shapeshift your essence and your life.

There are a variety of energy fields surrounding and emanating from the physical body. These fields include - but are not limited to - light, electrical, magnetic, thermal and electro-magnetic. They are scientifically measurable and help demonstrate how the human body is an energy system.

**"Within the body,
all of the energies of the universe -
heaven and earth - play themselves out.
As we learn to use the body in a more
consciously directed manner,
we open ourselves to the universe,
and we awaken and manifest its powers
within ourselves and our lives.
We become the living universe!"**

How Shapeshifting Works

There has developed in modern times a great mystique surrounding the occult practice of shapeshifting. For many groups and individuals, it is perceived as the be-all and end-all of magical skills. The truth is that there are variations of shapeshiftings performed at some time by most people who meditate and who practice spiritual/magical development in any of its many forms. Visualizations alone though are not shapeshiftings. They are an aspect of the entire process – as can be daydreaming. Shapeshifting does incorporate the use of the symbols and images in an imaginative manner, but without the other primary element of dance and movement, the shapeshifting will not happen to any great degree. The results will be greatly limited in comparison.

Shapeshifting is natural to humans. We are in a constant state of change from the moment we are born and throughout our entire life. Cells grow, die off and are regenerated constantly within our bodies. But shapeshifting is much more than transforming our cells into a beast. Everyday, we shift our energies to meet our daily trials, obligations and responsibilities. We learn early on when to smile, when to be serious, how to appear apologetic or how to express a wide variety of personas according to need. Shapeshifting is not just transforming into an animal, as often described in ancient myths and tales.

Today we must do things differently. Today, most magic – including shapeshifting – takes place in the mind at a different level of perception. That doesn't make it any less real or useful to our outer lives. Although the skill of shapeshifting takes time and practice, the formula for shapeshifting is simple:

Creative Imagination

+

Directed Dance or Movement =

Shapeshifting

Creative Imagination

The first capacity that must be developed for true success with shapeshifting is **creative imagination.** This faculty - when truly developed - will lead to higher forms of inspiration and a fully conscious perception of the spiritual realm. Creative imagination or imaginative cognition is a powerful tool for opening the doors to the spirit realm. Through it, we begin to see the spiritual essences and energies surrounding and interplaying with our physical world at all times.

Keep in mind that what we consider imagination is a reality in some form on some level beyond the normal sensory world. Through creative imagination, we open to a new kind of experience in form and color. Through creative imagination, we build up the significances of the images and symbols and imbue them with greater relevance to our life. Then we assume a union with them through shapeshifting movements. Through repeated shapeshiftings, we connect more and more fully with the image's archetypal origins, releasing its energies more dynamically and tangibly into our life. It is like turning on a faucet that allows a flow into our everyday life.

An old axiom states: "All energy follows thought." Where we put our thoughts is where energy goes. With practice, we can strengthen the imaginative faculty and consciously shift and direct our energies along any lines we desire. We can shapeshift the imagination so that for all intents and purposes, we become the shape we imagine. For this to occur though, visualization and concentration skills must be developed to some degree.

Visualization is the ability to create a mental picture and hold it steady within the mind for a reasonable time. The image should be as clear as anything seen within the physical life. It should be made as lifelike as possible - in color, texture, fragrance, etc. A simple exercise is to visualize an orange. Clearly visualize its shape, size and color. Feel the skin on it. Experience how it feels as you press your finger into it and begin to peel it. Notice the fragrance as the juice squirts out. Then create the image of its taste.

Now some individuals are not visual and thus may feel that their work with shapeshifting will be hindered. Nothing could be further from the truth. Even if we can't picture in our minds, by simply bringing the thought or idea of an image or symbol to mind, we open the doors that will elicit the same result. And when we incorporate it with the movement aspect the process will work.

Concentration is the art of holding the thought or image that you have created within your mind without the mind wavering or wandering to other things. We should develop a concentrated focus that is strong enough to hold one image or thought to the exclusion of others. This takes practice. If we find our mind wandering, bring it back to the image or thought - no matter how often it wanders. By doing so, we train the mind. In time, it will respond with increasingly concentrated focus when and how we wish. And when we incorporate movement or dance – a physical activity with it – our concentration is strengthened.

Directed Dance and Movement

For shapeshifting to occur though, the creative imagination is not enough by itself - unless we are working with shapeshifting in dreamtime. (And this we will cover in Part II.) Without physical expression of those energies, the shapeshfting effects are limited. We must take those concentrated imaginative energies and release them into our physical life.

The Magical Power in Make-Believe

When we were young, the world was filled with enchantment. Each day offered new adventures. Anything we could imagine was real – be it a ghost, a space ship or the wonderful beings of the Faerie Realm. We could be anything we wanted. We could be hunting buried treasure in the morning and playing with a unicorn in the evening. We could be anything we wanted. Everything was possible.

Creative imagination is one of our most powerful abilities. It is a key to opening doors to magical realms and abilities. Most people have played make believe, but few people realize what a powerful magical process it can be. It is drawing to beings of the Faerie Realm. It awakens our hidden abilities and it helps free our magic. Think about all of those times when you were playing make-believe and lost yourself in the game, losing track of time. You shifted into a Tween Time. For a brief period, you became what you imagined.

Playing make-believe to act out some of your favorite fairy tales or adventure frees up our imagination. It removes blockages to our creative energies. We reconnect with our beliefs and we release our magic. When I am feeling a little stuck in my writing, I will choose a fairy tale and go to a special place in my woods to play. And within 24 hours my creative juices are flowing again. It is a magical way of shifting energies in and around you.

This is where dance or movement comes into play. The physical movement is a dynamic catalyst for the physiological and spiritual changes that we are seeking through the imaginings. It is what makes the shapeshifting possible.

When we incorporate consciously directed movement to reinforce our imagination, the results can be phenomenal. We create dramatic shifts in consciousness that brings great illumination and personal empowerment. We connect deeper levels of our subconscious mind to our normal waking consciousness. More importantly, we create shifts in the bio-chemical and electro-magnetic aspects of our body. We ground and release the energies from our creative imaginings into our physical life more tangibly. So for example, if we need to be more bear-like in a situation, just imagining ourselves as a bear is not enough. By imitating the movements of the bear or standing and posturing like a bear though – in conjunction with the imaginings – we are able to express those bear qualities more effectively in situations around us. It creates a change in our body and even more dramatic changes in our aura and our personality. We create a physical link and resonance with the bear.

Movement triggers the metamorphosis, giving the creative imagination expression in the physical. With shapeshifting, we are choosing and directing the movement of energy within our lives, based upon the energies invoked through our imaginings and the movements necessary to release them. When we control, direct and focus the inner energies consciously through creative imagination and movement, we are doing what the teacher and mystic Rudolph Steiner referred to as "grabbing the serpent of wisdom by the neck". We make the energies work for us - when we wish and how we wish.

The key to empowering our life is setting up conditions that create a new way of tapping and working with our potentials. Through the techniques in this book, we learn to do this in a powerful way. They enable us to delve into deeper parts of our being, access hidden potentials and give them more tangible expression. Shapeshifting reminds and teaches us that we are always more magical than what we believe and more than what others think. As you develop your skills through the progressive exercises and practices in this book, you will find greater and greater possibilities manifesting in your life. When we open the doors properly to a magical life, it does nothing but grow. And eventually, it becomes more wonderful than even we imagined.

But remember: To have a magical life, you must seek a magical life. Shapeshifting is not a hobby, a past time, or a path to weekend thrills. It is a path of self-discovery. It is a way of life – a commitment to a life of enchantment, wonders and possibilities. It is when we merely dabble in it for fun that troubles unfold. That is where the precautions come into play.

Guidelines for Shapeshifting

1. In the beginning of shapeshifting, do no more than one per day, unless specifically directed otherwise by the information on that exercise.

2. There should be no interruptions when performing your shapeshiftings.
Make sure the phone is off the hook and that you will not be disturbed. Altered states of consciousness induce a hyperaesthetic state in us. Sounds are more shattering, and lights are more penetrating. Unexpected interruptions are upsetting to the nervous system.

3. All meditations, journeys, and shapeshiftings have a beginning, middle and end.
If your work or exercise is interrupted, simply take moment and then slowly perform the physical movements of the exercise or the grounding movements to restore your balance and then perform it at another time. It is usually best not to try and continue.

4. Use as many aids as you find comfortable to help you.
Incense, candles, crystals and music set a tone and energy that facilitates our work. Specific guidelines for their use will be given later. The atmosphere in which we operate is extremely important to a successful performing of a shapeshifting.

5. There may arise a time during an exercise when you feel you cannot complete the shapeshifting.
Honor that feeling. Maybe you are uncomfortable, a little fearful or doubtful. Do not be upset by this! Ultimately you know what you can handle and at what rate. Simply visualize yourself back solidly in your body. Work on the preliminary and developmental exercises found in the earlier sections throughout this book until you feel comfortable working the more complete shapeshiftings. Emotional upset can occur during a shapeshifting and although it often reflects that we have successfully accessed the dynamic archetypal forces of Nature, part of our development requires that we honor ourselves by not traumatizing ourselves in the growing process.

6. Some of the shapeshiftings will have immediate effects upon your life.
Others may take weeks or even months before their manifestation and impacts will be fully recognized. *Be assured, they will have an impact. They will affect your life on all levels.*

The energy released and its effects are often stronger than we imagined. The energy released will play within our lives in a unique manner. But every word, phrase, picture and movement can trigger chain reactions which will rise to the surface within our life.

7.   Most importantly, do not make the mistake of thinking that these techniques are an excuse for daydreaming and psychic thrill-seeking!
They are so much more than mere fantasy, and such assumptions will be devastating when the truth of their power is driven home!

8.   Employ various grounding techniques if you find yourself hypersensitive following a shifting.
Use grounding postures, such as is depicted below, before and after exercsies. Take a few minutes to stretch and then eat something light. If still sensitive, have someone stroke the spine downward from the crown of the head. It stabilizes the chakras and it draws the consciousness back into present reality.

This modified horse stance provides balance and it softens the impact of energy activated when used at the end of exercises. Feel yourself connected to the Earth.

This posture places you in solid contact with the earth and stabilizes energies. It prevents disorientation and that "spacey feeling". While in this position, feel yourself, solidly in your human essence. In aikido, this is known as the immoveable posture, meaning "imperturbable". The chin is in, the spine straight and you sit solidly on your buttocks. The right toe is crossed over the left big toe.

Preparing for the

Although shapeshifting may seem like a fantasy of the mind or an innocuous - if not fanciful - daydream, it is dangerous to assume it will have little effect upon our lives. We are working with powerful imagery that generates and releases Nature's archetypal forces. We combine imagery with movements that ground that energy into our physical life. This impacts the subconscious mind and awakens what is hidden there. And although the situations, experiences and shapeshifting may be symbolic, they will strongly impact the physical world in which we operate daily.

We must remember that whatever we do on one level of our consciousness will flow down and manifest similar expressions on a more mundane level. We are learning to use symbols and images with directed movements to activate and experience specific energies and potentials more quickly and powerfully within our life. This will occur within our normal, day-to-day circumstances. Those who doubt that such connections and relationships exist have only intellectualized the process. These individuals will come face-to-face with what will be for them a harsh reality of the interrelationship between the art of shapeshifting and its impact upon our lives.

Shapeshifting is an agent for transformation between the inner and the outer, the upper and the lower, the past and the future and for all levels of consciousness. The raising of matter and awareness from an ordinary level to one that is extraordinary is the task of the true seeker. And although difficult at times, the epiphanies that come from each shapeshifting are worth every difficulty. Without techniques like shapeshifting, the tasks and the successes of the seeker are often random and atavistic.

1. Setting the mood (preparing for the exercise)

Begin a magical practice by finding a time to be by yourself, when you will not be disturbed or interrupted. You may wish to set the mood by using candles or fragrances.

2. Physical Preparations

Most of the shapeshifting exercises throughout this book will have physical movements associated with them. These movements and postures create electro-magnetic shifts within our own physiological systems so that

Shapeshifting Exercises

we can accomplish the task of the exercise more balanced and effectively. These should always be performed in the beginning and at the end.

3. Relaxation (beginning the exercise)

There are two simple kinds of relaxation techniques that will help with these magical practices. Use the one that works best for you:

Progressive Relaxation

Make yourself comfortable. Take a few slow deep breaths and imagine sending warm, soothing thoughts to every part of your body, starting with your feet and moving to the top of your head. Visualize warm, soothing energy, melting up over you from your feet to your head. Take your time with this. The more relaxed you are, the more quickly and easily you will succeed.

Rhythmic Breathing

Inhale slowly through your nostrils, hold the breath and then exhale slowly out your mouth. Imagine warm, soothing energy flowing to every part of you body with each breath. As you relax, allow your attention to be focused entirely on yourself

4. Grounding Ritual (ending the exercise)

Altered states tend to draw us away from the physical, so after our magical practices, we need to ground – to reconnect with the physical world. Grounding should always involve a little stretching. Eating a few crackers is also helpful. By eating something light, the body begins to focus on digestion, which also helps us to ground. If there are physical movements associated with the exercise, perform them slowly. It shifts the energy and helps ground it.

One of the most important aspects of grounding and releasing the energies awakened through a shapeshifting exercise is the pohysical movement. Most exercises have some form of physical movement associated with them. They should be performed at the beginning and at the end.

Writing in journal about your feelings and observations after a magical practice also grounds those magical energies into the physical, helping to release them into your life.

The grounding should also involve some vocal expression of affirmation and gratitude. This can be a prayer of thanks for what already is and for the magic of your life.

Shapeshifting
Exercise
(developmental)

Activating the Microcosm

Skills & Benefits:

- **activates energy around us**
- **grounding**
- **helps combat fatigue**
- **develops sensitivity to the flow of energy**

We are each a microcosm of the universe. We have reflections of all the universal energies within us. By learning to activate them, we create a magickal existence.

Most movement creates spirals of energy. In essence, the energy spirals around us, linking the earth and heaven. We become a bridge between the two. In traditional dance training, the individual is taught basic positions. These body positions are basic to dance all over the world. The first five positions activate a spiral of energy that forms around the body and links it to the earth below and the heavens above. The number five, in traditional numerology, is the number of the microcosm, of the universe expressing itself through the human being.

These positions are effective to do periodically throughout the day, as they are energizing. Assuming these positions, especially the positions of feet in figures three, four, and five, helps strengthen us in tense situations and gives us greater energy. Often, when I am lecturing, I will stand in positions three and four. This gives me a solid base of energy to draw on throughout the lecture or workshop. Then, as I gesture, speak, and move, that spiral of energy is drawn up and used to help touch and teach the audience more effectively.

Practice assuming the five following positions. Feel and sense the spiral of energy rise up as you move from one position to the next. Remember to visualize the spiral forming and drawing upward, encompassing and energizing your entire body. They have an energizing and yet grounding effect. They are good to use as a prelude and conclusion to any meditation.

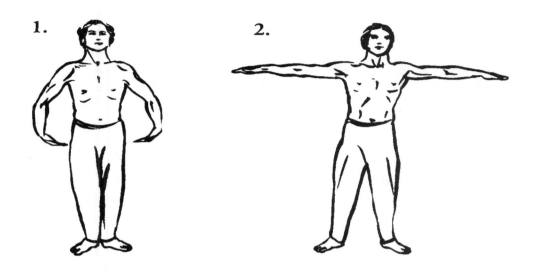

Creating a Spiral of Energy Through the Five Basic Positions

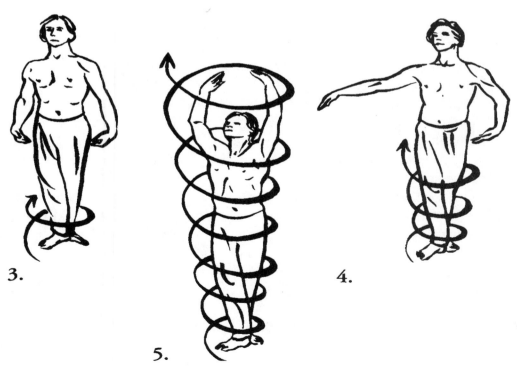

1. In position one, the legs are turned out from the hips. The arms are in a long shallow curve, and the palms face inward. The head should be up and the shoulders back. This will enable the spiral of energy to rise strongly.

2. In position two, the feet are about shoulder width apart. Raise your arms slowly and smoothly to shoulder height. See and feel your body expanding and stretching. At this point, you are filling up two-dimensional space.

3. In position three, the arms are again lowered and one leg is placed in front of the other. The heel of one foot just crosses the ankle of the other. This initiates and activates the energy spiral for the creation of intersecting space and dimensions.

4. In position four, the spiral of energy is extended, pulled upward, and strengthened. The feet are separated a little more, by a distance that is comfortable for you to stretch and point the front foot forward. Point it forward and draw it back, heel to ankle. Feel the spiral draw up and soften as you do.

5. In position five, the spiral is pulled all the way up and tight around the entire body. The heel of the front foot is placed against the big toe of the back foot. With the arms raised and curved up, the spiral is drawn more tightly around the body. With the arms remaining in a shallow curve, the spiral rises more gently and not as tightly around the body.

Experiment with these exercises. Pause after each position. Feel the energy and space around you as you do. Be aware of the spiral energy as it is activated and rises up and down. With practice you will learn to recognize it and control it whether you use these stances or the two more natural ones described below. Whichever you use, visualize yourself standing in the center of a vortex of energy, about to release it through the dance in a determined manner.

These ballet positions can be very unnatural to the untrained body. Turning the feet out can actually cause imbalance. A more natural way of standing for initiating dance/ movement in ritual and magic is by using an open stance, as in modern dance and in the martial arts. Two of these more natural stances are depicted in the photographs on the following page. These two positions will not change the magical intent of the movement; rather they will reinforce the simplicity and ease of the ritual movement. They are effective for those who may be less flexible.

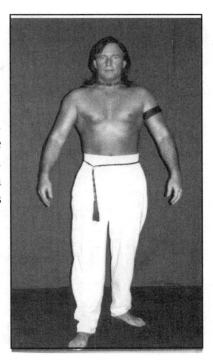

The first position is an open stance. One foot is placed straight forward and one is back and angled at no more than 45 degrees. They should not be on the same line with each other, but should be six inches to a shoulder's width apart.

The second is a simple parallel stance. Both feet are placed about shoulder-width apart, with toes directly straight. This activates a strong sense of balance and stability. With a slight angling, there is an ability to move with ease. Most often, the simpler and smoother the movements and postures are, the more effective they will be. Remember, the significance you give your movements is the most important aspect of magickal dance and shapeshifting.

Shapeshifting
Exercise
(experiential)

The Phoenix Rising

Skills & Benefits:

- **stimulates dream activity**
- **strengthens the astral body for travel**
- **invites healing and resolution of past issues**
- **improves communication with animals**
- **initiates rebirth in some area of your life**

The phoenix is the great bird of rebirth. Like its companions the unicorn, dragon and tortoise, the phoenix is a mixture of different animals and its significance is quite complex. In China, the phoenix was married to the dragon. The phoenix was female and represented the empress, while the dragon was male and represented the emperor. It is the sacred animal that rules all of the creatures that are feathered.

In the western world, the phoenix is the bird that sacrificed itself to fire and then rose from its own ashes. It is found often within western myth and lore. In Egypt it was linked to the worship of the sun god Ra who died every night and was born again the next morning. In Christianity, it is a symbol of the death and resurrection of Jesus. Many legends and myths contain common threads that link heroes to this creature. The hero lives a long life, and then the phoenix appears either just before or just after the hero's death. The hero is thus born again.

The phoenix is the symbol of the sun and resurrection, of life after death. It is a symbol of the immortal soul, love and eternal youth. In its form as the peacock, it is a guardian of the forest for the unicorn and sacred beasts.

For many people, the phoenix is one of the easiest of the fantastic creatures to encounter in Nature. Myrrh is a fragrance that is drawing to it, as well as signaling its presence. When the early morning sun is at its peak or at that time when the last of the evening sun can be seen are also great times to seek it out. Coincidentally, these are times when the pheasant is more active and about, and the pheasant is one of the animal forms that the phoenix will take upon occasion.

A phoenix encounter always heralds a time of new beginning, of new life. In our search for our true magical and spiritual essence, a phoenix encounter can signal the beginning of success in that Holy Quest.

Preparation for the Exercise

Most animals in nature have had dances associated with them. It was a powerful way of aligning with and invoking the energy and essence of the animal. This had many healing and magical applications. This practice also involved the creatures that most think of as mythical or fantastic.

The movements and postures of creatures, real and fantastic, are a source of great power in the East. They are incorporated into the martial arts, spiritual dances and celebrations, sexual activities and a variety of mystical healing practices.

Part of the purpose of all the exercises in shapeshifting involves learning to shift awareness more consciously from the physical to the spiritual. For this to occur, we must develop the right muscles and energy states. This exercise works strongly on both aspects.

In this exercise, you will use the posture for the phoenix to awaken its energies in your life. It will also help you to attune more to animals and to recognize the presence of nature spirits. It will strengthen healing of the entire body. It will help eliminate blockages and free up energy. It helps open all aspects of the natural world because the phoenix was one of the four sacred beasts – along with the dragon, unicorn and turtle. This exercise will assist you in any work with animals, especially in understanding their communications.

This exercise energizes the astral body so that it can be used as a separate vehicle of consciousness. As we will learn in Part II, there are ways in which we can take the form of an animal to travel out of the body or to move within the dream world. This exercise helps develop a readiness for this practice. It also assists in developing lucid dreaming and an awareness of out-of-body experiences. When performed before sleep, it can stimulate dreams that show us where people and situations are tying us down and where transition is needed in order to free our more creative aspects.

This exercise is also beneficial for stimulating dreams that reveal past issues we have not fully dealt with and resolved. It can awaken dreams that you had in your youth and had forgotten. It stirs long forgotten memories so that we can see their effects upon who we are now. It can stimulate dreams that show old issues playing themselves out in our present life. This is going to be a time of examination, a time to discover how to resurrect yourself through shapeshifting your energies.

1. Make all of your preliminary preparations, as discussed previously in this chapter.

2. Pause and move into the pose of the phoenix that is depicted.
See and feel yourself becoming the phoenix. See and feel its energies of rebirth awakening within you and your life. Imagine all that is manifesting for you as a result of this exercise. Hold, visualizing all that it represents for you.

The Phoenix Pose

Raise the arms sideways to shoulder level, palms down. The right knee is raised at the same time, while the left heel is lifted off the floor. Then lower the arms and legs back down. Repeat. Raise the arms up, but this time, the left knee is lifted and the right heel is off the ground. Repeat the entire cycle three times (right, left, right, left, right, and left). Keep your movements slow and smooth. Imagine yourself as the phoenix rising from the ashes and taking flight through infinite space. See your life moving forward.

3. After performing the posture, sit and focus on relaxing.

For this exercise you may wish to sit so that a candle burns at eye level before you. This is often more effective if you are still having difficulty with visualization. It is extremely effective when performed in front of a fireplace.

Focus upon the candle flame in front of you. See it dance and shimmer, creating form after form after form. Its light and energy is hypnotic and comforting in the darkness.

See before yourself a circle of fire. The flames dance and twist, each seeming to have a life and purpose of its own. You can feel the warmth it generates, and the flames create a myriad of shadows and shapes upon the walls surrounding you.

You watch the shadows. Memories are very much like shadows. You know they are there. They are a part of you and your surroundings, but they dance about you, haunting you at times.

You begin to reflect upon major incidents in your life. They begin to replay themselves within your mind. Some are the important incidents, and some you remember as trivial. Then you realize that because they are memories and have come to mind, they have also created change within your life.

You examine several of these. You think back to the time prior to the incidents. You remember how you were feeling, what you were doing and who was a part of your life then. You see these incidents occurring, interrupting those other energy patterns. As the flames dance, almost mocking you, you see and feel how you were never quite the same again. You understand that anything that created an emotional or mental response in you changed you by becoming a part of your very fabric.

As you review these incidents, the shadows upon the walls grow larger, as if taking on a life of their own. They are the ghosts of your past. They are the shadows of events that changed you in great and small ways. And they still haunt you.

You wonder how things would have - might have - turned out differently had you responded differently to those situations. If only you had only had some guidance. If only you had done something different. If only... You realize that you could "if only" yourself forever. It would not change a thing. You stare into the flames, and they continue their mocking dance.

Suddenly they calm. The flames are no longer dancing and mocking. They shift, pulling away from the center, creating a circle around a black hole. A single, yellow flame appears in the middle of the blackness. It shoots up a column of golden light that pushes back all shadows within the room. A sound builds with the light, until a roar fills the entire room and vibrates every cell of your being.

Then with a blinding flash, the column of light disappears. Where the column once stood there is now a beautiful golden Phoenix, the mythical being of light. Out of the ashes of the fire it rises up before you. The fires are gone and the room shines with crystalline light. You shrink back a little at its intensity. As if in response to you, the lights surrounding the Phoenix soften.

It fixes you with a stare and its voice fills your head in a manner that makes it impossible to determine if the sound is from without or from within. As the words echo within your mind, the plumage shimmers and changes colors, each more brilliant than the next.

"There is no 'if only'. We live our life and we grow from it. There are no right or wrong decisions or choices. Yes, some are easier than others, but all bring growth. All choices are gifts, gifts which create and shape you. You wish for guidance. What you wish for is someone or something to choose for you, to decide for you. Even no decision is a decision and even this will shift your life into certain patterns.

"The gift of experience is the gold of alchemy. It should be your guidance. It enables us to mold and shape and alters who we are and where we go. It alone provides true discernment.

"I am your mirror. You are seeing yourself in me. The Phoenix does not exist without you, for it lives within you. As you learn to see the Phoenix within you, as you learn to form the Phoenix about you, its energy will guard and guide you. You too will then rise from the ashes of your past to take flight within the heavens."

The Phoenix shifts and shimmers, and where it stood, there now stands a mirror. It reflects your image. As you gaze into the mirror, the outline of the golden Phoenix overlays your own image and you feel old fires of inspiration coming to life within you.

"As you come to recognize me in all that you do and have done, you will see the gold by which you can shape the future and mold yourself anew." The image of the Phoenix disappears, followed by the mirror. In the circle of flame now lies a golden egg. You extend your hand through the flames, reaching for it. The flames are warm and give off light, but its fire does not bum. It is something you know you must meditate upon.

As you lift the egg, the circle of flames contracts and begins to dance and bum as it did initially. In the light of the fire you examine the gift. It really is a golden egg. In exquisite detail, it is engraved and set with jewels. It is an engraving of a Phoenix, rising forth out of the fires of life. It feels warm and smooth, and it causes a tingling to run up your arms and through your body. "Out of the egg comes new life. Out of experience comes anything you desire yourself to be, anytime you desire to be!"

As the words echo within your mind, the fire melts down. There is only the initial candle that you lit. You are left to your own inner fires and to the Phoenix that resides within the heart of you.

4. Perform the phoenix pose once more to ground yourself and release the energies of the exercise into your life.

5. Follow this with the usual grounding as discussed earlier.

Chapter Three

The
Forgotten Key

The most often neglected aspect in the realm of magic is sacred movement and dance. It is a forgotten key that is essential to the success of many magical and spiritual endeavors. Dance itself is one of the most ancient and powerful forms of magical ritual. It is a dynamic tool for awakening and stirring the subtle forces and energies of life. True sacred dance and movement is a means of focusing and directing spiritual or magical consciousness through physical behavior. It is an outer expression of the inner spirit. And in the art of shapeshifting, sacred dance and movement is critical to success.

Now this doesn't mean that those of us with two and three left feet are out of luck when it comes to shapeshifting. Magickal dance can be performed by anyone. No formal training is required to utilize the powerful effects of sacred movement. Dances for higher states of consciousness are simple, individual, and passionate. They do not require great space because when a dance pattern is created for specific effects, it will also create an illusion of great space, power, and time. It is simply a matter of imbuing movement with greater significance and focus. It is not the talent that invokes the energy but rather the participation.

Dance and movement is natural to the universe. Plants will move in graceful and rhythmic ways. They turn to face the sun; they wave in a breeze; they grow in spirals and other exquisite forms. Birds have their own movements and dance, spreading their wings and plumage in magnificent displays of courtship or strength. All animals have unique dances as well to show strength, aggression, or just high-spirited fun.

The human body is designed for movement. Movement is as natural and as important to life as breathing. Like breathing, it fills us with energy.

It enables us to transcend our usual perceptions and consciousness. Movement balances, heals, awakens, and energizes. It generates psychic energy for strength, for enlightenment, shapeshifting, for life, and even for death.

In the modern world, the magickal power in dance has been diminished. Actual energies are created and awakened in all forms of dance, even in modern social settings. In these, magnetic energies are stimulated, but the result is a touching of the romantic rather than the sacred realms. Many of the ancient societies stressed continual watchfulness and control over dance energies. They recognized a therapeutic and an educational value to dance, but they focused upon its sacred aspect. They knew that the male and female participants were not just dancers; rather, by dancing, they became priests and priestesses.

Magickal dance is a means of transcending our humanity. Through it, you can gain control over normally automatic responses by evoking lower emotions and energies and then channeling them through the dance. Magickal dance is an art that fires our vitality, revives depleted energies, and awakens individual creativity and improvisational abilities. And it is the forgotten key to shapeshifting.

All human activity is a dance ritual, but we still must learn new approaches to it. Non-believers and non-participants will never understand the true ritual power of dance. For these individuals, the magickal dance will be little more than a window display. The dervishes will only be entertainers. The Catholic mass becomes little more than a spectacle. We must remember that religious ritual of any kind is not, and should never be, performed for its own sake. This may be the primary problem with the weekly mass. Ritual - especially magical and shapeshifting dance rituals – should be performed as a way of reaching another level of consciousness or being. It should be a way of releasing spiritual meaning into our lives. We must participate in and become the priests and priestesses or shamans of the dance ritual.

Our participation in magickal dance requires us to remember that energies are not created by the dance but simply invoked and challenged by it. We must remember that the energies function less through our talent for dancing than through our participation! Thus, anyone who can move any part of his or her body can participate in magickal dance, even if only through the flickering of eyes or the rhythm of breath.

Magickal Dance Yesterday and Today

In our recent history, we find sacred dancing taking place within churches and temples. Earlier groups created dance temples by marking off sacred circles for the dance on the Earth herself. One common theme was the imitation of angels dancing in heavenly rings around the throne of God. This led to many of the circle dances.

Sacred and magickal dancing has been a functioning part of every society and civilization throughout the world. The shamans and priests/priestesses used music and dance to induce trance states. In all of the dances, intense feelings and bodily movements were related. In many cases, such as in the ancient Kachina rites, the participants became reflections of different powers in the universe.

A basic premise behind esoteric teachings around the world is that we all are a microcosm - a reflection or miniature of the macrocosm or universe. We have all the energies of the universe within us. Sacred dance was a means of stimulating them and bringing them into expression from the deeper levels of our consciousness.

The Kachina dancers used round or circle dances to imitate the path of the sun. Chain dances were used to link male and female energies, to stimulate fertility, and to bind Heaven and Earth. There were thread-and-rope dances, as with the threads of Ariadne, threads that lead the dancer to the secret knowledge within the maze of life. And there were dances of transformation.

The power of movement and dance was even infused into the martial arts, especially in the Eastern world. A kata is a series of movements in the martial arts. While some interpret it as a combat discipline, it can also be seen as a martial arts dance. A kata can be translated as "how one behaves" or a "moving book." The practitioner, in more ancient times, would record what he learned in a sequence of moves. The outer form expressed an inward movement or purpose.

In Kung Fu the forms and movements are based upon animals - praying mantis, hawk, eagle, a tiger, etc. This facilitated the study of nature and helped attune the student to animal aspects of Nature. The mimicking and imitating of animals will be explored more fully later in the book.

In the Ninja tradition, postures and hand poses have great significance. The Ninja could generate power based on the mystical idea of redirecting the intrinsic energy of nature through their hands. Each hand and finger symbolizes an intrinsic force and attribute of the body.

In India, the sacred dancing girls, or devadasis, were married to the gods. Their dances represented the life of the god to whom they were married. Ancient Egypt was also a great dancing center. The importance of dance to the ancient Egyptians is illustrated in the hieroglyphs, where dancers are extensively depicted. The Egyptian love for dance was widely felt throughout the ancient world. The Cadiz, the sacred dancing school in Spain, was another great center of ancient dancing and was Egyptian in character.

The Greek and the Roman mystery schools were strong in dance ritual. Dance, along with music, formed an essential part of the magical and healing arts in the Orphic, Eleusinian, and Bacchic mysteries. The snakelike winding of the Greek farandole dance of Provence symbolized the journey to the middle of the labyrinth - the pattern of the passage of the dead to the land of the afterlife. This journey was a common theme in many areas of the world.

Sacred dance revolves around themes and patterns that stimulate multiple responses. A dance for higher states of consciousness is simple, personal, and passionate - fusing the mind and body. The degree to which energy is invoked is determined by the participation and the significance associated with the movement. Every gesture and movement must be symbolic. The more meaning we attach to movement, the greater the release of power - the greater the shapeshifting.

Sacred dance helps us to transcend our humanity. The transcendental aspect of dance has been neglected for centuries, yet each of us has the ability to re-awaken it. Magical dance is more than just a symbolic expression of an

individual's personal beliefs. At the root of most ceremonial use of dance is sympathetic magic. The movements and gestures create thoughtforms, vortices of energy. The fusion of thought and action manifests a particular pattern of energy in the physical realm.

Throughout the rest of this book, you will awaken your own creative energies through dance and movement specific to the art of shapeshifting. The exercises and dynamics in this book are only a foundation. They are starting points. Do not allow the movements to become rote and always allow for individual expression and variation. As you do, you will find yourself dancing the Tree of Life, which joins Heaven and Earth within you.

The dancer celebrates life.

Understanding How It Works

The purpose of all physical, ritual behavior is to direct and focus the consciousness. Humans have a unique ability to block their own growth process. Directed physical behavior, such as dance, can help us overcome this tendency. It aligns our physical responses and energies with our spiritual goals and helps us maintain contact with the higher forces of life.

Dance links the hemispheres of the brain, joining the intuitive and the rational. Every movement and gesture creates electrical changes in the body and the mind. Through magickal dance, the movements and their essence are experienced on subtler levels. The central nervous system and the neuro-muscular systems transform musical rhythms into a movement pattern. We can become driven by it and led away from our traditional perceptions of the world. In the past, individuals would surrender to these rhythms and be possessed by them. Examples of this can be found within the Voudon religions of the Caribbean. Today, we must learn to ride the rhythms in full consciousness to those inner worlds.

Frequently, the student of the metaphysical and psychic world will have difficulty achieving tangible results through mere meditation. Often individuals will sit to meditate, but they may still be thinking of that last phone call, the argument with the boss, or troubles with the kids. These kinds of mundane energies can block our higher perceptive abilities. Physical movements enable a person to move from outer world consciousness, with all of its hassles and distractions, to the inner world more fluidly.

Working with the physical movements will deliver results more quickly and effectively than passive meditation. Movement creates electrical changes in the body and mind, which facilitate the accessing of subtle energies. Physical activity causes the mind to shift gears. It has to concentrate

on the movements and gestures. The postures, positions, movements, and gestures throughout this book will help you make transitions from the outer to the inner world, and back again, more easily and effectively.

Some physical movements, gestures and postures stimulate different levels of consciousness. And there are some which even activate celestial energies, drawing them more emphatically into play within the physical realm. We can learn to use these movements and postures to create a mind-set that enables easier access to these energies.

Gestures, postures, and movements express the inexpressible. They utilize both aspects of the brain, especially when we imbue them with significance. The more meaning we ascribe to them, the more empowered they become. They are direct, potent ways of communicating with the divine forces operating around us and within us. They aid us in concentration, so we can manifest our highest capacities.

All dance is gesture, and we each have gestures that are uniquely our own. They give us color and individuality. Gesture links the outer person with the inner and serves to bridge us to our more divine aspects. They can also link us to our totems and animal guardians. For gesture and movement to become empowered, they must be consciously directed and infused with significance.

The Eastern world has recognized the spiritual value of movement for ages. Fortunately, there is a growing integration of Eastern and Western philosophies and techniques. We can apply some Eastern methods of movement specifically to Western forms of magic and mysticism. The Eastern yoga movements and postures are simply outer expressions, stimulating and representing inner degrees of consciousness.

Yoga asanas are designed to be meditations themselves, leading to greater depths of energy. Applying them to Western mystical and magickal traditions reinforces the idea that there truly is nothing new under the sun. There are simply different variations. All gods are aspects of the same god, and we each have the responsibility of finding the methods or combination of methods which will most effectively awaken the divine within ourselves.

In yoga, kriya is a movement, asana, mudra, or exercise to produce an altered state of consciousness. There is an outer kriya which involves asanas and mudras (postures and gestures) - basic physical expressions, as well as an inner aspect. When we learn to dance magically – especially in shapeshifting, we are using an outer form to express an inner energy. We learn to apply physical expressions to inner realities. These physical movements awaken and draw out our inner spiritual energies. Different movements will activate different energies - whether they are intuitive, creative, protective, healing or shapeshifting.

Postures are a way of physically communicating with the divine within us. As we will see in Part Three, many postures and movements arose from a ritual mimicking of animals and Nature to establish a magical contact with its forces. Different postures and movements will activate different energies and forces. Learning to combine, control, and direct the forces and energies through dance is an individually creative process. Movement is basic to our body's shape and function. Dance allows the body to worship. Magickal dance releases tremendous power. It intoxicates you and helps you become more aware of where your body is in a given space and time. Movement will stimulate a tangible awareness that the body houses the divine spirit.

Make the most of these exercises. Keep in mind the following points throughout them:

1. Allow for individual expression and variation while performing the exercises.

2. Do not allow the exercises to become rote. Imbue your magical dance and movements with greater significance and power each time you use them.

3. Keep your movements simple and fluid.

4. Shapeshifting dance movements are tremendously empowering to meditations when performed before and after the meditation.

5. The more we work with the movements, the easier they become, and the more energy is released to us.

The Key to Magic is Movement

All traditions had a means of using movement to invoke and manifest energy for various purposes - including shapeshfting. In Eastern traditions, it is the power of kundalini that is awakened through yoga. In the ancient Hawaiian tradition of Huna, it is called mana. In Asia, it is called chi or ki - developed most often through the martial arts. This energy is called psychic energy by modern metaphysicians. Every mystical tradition used movement to move, direct and shift the energy of themselves and the world around them.

Occult Significance of the Body in Shapeshifting

Dance and movement actualizes energy. Magical dance – especially in shapeshifting – is the art of ritual and ceremonial movement, which has the power to unite body and spirit. In other words, it is the catalyst for the shapeshifting of energies. Anyone participating in shapeshifting must begin to recognize the body as a medium for invoking and expressing energies, keeping in mind what he or she wishes to express with the body. Shapeshifting movement must be approached in a manner that facilitates the union of body and spirit, the linking of human and nature. With dance and movement in shapeshifting, we induce energy changes along specific definable avenues. We invoke and direct very subtle, yet very real changes within our energy system by using movements.

Our body has much greater significance than what we often imagine. And understanding this is an important element to a successful shapeshifting. All energies upon the Earth and those of the heavens play themselves out through our body. Seeing the body as more than just a physical instrument that enables you to move around during the day is crucial to empowering yourself and especially your shapeshiftings.

Remember that the body is a microcosm. It is a universe of energies unto itself. It reflects the greater energies of the universe, the macrocosm. This does not infer that we are just a part of the universe; rather, we are a miniature of the universe.

This means that our hands are not just instruments for grabbing and holding. Our legs are not just for standing and walking. Our hearts are not just for pumping blood. Every part of our body has significance much greater than its physical responsibilities. They are instruments of greater power, a power and significance that are often hidden (occult). They are the points through which the energies of the universe flow - energies which can be manifested dynamically in our daily lives.

Our spirit has access to the entire universe and all of its forces. The physical form is an embodiment of our spirit. Thus, it must use the physical form to reconnect with those universal energies. It does so through the various organs, centers, and activities of the human body. Through magickal dance and movement, we awaken ourselves to the hidden forces which play upon our lives on subtle levels.

When it comes to shapeshifting, three parts of the body are most significant for initiating the changes we seek: the legs, hands and eyes.

The Legs

The legs have powerful significance. They represent our ability to progress and evolve. The fact that we stand erect indicates much about our evolutionary status in relationship to other animals. The legs symbolize lifting and raising ourselves higher. They symbolize movement into new realms.

Legs are also symbols for the pillars in the Great Tree of Life. The tree is an ancient symbol, representing things that grow, things that are fertile and new life in general. To some it is the world axis; to others it is the world itself. Its roots are within the Earth and its upper branches extend toward the Heavens – bridging the two worlds. In shapeshifting, we are moving into a new expression of energy. We are bridging our old energy with something new.

Assuming the position of the Tree of Life at the end of a shapeshifting or any meditation is a means of empowering it. The Tree of Life pose is a physical affirmation of the energies of the Heavens being channeled through you and into your activities upon the Earth.

Stand with your legs firmly on the ground. Place your feet shoulder width apart. Imagine and feel as if roots are extending down through them, out the soles of your feet, and into the heart of the Earth. Feel yourself being anchored and attuned to all the Earth's energies and rhythms.

Now, slowly and deliberately, extend your arms up over your head. Visualize them as branches, extending up toward the stars. Imagine and feel yourself becoming the great Tree of Life, with your roots in the Earth and your upper branches in the Heavens. Feel the energies of both realms flowing through you and empowering you. Imagine and know that you will bear great fruit and will grow stronger and fuller each moment thereafter. You have become the Tree of Life!

The Hands

The hands are one of our most expressive tools. We can use them to grip and to release. We use them to caress and to fight. They are symbols for giving and taking. They reflect many of our physical, emotional, mental, and spiritual characteristics.

The sciences of reflexology and palmistry focus on the hand and its powerful characteristics. Reflexology, in part, involves understanding that there are points on the hand that are tied into every organ and system in the body. Most of the body's energy pathways, or meridians, terminate at the fingers. Palmistry is the study of what the shapes, lines, and mounds of the hands and fingers indicate about a person physically, emotionally, mentally, and spiritually.

Hand movements and gestures are important to magical dance and shapeshifting. The hands are sometimes referred to as the true universal language. From signing for the deaf to the expressiveness of the hula dancer, the hands and fingers are a dynamic tool of communication with others and with higher aspects of our own consciousness. Learning to position the hands in various shapes and forms will activate certain kinds of energy patterns around us.

To the ancient Hermeticists, every action had a specific purpose and significance. Our hand gestures should have their own significance and should be associated with a specific dance. There should be no purposeless movement. The ancient practitioners of ritual and high magic used specific hand postures even when stationary. Refer to the chart, Dances for Hands, for a few examples. Later, we will learn to use the hand gestures of various animals to assist us in aligning with and manifesting that animal's energies more dynamically within our lives.

Hand Postures of the Odissi Temple

Positioning the palms of the hands is a simple and common way of directing energy in magickal dance. Three common hand postures in the Odissi temple dances were:

1. Palms up with the sides of the hands touching as if preparing to cup, a symbol of the yoni or feminine energies
2. A fist resting on the open palm of the other hand with the thumb of the fist pointing straight up, a symbol of the lingam or masculine energies
3. The hands in prayer position, a symbol of obedience to the higher.

In general, when the hands are held with palms up you become more receptive to outside energies. This position activates the feminine aspects within you-intuition, creative imagination, and illumination. The palms downward indicate more of an activating flow of energy. It stimulates the masculine aspects within you-the assertive, strengthening, and directing forces. Palms up activates form; palms down activates force. Form and force together, one palm up and the other down, creates a stress for growth.

When our palms are down, the energy radiates outward from the hands. When the palms are up, the energy is drawn in through the hands more easily. When alternated with one palm up and the other down, the flow of energy through and around the individual is balanced and more easily handled.

Experiment with different hand movements and gestures. Feel the differences. Experiment with the way you hold your hands around other people. Pay attention to the way they respond. Our hands are tools for magickal communication.

Dances for Hands

Fires energy outward.

Sends love and protects.

Palm Up—receptivity.
Palm Down—Activating and sending energy.

Closes aura to outside influence.Calms and balances.

Strengthens, used to gain power.

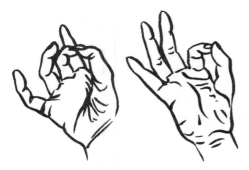

Activates specific energies during meditation.

The Eyes

There are powerful ways we can dance with our eyes. They have been called the windows of the soul, and they are symbolic of vision and power. Focusing the eyes on the tip of the nose stills the eyes and the mind. This allows vision to be turned inward, stimulating clairvoyance.

The eyes reflect and project inner states of energy. In Tantra, the four predominant gazes, or ways of using the eyes to direct energy, are petrifying, subduing, overthrowing, and conjuring. In the petrifying gaze, the eyes look toward the tip of the nose while the breath remains relaxed and motionless. In the subduing gaze, the eyes look to the left while the breath is inhaled. In the overthrowing gaze, the eyes are turned upward while the breath is exhaled. In the conjuring gaze, the two eyes are turned to the right and slightly upward while holding the breath. It is also a very seductive gaze.

Practice these gazes on people around you and watch their reactions. This will tell you much about the energy that can be directed by eye dances. Then try to incorporate them into your magickal dance ritual as well.

Owls have always had great mysticism about them. Their ability to blink by closing the upper eyelids like humans gives them a human expression and has added to their mysticism. They can, in fact, blink both eyes and each eye singly. In my work with owls, I have found that repeating their blinks back to them helps calm them and establishing some rapport with them. There is a theory that they communicate with others of their species partly through the blinking patterns.

Other Body Part Significances

HEAD	Higher mind; place of heaven
MOUTH	Power of speech; the creative word; creativity and destruction
BONES	The support system; structure of the universe; seeds of life; resurrection
SKIN	Protection and higher sensory system; rebirth
ARMS	The ability to embrace and hold life experiences; activity
FEET	Support and uprightness in movement
HEART	The seat of the soul; center of love and healing; the sun
BREASTS	Nurturing; mothering; nourishment
LUNGS	The ability to experience and enjoy life; freedom
STOMACH	Assimilation of experiences and ideas
SEX ORGANS	The creative life force; the perpetuation of life; the cosmic forces
HIPS/BUTTOCKS	Balancing; sexuality; power

Heavenly Associations with the Body

Planetary Associations

SUN	Heart, back
MOON	Stomach, breasts, digestion
MERCURY	Hands, arms, nervous system, solar plexus
VENUS	Throat, voice, loins, veins, kidneys
MARS	Head, sex organs, muscular system
JUPITER	Hips, thighs, liver
SATURN	Skeletal system, knees, teeth
URANUS	Ankles, shins, cerebrospinal system
NEPTUNE	Feet
PLUTO	Generative organs

Atrological Signs

ARIES	Head, face
LIBRA	Kidneys, ovaries
TAURUS	Neck, throat
SCORPIO	Sex organs
GEMINI	Hands, lungs
SAGITTARIUS	Hips, thighs
CANCER	Breasts, stomach
CAPRICORN	Knees
LEO	Heart
AQUARIUS	Ankles, calves
VIRGO	Intestines
PISCES	Feet

Elements of Shapeshifting Dance

Shapeshifting is a gesture of the whole body, which allies the body with the soul for specific purposes. It is the becoming of energy - not just becoming conscious of energy. Shapeshifting movements induce electrical changes in the body, which induces specific states of consciousness. When we employ dance in the shapeshifting process, we are using purposeful physical behavior to activate real energies.

For dance to be magickal, we must learn to move with intent. Dancing compliments the intent and grounds our energy so that we can more fully experience it. We can then more easily integrate and apply it to aspects of our life.

Each hemisphere of the brain possesses its own abilities and each provides access to a force we can learn to use. When the two forces of hemispheres are integrated, they create a third force that we can access. It is a force that goes beyond personal expression by aligning our personal energies with the rhythms and forces of the universe. This force can be effectively manifested through dance. But for dance shapeshifting movements to work their magic, we must learn to employ five predominant elements - Centering, Balance, Posture and Gesture, Space, and Creative Imagination. They are fully described below.

Centering

Centering is the ability to activate, move, control, and direct energies around a central focal point. Most of the time, the energy is activated around us. We are the center of the universe. All the energies will play themselves out uniquely within our lives. Learning to maintain focus is crucial to employing magickal and shapeshifting dance. If we are scattered in our focus, our movements will also be scattered. This, in turn, will bring chaotic and unpredictable energy into our lives.

Part of the centering process occurs by paying attention to the preliminary preparations of magickal dance ritual or meditation. This includes determining the theme and purpose of the dance, taking a ritual bath, and properly incorporating fragrance, music, and costume. All of these preparations help focus and center the mind and the movement for the greatest magickal effect. These preparations will be elaborated upon in Part Three.

Balance

Balance is not just an ability to stand posed on one leg without falling over. It is the relationship between the inner and outer. It is maintaining harmony and recognizing that the outer movement reflects the inner realities and those outer realities will affect inner movements.

View balance as a circle. There are outer and inner parts to the circle. Without one or the other, there is no circle, so there is no balance. This is why the circle and circle dances are so powerful and effective in ritual. They not only create a point of sacred space, but they also awaken a perception of inner and outer balance.

Balance is movement, it is active. We are constantly exposed to situations which test our ability to maintain balance. Dance forces us to move, shifting energies into new patterns, all within the circle of our own essence.

Posture and Gesture

Posture and gesture not only reveal our feelings, but they will produce them as well. This is especially important to understand when we apply posture and gesture for magickal and mystical purposes. If we have poor posture, we are unable to move and we become less flexible in our movements and in our thoughts.

Gestures not only reflect certain moods and energies but can activate them as well. Someone who stands with his or her arms folded across the chest is being very protective. Hands on the hips indicate a *show me* attitude. The palm of the hand held to the face expresses sympathy or concern, while curling that hand into a fist against the cheek indicates thoughtfulness.

Take a moment, close your eyes, and relax. Now place your fists on your hips and hold that position for thirty seconds to a minute. What are your mood and temperament like now? What does it make you think of? Now place the palm of your hand against the cheek? How does this make you feel? Do you notice that these gestures activate certain moods? Reading and studying books on body language will give you many ideas of how to incorporate gesture and posture into your magickal dance.

Space

Dance makes us aware of the *space* in which we move. Magickal dance in shapeshifting doesn't require great space, nor should it. In part, magickal dance creates an illusion of great space, time, and power manifested within the area of your movement. Humans have a tendency to view things from a limited perspective. We rarely think about the space where we move and act out our lives.

Space is not just empty air. It is the element we move through, just as water is the tangible element that a fish moves through. Periodically, see yourself performing activities in the space around you as if the space was not just empty air but was a tangible element such as water. Walk across the room consciously, as if you are walking through water. Try to sense what the space feels like. As you learn to see yourself consciously moving through space, you open your perceptions to the more ethereal energies and beings that share that space with us.

Creative Imagination

Creative imagination is essential to opening the doors to spiritual energies and beings and should be used in conjunction with dance. We talked about it in the previous chapter, but it is important to repeat here. Creative imagination is the ability of the mind to create images and scenes associated with a seed thought, purpose, or idea. You should visualize these images in a three-dimensional form.

Creative imagination, when used with shapeshifting, places the shapeshifter into a scenario or essence that helps him/her release a specific kind of energy. This can be as simple as a visualization of you in an ideal magickal image or body. It can also take the form of a highly concentrated daydream or actual dream, in which you become absorbed into the framework of the unfolding scenes. Through movement, the shapeshifter is immersed in energy beyond the physical realm.

Dancing with creative imagination involves seeing yourself with the ability to touch all worlds through movement. You are the dancer at the gateway of all dimensions. With the right movements and visualizations you can enter and exit all of them.

Employing the creative imagination in shapeshifting dance facilitates our journey beyond the normal sensory world. We create a new awareness, a new kind of experience relating to this world. As we imbue our movements with proper imagery and significance, we empower them to gain entrance into the spiritual realms. We assume a union with those realms and find a new expression of our soul power within our lives.

Ghost Dance

Dancing always
calls the spirits.

It jiggles and frees the soul.
Spirits hear this
and
becoming curious,
they draw close.

And when we dance
to the animals,
their spirits respond
and
they come to us
as well.

Shapeshifting Exercise (developmental)

Two-Week Enhancer

Skills & Benefits:

- **develops sensitivity to changing energies**
- **improves control of shifts in the body**
- **develops flexibility in thought and in energy**
- **enhances focus and concentration**

This may seem like one of the easiest exercises, but it is one of the most important. And if done correctly and consistently, it will make all of the other shapeshifting rituals and meditations more powerful with quicker results.

Different postures and different body positions alter the energy inside of us and surrounding us. Learning to recognize subtle shifts created by postures and movement is a skill that must be developed by all shapeshifters. The easiest way of developing the ability to recognize and initiate energy changes is by using four foundation positions.

These positions are effective to use anywhere in magickal dances to help assimilate and shift energy more effectively. They help us to focus and release the raised energy so it can work for us.

Remember that these positions are guidelines. The important factor that we will stress throughout this book is to imbue every activity and posture with significance. Through the physical movements, gestures, and postures, we are learning to transcend the physical world to link with the spiritual world.

Sitting or Resting

The first position is the *Sitting* or *Resting* position. This is a position of outer quiet with great inner activity. This activity is the result of the energy stimulated by the dance. The dance stimulates inner levels of consciousness. This position is representative of the changing energy from one state to the next. It is a position of closure and receptivity. It is especially effective for absorbing the energy patterns created and released through the dance.

Kneeling

The second physical attitude is that of *Kneeling*. This position, when done on both knees, represents the human ascent toward divinity while still attached to the earth. When assumed on one knee, it indicates an increase in freedom, a partial resurrection through the divine energies stimulated by the dance.

Prostrate

The *Prostrate* position grounds the energies activated by the dance. With outstretched arms, it becomes serpentine, as in the Serpent of Wisdom, which dances around the Tree of Life. The prostrate position can also be semi-prostrate, as in the yoga position of the cat stretch. In this, the arms are outstretched and the knees are tucked under the body. Womb-like in appearance, the dancer gives birth to new energies through the dance. It is a position of personal negation - an acceptance of divine authority. It is also an excellent position to use when reaching for the purpose or bindu at the center of your sacred space.

Standing

Standing is the fourth physical attitude. This position signifies that we are now able to be upright, through the energies we invoked. We are now able to move. It signifies the emergence of light into the body and the manifestation of the magickal body. Both are accomplished through the energies of the dance. It is also symbolic of being able to move on to higher levels and achieve greater heights.

1. Begin by creating ten minutes of quiet time at some point in the day.
It can be anytime during the day as long as you give yourself approximately ten minutes. By performing this exercise for ten minutes everyday for two weeks, you will begin to feel the subtle shifts of energy in and around you with each change of position – stimulation, calm, excitement that occurs in response to the position. And you will also notice at times during the day – when you are not performing the exercise.

2. Take the sitting position.
Allow your eyes to close and relax. Feel yourself connected to the Earth. Allow your mind to quiet and just feel yourself calming. Feel the area around your calming as you become calmer yourself. Maintain for about two minutes.

3. Slowly shift into a kneeling position that is comfortable for you.
Feel your energy becoming less calm. Feel the building nudge to get moving and active. Your heart beats a little faster. The mind starts turning its wheels again. Pay attention to any emotions you feel. Feel the area around you shifting from a place of calmness to one of preparedness. Maintain this position for about two minutes.

4. Slowly shift into the prostrate position.
Lay flat on the ground with your arms outstretched. Imagine and feel yourself sinking a bit into the ground as if laying upon a foam cushion. Feel the heart slow down, the muscles untense. Feel the area around you shifting from that feeling of preparedness to one of safeness and groundedness. Pay attention to what your body feels and any emotional changes. Maintain this position for about two minutes.

5. Slowly roll to your side and then stand.
As you stand, keep your feet about shoulder width and arms at your side. Pay attention to how your body responds to standing. Mentally note the changes. Take a few deep breaths and pay attention to any emotions. Feel the area around you shifting from one of groundedness to one of preparing for activity. Sense your body shifting for activity. Maintain this position for about two minutes.

6. Make note of what you felt and then go on about your activities.
You may wish to jot down some responses to each position in your journal at this time. Then just go on about your regular activities. After two weeks of doing this simple observation technique, your awareness to energy shifts in you and around you will increase dramatically.

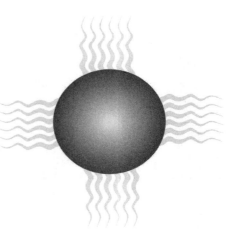

Shapeshifting
Exercise
(developmental & experiential)

The Sun and Moon Breath Dance

Skills & Benefits:
- **amplifies and balances energy**
- **directs energy with breath and movement**
- **heightens sensitivity to the aura**
- **strengthens your energy levels**

This meditative dance is taken partially from the oriental art of tai chi chuan and employs breathing techniques, called *the Sun and Moon Breaths.* This exercise will balance the hemispheres of the brain and will shorten study time. It heals and strengthens all systems of the body and is an effective tonic for recuperation after illnesses. It activates the heart chakra while balancing the male and female polarities of the body to stimulate creativity, fertility, and intuition.

Because we will incorporate movement with it, the effects are amplified. It will enable you to feel energy moving in and out of you. Through this exercise you begin to learn how you can control and direct energy in and around you.

1. Familiarize yourself with this exercise.
Choose incense or a color candle that is effective. Red and blue candles can be effective (red = masculine, blue = feminine). A rose fragrance is very effective.

2. Perform any of the balancing positions to harmonize yourself with it.

3. Calm and center yourself

4. The sun breath is a slow exhalation.
Extend the arms forward in front of the chest, with the palms facing outward.
By exhaling audibly, the energy level is increased. We are pushing the energy
of the inner sun (the heart) out into the auric field.

5. The moon breath is the inhalation.
Draw the arms and the energy into you with the palms facing inward.

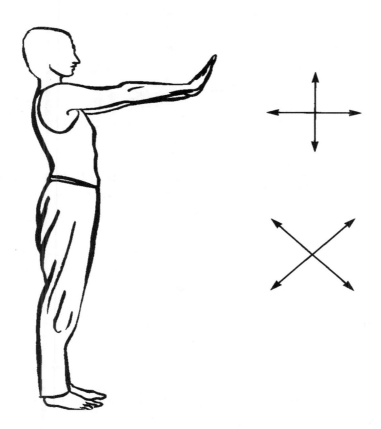

The Sun and Moon Breath

*As you exhale, slowly push your arms out in front of you. Now turn the palms
toward you, and as you inhale draw the arms slowly back and fold them across your
heart. Then repeat the movement up and down.*

*Next, the right arm is extended to the right and the left to the left as you exhale and
then drawn back together at the heart as you inhale. Then with arms moving in
unison, push one arm up at a diagonal and the other down at a diagonal as you
exhale. Then bring them back to the heart as you inhale.Then repeat in the opposite
direction. Visualize yourself as the Sun, radiating in all directions around you.*

6. On the inhalation, always bring both hands back to the heart or solar plexus area.
Take a few moments and practice both before using it in the meditation form. You will feel the energy moving out from you and drawing in through you. During the dance ritual, we will radiate this energy in six directions: forward, up, down, both sides, and the diagonals. It is performed using moves a - f. Keep your movements and breathing slow and deliberate.

a. Raise the arms up, pushing energy up, and out. Draw the arms back, inhaling and bringing the hands back to the heart.

b. Now push the arms and the energy down in front of the body, and then draw them back to the heart.

c. Next, the right arm is extended out to the right and the left arm is extended at the same time to the left. Inhale and bring both arms back to the heart area.

d. Now the arms are moved in a diagonal direction with the breathing. Let one arm push the energy up at a diagonal while the other pushes down at a diagonal. Draw them back together at the heart.

e. Then reverse the positions of the diagonals. The arm that moved down at a diagonal will now move in an upward, diagonal direction. The one that moved down will now move up. Move the arms in unison.

f. Finally, the arms are extended together in front of the body. Feel and see the sun inside you burst into brilliant light that radiates out in all directions around you. Draw the arms back with the hands together against the heart.

7. Take a few moments and feel the energy alive and vibrant in and around you.
See yourself as energized, healthy, and strong. Offer a prayer of thanksgiving or an affirmation.

8. Take several deep breaths, and then perform one of the balancing exercises so the energy you activate will manifest itself harmoniously.

Chapter Four

The Magical Body & Weaving Glamour

I t has been said that prayer is a state of heightened awareness and communication. I treat shapeshifting as a sacred process – like a very special prayer that unites us to the spirits of Nature – creating a state of heightened awareness and communication with some aspect of it.

All traditions taught at some time that the only way that the Divine – no matter how you define those Divine forces in the universe – could communicate with humans was through Nature. And the only way humans could understand what the Divine was trying to tell them about their lives was by studying Nature and connecting with her elements more directly. When we attach special significance to our movements, especially when attempting to touch and communicate with the Divine, we are praying through movement. These prayers can be simple or complicated, but their effects are dependent upon the import we attach to them. When we pray through movement, we are using all aspects of ourselves for growth and enlightenment. We are shapeshifting our consciousness to communicate with the Divine forces of the universe more effectively.

Working with shapeshifting is a creative process that serves as a means for transcending our ordinary humanity. It must involve body, mind and spirit. Without any one aspect of it, we will not succeed. Thus, movement must be joined with creative imagination and then linked to a particular purpose. The movements and postures help us to direct and focus our consciousness. They align physiological responses with our spiritual goals. They make the world of subtle energies and powers more physical. We develop control over normally automatic responses by evoking emotions

Awakening our Dormant Magic

Sacred movements enable us to move from the outer world and all of its hassles to the inner realm — where our dormant magic resides - much more easily. It creates a shifting in our normal mindset - a rebirth. The physical activity stimulates nerves that subtly cause the mind to shift gears. Gestures, postures and movements express the inexpressible. They utilize both aspects of the brain, especially when we are aware of their significance. They are direct and powerful ways of communicating with the Divine within us. They assist our concentration and they help us to ground the energies that we awaken. The postures and movements are kept simple throughout this book but do not let their simplicity mislead you into believing they are not effective. When we incorporate physical movements with shapeshifting imagery, the impact will be intensified. The movements employed throughout the rest of the book are designed to help you make that transition from the outer to the inner and back again more easily - to extend yourself into new realms.

and hidden magical potentials deep within us and then channeling them through the movement. We begin to re-express those less tangible energies upon the physical plane – using our own body as the medium for that expression. And the extraordinary begins to manifest. Shiftings in us and our life begin to occur.

We are physical beings, and as such, everything we experience must ultimately be expressed and experienced through the physical. When we incorporate physical movement and postures with shapeshifting imagery, we awaken archetypal energies and inner potentials to manifest them within some aspect of our lives. In this book, we are focusing primarily upon simple physical activities that enable us to invoke, activate, touch and express Nature's forces more powerfully – specifically the spirits of animals - but it has applications far beyond this.

Remember throughout that it is not the movement, but what we believe of the movement, that gives it power in the shapeshifting process. Physical movement with intention is freeing and strengthening. It awakens our bodies to the spiritual and magical within us, while freeing the spiritual and magical to nurture the body. In our daily life, our movements have no power or little direction and focus. When we dance our prayers - and shapeshifting is a form of prayer - we empower our lives. We begin to shapeshift out of the old and into the new.

Life brings many situations where it is necessary to use all aspects of ourselves to be truly successful. We must learn to shift and adapt as circumstances warrant. We become most magical in life when we recognize all of our aspects and the gifts that they add to our daily lives. Shapeshifting is learning to weave these aspects into our outer life circumstances. That is all well and good, but where do we begin though? Well, we begin by looking at ourselves a little differently. We begin by awakening the magical body and the magical essence that is the true us. While the previous activities and exercises begin to open us up to our possibilities and how to work with energy, awakening and developing the magickal body is the first major step toward you actually shapeshifting.

The Magical Body

One of the greatest benefits of working with techniques of shapeshifting is the creation and manifestation of the magical body. The magical body is the new, more conscious you that is created through the art of shapeshifting. When we work with the art of shapeshifting, we bring to life our inherent and unexpressed abilities. We transform that which we find less suitable, and we awaken our higher, more powerful selves. We awaken our innate abilities and begin to release them within our lives.

The magical body is the ideal you, with the ability to manifest and appear in the manner that is most powerful and most effective for you in your life or in a particular situation within your life. The magical body is a reflection of the divinity that is inherent within us. The magical body enables us to assume the manners and powers that are necessary for whatever the task may be. In order to do this, we must first have the energies, abilities and powers at hand. This is what shapeshifting helps us to accomplish.

Through shapeshifting, we create the new rather than change the old. This must be kept in mind at all times. Through shapeshifting, we turn our focus to the images and abilities of the ideal that exists within us - physically, emotionally, mentally and spiritually. And these images are strong, vital and flexible.

As we develop the art of shapeshifting, mind and matter become more malleable. In fact, the world becomes a canvas of ever shifting scenes, colors, and roles. We not only shape and color the world around us, but we also continually transform the role we play within those ever changing scenarios.

This is why shapeshifting begins with the creation of the magical body. What is the highest, brightest, most creative image of yourself that you can create? What characteristics could you have? What abilities and energies would you be able to express? How would you ideally like others to see you? How would being that way change your life at home and at work? If you could manifest those abilities now, what are some ways that you could use them so that no one would ever know? How would you be able to help others without them ever knowing? Imagine it, envision it, know that it can be real. *Remember that if we can imagine it, it can be! When you change your imaginings, you change your world!*

All energy follows thought and the more intense and focused that thought, the greater the energy becomes. The more you practice something, the better you get at it. It must be practiced! There are no short cuts. The more you practice anything, the easier it becomes. Just as muscles of the body will adapt to different exercises, so will our psychic, magical and spiritual "muscles" as well.

I liken it to learning to read. Anyone can be taught to read. Some may pick it up more easily, but everyone can do it. Regardless of the individual though, the basics must be learned. You must learn the alphabet, phonics and pronunciation. You must develop a basic, working vocabulary to become a functional reader - not a scholar, but functional! In modern society, a functional reader will have opportunities in life that may never open to one who is illiterate. The same holds true for the art of shapeshifting. Becoming just the least bit functional in it will enhance your life tremendously.

For some, the release of such internal abilities and capacities is very subtle, but for others. it is quite apparent. *For everyone, it is possible!* If we are to truly empower our essence, we must first become more aware of the process - especially in the western world where we have been raised with the rational approach to life.

That is the wondrous journey this book will begin for you. It will provide practical and safe techniques for learning to shapeshift your consciousness and your world. It will provide new insights to the ancient tools and techniques applied by mystics, shamans and seers from around the world. It will combine science and mysticism to help you bridge to new realities and creative possibilities, hidden within the limitations of life. It will help you to reconnect with all of Nature - including your own nature - in ways and on levels that will amaze you and fill your life with renewed wonder and reverence. It will lead you through the many masks - both real and fantastic - that make life a true joy to live. It will help guide you to the magnificent power of transformation that is the core of your essence and the purpose of your soul!

Begin with the Imagical You

When we work with shapeshifting, we bring to life the unexpressed, inherent energies and abilities within us. We use shapeshifting to awaken our higher, more powerful selves. For some people, the awakening of these internal abilities and capacities is very subtle, but for others, the awakening is quite apparent. If we are to truly empower our essence, we need to be aware of this process.

What we are working to accomplish is to consciously bring to life those aspects of ourselves that we wish, dream and hope to manifest. The magickal body is the ideal you, with the ability to be the most powerful and effective that you can be in your life. Through work with shapeshifting, we develop the ability to assume the powers and potentials for whatever a task may require within our life.

The creation of the magical body begins with the creation of the imagickal body – how you imagine your true magical self to be. Imagine the ideal you. What would the ideal you truly be like? All energy follows thought. Where we put our thoughts that is where energy goes. Form follows idea, thus thought and image create an energy matrix or blueprint by which the form will manifest within our life.

When we use symbols and images - including the magical ones of ourselves - in the proper manner, we are opening to the creative powers of the universe. The amount of energy available to each of us is limited only by our capacity for realization. If we increase our awareness, at the same time removing our inhibitions and limitations, we increase our intake of universal or cosmic energy. Whatever we are or are becoming is intensified. Every aspect of our nature is intensified!

The process is rather simple. Visualize exactly what it is you wish to be, with all of its variations and in as much detail as possible. Visualize it as if you are already it - as if it is already accomplished. Write it out in your shapeshifting journal. Leave space to add to it because as you change and grow so will the magical you.

Begin by asking and answering some basic questions:
1. What is the highest, brightest, most creative image of yourself that you can imagine?
2. What characteristics would you have?
3. What would you most ideally like to be able to do?
4. What abilities would you be able to express?
5. How would you ideally like others to see you?
6. How would being this way change your life at home and work?
7. If you could manifest those abilities now, what are some ways you could use them to your benefit and that of others?
8. How would you be able to help others without them knowing?
9. What would you be able to accomplish and how would you do it most effectively?
10. What new possibilities would unfold for you?
11. What would you change and how would you do it?
12. How would being this way change your life at home and school?

Then do whatever is necessary in the physical to help it along. Act according to the way you have imagined. The key to magic is being who you truly are. Our magical essence is merely a reflection of our higher, truer essence.

We are physical beings. This means our primary focus should be within the physical world, but we can use other dimensions and levels of consciousness to create more productivity within our physical lives. If we are to use other, deeper levels of consciousness for our betterment, then we need to transform the energy potentials of the inner to the outer life. It is the magickal body that assists us with this. With each shapeshifting exercise, we release energy that assists in molding, creating and empowering the ideal self - the true magical person that lives within us. It enables us to weave glamour into our life, helping us move from merely developing a magickal body to becoming a very real magickal being.

Assumption of the God-Form

Costume, posture and props can be used to align oneself more easily with archetypal energies represented by mythological gods or goddesses. In this photgraph, I am aligning myself with the energy of Apollo, the Greek god of prophecy, music and art.

Weaving Glamour

Imagine if we could shapeshift ourselves to relate to all people more successfully. Imagine if we could shapeshift our presence more effectively to succeed at school, home, work, or wherever we are. Imagine if we could shapeshift to accomplish our goals and achieve our dreams more easily. Well, the truth is that all of us shapeshift. It is natural for us. Everyday on some level, we all shapeshift to help us through the day. We learn early in life how and when to smile, when to be serious or studious. We know how to present a particular image. What we haven't learned is the next step.

It is something though that we can all do, and it begins by learning how to first create a magical body and then use it to weave a little glamour. *Weaving glamour* is a form of shapeshifting. It is an old term that applies to working your magic so that you and things around you appear to others as you wish them to.

When I was in school, I would raise my hand in a way that I would be noticed but not actually called upon to answer the question. I used a little glamour to give the appearance that I knew the answer. And most of the time it worked. The teacher would have the impression that I was doing my work and was trying to participate in class. This is not the best use for this ability, but it is nothing new. Kids do this in school all of the time. Some are just more successful at it than others.

A good salesman weaves a little glamour around his product to make us want it or feel that it is the best buy for the money. TV commercials weave glamour through music and images to manipulate us to buy products. They want us to feel a certain way. They create a mood to influence us.

And yes, such abilities can be misused. The truth is that we have all experienced aspects of glamour and have had it used against us at times Take a look at the commercials we see on TV everyday. Advertisers use images and music to manipulate our thoughts and feelings. They make us think and feel that our homes aren't clean enough, our breath isn't fresh enough, our hair isn't full enough or the right color, and let's not even get into the smell of our underarms. They weave a little glamour to make us feel that we aren't good enough without their product. And what do we do? We go out and buy them – even when we don't need them.

Weaving glamour is a process for bringing out the magical and more powerful aspect of you to influence a situation. We draw upon our creative imagination, shifting our consciousness to shape what is going on around us and to affect how people respond to us. We learn to tap and project a particular energy around ourselves.

It is said that Merlin practiced shapeshifting throughout his life, continually weaving glamour. When kings summoned him, he disguised himself as a poor shepherd, a woodcutter, or as a peasant. He could present himself to others in any way he desired. People would believe he was just as he appeared. Because of this, he was able to accomplish much more within his life.

We are the shapeshifters of our life. We will all wear different masks at different times. The masks and forms we put on though should be ones that reflect the most creative and magical aspects within us. That is when glamour and shapeshifting take on great power. It affects how we feel and if allowed to grow, it affects how others respond to us and influences what happens or doesn't happen for us in life. When we learn to do this, we can re-create our life and how people respond to us. We can weave our life into anything we hope, wish or dream.

Veils of Magic

But is that magic? Sure it is. Magic is simply a word that means "wisdom". It is the wisdom and ability to work with energy to make things happen. Understanding how to make energies work for you takes a lot of time and practice, but when we combine believing with effort and wisdom, magic does happen. Shapeshifting and the weaving of glamour occur. But it must be practiced everyday so that it becomes second nature. This is why so many of the exercises in this book are experiential. They strengthen your beliefs and our ability to shift into the magical essence that is the true us.

The magic of shapeshifting is natural, even though aspects of how it actually happens are still somewhat occult. I know that's a trigger word for some people, but it simply means "hidden". It is veiled. The truth is that we just do not yet completely understand how most magic works – including shapeshifting. Think of it like electricity. Most people still do not know how it works, but we do know that it is real. We also know there are tools that help us to control and direct electricity to make our lives much more comfortable. Through the exercises in this book, you will develop the skills necessary to control and direct the hidden energies of your own life.

Shapeshifting magic is the wisdom of directing energy to produce specific effects. It is the art of using our imagination and movements to create changes in us and the world around us – to better direct the energies of life. True magic is a craft that involves doing something to awaken, strengthen, control and direct the energies of life.

Of all the tools that we can use to help ourselves, none is more important than our own belief. **No magic ever happens without belief on some level.** Magical believing begins by changing ourselves – by realizing who we truly are and what we truly can do. The art we will teach you in this book is how to believe once more and how to use that belief to weave magic into your life more fully.

*Shapeshifting
Exercise
(developmental)*

The Dancer's Pose

Skills & Benefits:
- **develops psychic and physical balance**
- **creates shifts in consciousness**
- **helps awaken the inner magical self**

Movements and postures for balance are beneficial before and after any shapeshifting exercise. They stabilize the energies that are activated so we can experience them more effectively. This will be explored more fully in the Part Three, but this is a good introductory exercise for this aspect.

The pose of the dancer is shown on the next page.. This is what we are becoming when we work with the magickal aspects of movement. We are becoming the great Dancer of Life. We are learning to choreograph our life and our inner resources for greater expression. The dancer's pose is an effective way to begin any shapeshifting because it balances the hemispheres of the brain and creates a shift in focus and consciousness. It can also be effectively used before and after rituals or meditations that don't involve dance.

One of the most powerful ways of using this posture is in the creation of a magickal body. As I have stated, the magickal body is the ideal you - the new, more conscious you that is created through the dance. The magickal body is the you that is capable of manifesting and appearing in the manner most effective and powerful for your life. It is the ability to assume the manners and powers necessary for the life tasks you encounter.

1. Begin the pose by standing, facing straight ahead.
Choose one leg to balance yourself upon. Raise the foot of the other leg behind you, and hold it with your hand. Raise the other hand up, pointing it forward and up. (See the Illustration below.) Keep your eyes straight ahead; it will help balance you. Now lean forward, and raise the leg you are holding up as high as is comfortable for you. See yourself as a dancer, making great leaps of consciousness, dancing from one realm to the next.

2. Now relax and stand straight again, with both feet flat on the ground.
Now reverse legs, balancing in this pose on the opposite leg. You may find it easier to balance on one leg than the other; this can indicate you need to work at keeping harmony in your life. As you develop a greater ability to hold this pose, you develop a greater ability to maintain harmony in your life.

3. Now, as you assume this posture, see yourself becoming the ideal you with whatever form, image, and power you have imagined.
Feel and see yourself shapeshifting into the ideal, magical you that can work effectively in both the physical and spiritual world.

Within the magical dance, everything is possible. It creates an intersection between the physical and the spiritual, the inner and the outer. It is a point of power that encompasses you. It becomes a space where you can learn to be capable of anything-where the magic of manifestation begins.

Visualize this ideal, magickal you, as if you are already it. See yourself, calling the ideal you forward through this position. Use this visualization with the movements at the beginning and the end of your rituals and meditations to give them greater power. Our magickal essence is a reflection of our higher, truer self. The movements and the imaging enable us to bring this essence into greater expression.

Shapeshifting
Exercise
(developmental & experiential)

Creating the Magical Body

Skills & Benefits:

- **personal empowerment for healing and problem solving**
- **greater control in life**
- **preparation for shapeshifting and out of body experiences**
- **awakens inner potentials**

One of the most important practices in magical shapeshifting is creating the magical body. The magical body is a new, more conscious you. Through it we bring to life the unexpressed abilities within us. We awaken our higher and more powerful selves.

Through this process we awaken our hidden potentials and begin to manifest them in our life. For some people the effects are subtle and take a little time to be seen. For others, it will be quite apparent. It happens differently for every individual.

The magical body is the ideal you. It awakens the most powerful and effective person that you can be in your life. In order to accomplish this though, we first awaken the possibilities. Remember that through this exercise you are creating a new you, not simply changing the old. We must keep this in mind, applying creative imagination to the ideal within us – physically, emotionally, mentally and spiritually.

Imagine the ideal you. What would the ideal you truly be like? Remember that if you can imagine it, then it can be. Your thoughts, beliefs and images create an energy blueprint that will manifest in some form within your life. The process is rather simple. Visualize exactly what it is you wish to be, with all of its varieties and in as much detail as possible. Visualize yourself as if you have already accomplished it. Then do whatever is necessary in the physical to help it along. Act the way you imagine and believe yourself to be. When you change your beliefs, you change your world.

Review your shapeshifting journal and the answers to the questions presented to you earlier in this chapter. What is the most creative and brightest image of yourself that you can imagine? Once you have reviewed the description of your magical self, prepare to do the following exercise.

1. **Make your preparations. Light a candle and use some fragrance to set the tone.**

2. **Make sure you will be undisturbed and perform the dancer's pose, as in the previous exercise.**

3. **Breathe deeply and allow yourself to relax. As you begin to relax, the room around you begins to disappear and you find yourself inside a beautiful and ancient castle...**

You look around you as you stand in the midst of the great hall. Much of the castle is familiar and feels like this is your own special place. To your left, is an arched door and you walk through it into an outer hallway. In this hallway is a great spiral staircase and you head toward it.

As you begin to climb, you find yourself relaxing more and more. With each step you leave the worries, stresses and fears of your every day life behind. With each step you find yourself feeling free and light. Soft candles light the stairway, and as you climb higher, a soft golden mist swirls at your feet.

When you reach the top of the stairs, you find yourself in a long hallway with only one door in the center. At the opposite end of the hallway another spiral staircase descends. That gold mist swirls and shimmers hiding the floor of the hallway. As you walk through this golden mist, causing more swirls, a soft tinkling of bells seems to issue forth from it – sending shivers of delight through your body.

You reach down and swirl the golden mist with your hands. You laugh at the wondrous colors and forms you stir within it. You straighten up and move to the door. It is large and wooden, carved with many strange symbols and letters. You reach out with your hand and trace some of them. As you do, the door slowly opens inward, as if inviting you in.

Your eyes widen as you step across the threshold. You are standing in a large circular room that looks like an ancient magician's laboratory. Around the walls are shelves of ancient books, manuscripts and scrolls. There are shelves of herbs, oils and stones. Exotic plants grow in different parts of the room and seem to be watching you.

The ceiling is painted with a scene from the heavens, and you gaze at the glistening stars. Then you realize that the stars are moving, the sky shifting. The ceiling is enchanted so that if you wanted you could trace the movements of the planets and stars in miniature. You watch the night sky shift.

You move further into the room and you find a large desk. Scrolls and parchment covered in notes are scattered about the surface. Laying on top of them is your own Shapeshfitng Journal. And you realize that this is your magic room!

As you smile, you continue to move about the room, feeling even lighter and freer. You come to a full-length mirror. As you stand before it there is no reflection. This puzzles you, but then a faint outline of an ancient face appears in the mirror. Its appearance startles you, and you take a step back.

Then softly a voice speaks from that face in the mirror, "What is it you would see?"

You hesitate, unsure, and then you softly speak, " I want to see me."
"As you wish."
The mirror begins to be filled with misty clouds, and then as they shift and part, you are amazed at the image that appears in the mirror. A magnificent person is seen in the mirror, shining with great light. You tilt your head trying to see it more clearly, and the mirrored image tilts also. It is only then that you realize that the image in the mirror is the real you. It is the ideal you. The Magical you!

Your eyes are filled with wisdom. And there is a beauty, strength and wisdom that radiates from you. As you gaze in wonder at your true essence, flashes of your abilities and potentials appear around the outer edge of the mirror. So many possibilities.

As you look upon your true essence, the light grows stronger and to your amazement, your magical essence steps from the mirror. With your next breath, your magical essence melts into you. You close your eyes feeling your true essence awakening. You see yourself stronger and more blessed. And with each breath that you take your magical essence grows stronger within you.

Your heart is filled with great hope. There is no doubt that in the days ahead this magical essence and all of its potentials will start awakening more fully. You offer a prayer of thanks of this reminder of who you truly are and for who you are becoming once more.

You step away from the mirror and look around this wonderful room. So much to learn and explore! You smile, empowered, freer and more magical. You step toward the door and it opens. You step into the golden mist of the hallway and now it swirls up and around you like a golden garment of magic. The mist has recognized what has been awakened.

As you step down the stairs and the hallway disappears behind you, you breathe deeply, blessed, and as you reach the bottom of the stairs you find yourself back within your own room. You are balanced, healed, blessed and empowered. And as you look down at yourself and stretch, you see yourself shining brightly. Your magic is coming to life!

4. Breathe deeply, and begin to stretch.

Perform one of the balancing postures to help ground the energy and repeat the dancer's pose from the previous exercise. You may wish to eat something or have a drink of water.

5. Take your shapeshifting journal and write in what you felt and imagine while doing this exercise.

Over the next week pay attention to dreams and events around you as this exercise opens new learning and new fun. Pay close attention to how differently people seem to treat you.

If you BELIEVE,

then it can be.

If you don't believe,

it will NEVER be.

Shapeshifting
Exercise
(developmental & experiential)

Assumption of the God-Form

Skills & Benefits:
- **awakens inner potentials**
- **develops flexibility in your energy system**
- **develops ability to work with powerful archetypes**

Assumption of god-forms is a powerful tool for enlightenment, but the participant must understand the symbolism of the movements and dress appropriately. If you are working within a particular magickal tradition, learn as much about that tradition as possible. Read myths, and tales about gods and goddesses within the tradition.

Many of the ancient gods and goddesses had positive and negative aspects, and unless you are aware of these qualities, your magical dance may stimulate more than you can handle. See the end of the chapter for list of the aspects of some god and goddesses to help you get started.

One of the most common questions that arises in the assumption of god-forms is whether or not a male individual can assume the god-form of a female and a female assume the god-form of a male. The answer is *yes*, but it is more difficult. A female will more easily resonate and be able to take on the form of a female deity than a male and vice versa.

This does not mean that the female god-form cannot be taken on by a male participant. It is just usually more difficult. This is one of the benefits of magickal dance. Using movements, postures, and gestures associated with the deity helps simulate the changes in the body and mind necessary to shift to that new consciousness.

We also must remember that, although the gods and goddesses are usually depicted as male and female, they are divine forces which are actually more androgynous - neither truly male nor female. They are beings who assumed a form that was most representative of the universal force and power they possessed. Along this same line, we are all a combination of male and female energies. Because of this, we can develop resonance with male and female deities. The deciding factors are the purpose of the dance and our own personal desire to attune and resonate with the deity. Our own sex does not exclude us from invoking and assuming any divine force. In the beginning - to avoid confusions - choose a deity that is the same sex.

1. Begin as always by creating your sacred space.
As you do so you may wish to see that space filling with a color that has come to be associated with the particular god or goddess.

2. Perform your balancing exercise or the dancer's pose.
 As you do, see this influx of energy swirling around and filling you. Imagine yourself being transformed, becoming the god or goddess. If you are not wearing a costume symbolic of the deity, put it on at this time.

3. Balance yourself and assume a meditative position.
Take time to reflect upon the symbolism and powers associated with the deity. If there are specific poses and gestures associated with this deity, slowly and deliberately perform them at this time. Imagine and feel you becoming one with the deity.

If you are unsure of the various movements, gestures, and postures of a particular deity, examine art and literature of the particular tradition. Many of the gods and goddesses are depicted in very symbolic poses; these will help you to assume the godform.

4. To help you empower yourself once in the sacred space, you may wish to have learned something about the folk dances of that area of the world.
Often the folk dances carry remnants of the religious significance of more ancient dances. It also helps you to understand how the people move, for people dance differently in different parts of the world. In some areas the head may be the center of expression, while in others the hands and arms are. It will vary from country to country.

5. Take time near the end to see you absorbing the energy of the deity.
See this energy as being born within you, an energy that you will take out with you from the circle to empower your daily life.

6. Rebalance yourself.
The entire exercise does not need to last more than 15 minutes for its effects to be released and experienced.

The Mythical Traditions

Each mythology had its own tradition of rituals, music, and dance. Each tradition had its own means of awakening its members to the divine forces of that society. Each society had its own pantheon of gods and goddesses, symbolic of the universal forces and reflecting certain premises of that society.

What follows are some guidelines to forms that can be employed in shapeshifting dance and assumption of the god-forms, based on four ancient magickal traditions; Greek, Egyptian, Celtic, and Teutonic. You are by no means limited to these four. They are examples to use as a starting point. Use the mythology to which you have always been attracted. Read the myths and tales associated with that tradition. Study about the customs and costumes of the society. They will assist in attuning and invoking the energies when used in the shapeshifting ritual.

As you read the myths and tales associated with the goddess or god you wish to invoke, you may find that they involve energies completely foreign to anything you have encountered in the physical world. This may indicate a need for greater harmony and balancing at the beginning and end of your shapeshifting.

Most of the ancient gods and goddesses were fallible. They may have expressed and represented very divine characteristics, but many had human qualities as well. By assuming their form through dance and movement, you open yourself to their strengths, as well as any weaknesses.

Choose the god or goddess according to your personal goals and not according to which one seems the most powerful. Complete resonance and assumption of the form with a lesser god or goddess can do more for you than a partial alignment with a major god or goddess. Use their symbols and colors to help the attunement.

Stay within a single tradition, rather than jumping around. Don't start one week with the Greek tradition and then move to the Celtic. Start with the one that attracts you the most. Work with it for an extended period first in study, then in meditation, and finally in shapeshifting. At least six months should be given to developing a working resonance. Learn to invoke its energies effectively before working with another system. Changing too often and jumping around creates discordant energies and it is unbalancing.

Most of the gods and goddesses had working relationships with others of their pantheon. Learning how they related to each other will help you to understand the energy that is invoked into your life through assumption of the god-form in shapeshifting. And it will affect how you relate to others in your life and how they relate to you. Remember that what we do on one level always affects us on another.

Many myths are tales of great beings who may have actually walked upon the earth, serving as teachers and helpers to humanity. Do not confuse the mythical with the unreal. The tales may be a blend of both.

There is often more going on within the myths than is apparent. There is usually more going on within our lives than what appears on the surface. Assumption of the god-forms with these mythical images will uncover this. When you align yourself with a deity of a particular mythology, you may activate events within your own life circumstances that are similar to those of the deity. And this is all part of developing the ability to shapeshift and work with life circumstances more creatively and effectively.

The Greek Gods & Goddesses

This is the mythology of individuality, of becoming the hero or heroine of your life. The gods and goddesses work intimately with humans, providing weapons and tools necessary to accomplish the task at hand. As long as respect is paid, the individual will have awakened the powers to overcome hindrances.

The Orphic style of Greek ritual is filled with joy, music, song, and food. It was designed to develop closeness with Nature and with others. They are powerful dances when performed outdoors, clothed or unclothed. Others such as the Eleusinian dances were more formal.

Zeus (God of thunder, air, and sky)
  Color: purple
  Symbols: oak tree and eagle

Hera (Goddess of marriage and all feminine energies)
  Color: emerald green
  Symbols: scepter, cuckoo and peacock

Athena (Warrior goddess of wisdom)
  Color: red-gold
  Symbols: owl, helmet, aegis, shield, and spear

Apollo (God of sun, prophecy, music, and art)
  Color: yellow-gold
  Symbols: sun, archery, and lyre

Artemis (Goddess of forest and moo)
  Color: amethyst
  Symbols: bear and dog

The Art of Shapeshifting

Hermes (God of communication, initiation, and magic)
  Color: silver
  Symbols: caduceus, winged hat, and sandals

Ares (God of war, strength, and passion)
  Color: scarlet
  Symbols: all weaponry

Aphrodite (Goddess of love and beauty)
  Color: turquoise
  Symbols: dove, porpoise, girdle, and rose

Demeter (The mother goddess)
  Colors: brown and yellow
  Symbols: cornflower and corn

Hecate. (Goddess of the moon, magic, and psychism)
  Colors: black with silver flecks
  Symbols: black hooded cloak, dark of the moon, hellhound

Persephone (Goddess of new life, growth, and creativity)
  Colors: citrines, russets, and olive greens
  Symbols: corn and pomegranate

Pan (God of prophecy, nature, and healing)
  Colors: greens of the forest
  Symbols: Pan flute, ivy, songs, and pine cone

Other gods and goddesses are easily adapted to magickal dance in this tradition. Dionysus, the god of magic and healing, was the source of much inspiration and ceremonial dance. Even Hades, the god of the underworld, can be invoked through dance, although he is less likely to express himself in front of others. A study of the myths and the major personas will elicit much dance inspiration.

The Egyptian Gods & Goddesses

The Egyptian tradition is more formal in its ritual. It had effects upon almost every major society as a center of the mysteries. It is a tradition of alchemy, and the process of birth, death, and rebirth. Their ritual and dance often involved activating energies of mind over matter.

Ra (God of the sun)
   Color: golden sunshine
   Symbols: obelisk, hawk, and uraeus

Osiris (God of wisdom, justice, and strength)
   Color: white and green
   Symbols: tet (tree), crook, and flail

Isis (Goddess of the moon and magic)
   Color: sky blue
   Symbols: throne, wings, veil behind the throne, a buckle

Horus (Sun god of art, music, and healing)
   Colors: bright yellow and gold
   Symbols: hawk and all-seeing eye

Bast (Goddess of joy and animals
   Colors: yellow gold and turquoise
   Symbols: sistrum, the cat, and the lion

Thoth (God of medicine, learning, and magic)
   Colors: violet and amethyst
   Symbol: caduceus

Hathor (Mother goddess of protection)
   Color: coral
   Symbols: mirror, sycamore tree, and cow

Nepthys (Goddess of intuition and tranquility)
   Colors: pale greens and silver grays
   Symbols: chalice and basket

Ptah   (God of craftsmanship and science)
   Color: violet
   Symbol: mason tools

Anubis   (God of guardianship and guidance)
   Colors: black and silver
   Symbols: jackal and sarcophagus

The Celtic Gods & Goddesses

The Celtic tradition is one of romance, creativity and intuition. It is extremely adaptable and effective with magickal dance, especially outdoors around trees. It is primarily a matriarchal system and attuning to it tradition awakens inner intuition and creativity, allowing for very individualistic expression. The Celtic tradition helps you discover your inner fires and is rich in the magic of music, words, and dance.

Green is the predominant color. While forming the sacred circle during the dance ritual, visualize it filling with the rich, fertile green of Mother Earth. This will amplify any other dances, colors, and images used with this tradition. The assumption of the god-form in this tradition may reveal a color different than what is listed. Do not be surprised. When the energy manifests, it will often do so in a color whose energy resonates most closely to your own. Because of this, I have not provided a color for them.

Dagda (The nourishing patriarch)
  Symbols: harp and cauldron

Danu (Mother goddess of wisdom)
  Symbols: newly planted seed, all symbols of water

Morrigan (Goddess of magic and enchantment)
  Symbols: crossed spears and ravens

Cerridwen (Goddess of magic and prophecy)
  Symbol: the great cauldron

Morgan le Fay (Fairy queen of magic and higher wisdom)
  Symbol: hand extending sword from the waters of life

Brigid (Goddess of inspiration, healing, strength, and endurance)
  Symbols: torches, fire, and well of healing waters

Taliesin (God of prophecy, poetry, magic, and wisdom)
  Symbols: harp and staff

Rhiannon (Goddess of assertiveness, justice, and the underworld)
  Symbols: gray horse and three sacred birds

Lugh (God of artistry, sun, and magic)
  Symbol: spear

Gwydion (Guardian and guide)
  Symbols: images of science and law

The Teutonic Gods & Goddesses

The Teutonic tradition is one of awesome power, beauty, magic, and violence. This tradition teaches great personal responsibility and the transmutation of energies.

The Norse and Teutonic tradition is rich in the magickal use of song and rhyme. Scaldcraft was the Teutonic method of using names, words, and poetry for magickal purposes. It was used to control one's own destiny and the destiny of others. The runes, the alphabet of this tradition, and the rhythm of the poetry were sources of power that could be used in a variety of rituals and forms of magic.

Odin (God of knowledge, runes, poetry, and seership)
  Color: deep blue and indigo
  Symbols: ravens and wolves, spear, and eight-legged steed

Frigga (Goddess of abundance, weather, and herbal healing)
  Colors: deep greens
  Symbols: golden spindle and necklace

Thor (Warrior god of thunder and lightning)
  Colors: bright reds
  Symbols: hammer, magic belt, and cart drawn by goats

Freyr (God of plenty)
  Color: bright golden yellow
  Symbols: bright sword, ship, and golden boar

Freyja (Goddess of love, beauty, and prophecy)
  Color: soft reds and pinks
  Symbols: falcon wings and a chariot drawn by cats

Balder (Shining god of purity, healing, and mercy)
  Color: shining white
  Symbol: all flowers, especially the balderblum

Tyr (Bravest god and god of great strength)
  Color: dark red
  Symbol: sacrificed hand

Heimdall (Watchman god of the rainbow bridge)
  Colors: the rainbow
  Symbol: the trumpet horn

Idun (Goddess of beauty, rejuvenation, and youth)
    Color: gold and pastel blues
    Symbol: golden apples

Bragi (God of poetry and scaldcraft)
    Color: rich sky blue and sparkled with gold
    Symbols: all songs, poetry, and musical instruments

Songi of the Bantu People

Explore the mythology and folklore of your heritage. Do not limit yourself necessarily to traditions I have provided here. For example, the Great Mother of the Bantu people of Africa is a being by the name of Songi. Assumption of her form awakens the energy of nurturing, love and great protection. Her energy brings the gifts of great wisdom, strength, compassion and fulfillment.

Chapter Five

Shifting the Veils

I f you could change yourself into anything, what would it be? What animal would you change yourself into? Can you truly imagine what it would be like to be that animal? Good shapeshifters can shift veils to draw upon magic successfully for any situation that arises. They can shift the veils that allow them to awaken their own magic, connect with animals, travel in spirit, weave glamour and even develop invisibility.

The biggest difference between shapeshifters of the past and now is that ancient shapeshifters accepted that there are veils separating different realities from aspects of everyday life. Because of their belief in and knowledge of these veils, they learned not only to perceive them but also to walk through them. They moved between worlds. This enabled them to perceive animals differently than we normally do today. They would not fathom the modern idea of animals as mere lowly beasts. They knew there was a powerful and creative spirit in animals. They discovered that we shared this spirit in common and that this commonality is what helps make shapeshifting possible.

The truth is that there are veils that separate our everyday world from those that seem less substantial. They separate the physical from the spiritual, the mundane from the magical. There are veils that can prevent us from seeing the true essence and spirit of animals and plants. And there are even veils that prevent us from seeing the magical side of our own self. If we wish to walk between the worlds - to shapeshift and move from one dimension to another - we must be able to discover the reality of these veils. This requires that we learn to perceive in new ways. We must be able both to perceive and shift the veils that separate the physical from the spiritual, the dreaming from the waking, and the magical from the mundane.

Becoming Jaguar

To the natives of North and South America, the jaguar is endowed with great magic and power. It climbs, runs, swims, stalks – even better than tiger. It functions so well in so many areas that it is a symbol of immeasurable power – of mastery over all dimensions. To the Tuscano Indians of the Amazon, the roar of the jaguar was the roar of thunder. It caused eclipses by swallowing the sun. The black jaguar is a symbol of darkness, death and rebirth from it. It is a symbol of the power of the life and power of the night. Jaguar is the Dark Mother and thus, the dark of the moon is the best time to call upon its magic through shapeshifting activities.

The Olmecs created monuments to the jaguar and the Aztecs and Mayans taught about the power of becoming half-human and half-jaguar. One who can become a jaguar is shorn of all cultural restrictions. The alter ego is free to act out desires, fears and aspirations. To the Arawak Indians, everything has jaguar. Nothing exists without it. And to them, becoming the man-jaguar is the ultimate shapeshifting ritual.

Native shamans would perform rituals to draw upon and borrow jaguar power. One who could do such could perform great good or great ill. Stories abound of revenge, abductions and great cures of disease through the use of jaguar power among the Latin-American Indians.

Some animals have always been more effective for helping shamans accomplish these things themselves The polar bear is one such animal. It has great supernatural powers. It is Nanook, the spirit of the North. It is an animal shaman, a liaison with the spirit world and a keeper of wisdom. Polar bears can almost magically appear and disappear out of nowhere and thus are powerful guides between the veils of worlds. The Aztecs and Olmecs taught about the power of becoming half-human and half-jaguar. Native American medicine people often use bear, coyote and raven as the focus of their shapeshifting. Birds are often good totems for shapeshifting as they naturally move between realms – the earth and the sky (the physical world and the spiritual worlds).

Shapeshifting is the most powerful way of drawing upon and borrowing the power of animals. It shifts the veils, allowing us to establish a link between our spirit and that of the animal. And as a result we are able to awaken the animal's power and medicine within us and express it more dynamically in some area of our life. To succeed though, we must learn first to see and then to shift the veils of life.

Shamanic Quest

Another important step in the shaman quest is building a bridge between our world and the more subtle realms of life. This involves unfolding our intuition, creativity, and creative imagination. The individual learns to visit the heavens and the underworld. Many shamans employ mythic imagination to facilitate this, using any number of possible images: climbing a tree, being carried/led by an animal, becoming a bird or animal, and following a cave through a labyrinth.

The Veils

There was a time when the distances between our world and those often considered imaginary were no further than a bend in the road. Every cavern and hollow tree was a doorway to another world. The streams sang and the winds whispered ancient words into the ears of whoever would listen. Every blade of grass and flower had a story to tell. Shadows were not just shadows and woods were not just trees and clouds were not just pretty. There was life in all things and interaction between the worlds.

Through the ages, veils have developed that separate our mundane world from other realms, realities and dimensions, but they still exist. The veils separating dimensions have been described in tales and lore through the ages in a variety of ways - usually as doorways or openings into strange worlds. A shifting of consciousness allows these other realms and realities to be experienced to some degree by everyone. Dreamtime is one of the most common and frequent shiftings of consciousness that allows us to cross veils. The truth is though that most of us have brushed against or crossed these veils from time to time within our life outside of dreaming and often without realizing it.

Wherever there is an intersection, there is a thinning of the veils between worlds, realities and dimensions. These intersections occur frequently in Nature. Such intersections can be of time or place, and they can be stationary or shifting. When experienced, these places and times of thinnings automatically stimulate a shift in our consciousness – a shift away from our normal thinking and feeling. Our focus alters. This heightens our perceptions, stirs inner potentials and magic, and makes us more aware of other realities and dimensions. Shamanic practitioners learn to recognize, attend to and use these thinning veils consciously.

Tween Times and Places

A more traditional and magical way of putting it is that we have experienced a Tween Time and Place. Tween Times and Tween Places are in-between. They are neither one nor another. They are indistinct. They are neither one time nor another, neither one place nor another. They are times and places where a thinning of the veils between our physical world and those that are veiled from us occur. This thinning of the veils, these Tween Times and Places, makes us more sensitive to subtle things around us. They are doorways and windows through which we experience psychic, magical and spiritual energies and phenomena more clearly. Our psychic abilities become stronger and our ability to contact and experience spirit becomes more tangible. And they make shapeshifting easier and more powerful.

Tween Times are neither one time nor another. They are in-between. Dawn and dusk are powerful time intersections where this thinning of veils occurs naturally every day. They are intersections of day and night – neither being exactly one or the other. Until that shift from day to night and night to day is completed, the veils are thin and sometimes completely open between worlds.

When we lose track of time, we have slipped into the Tween Times. That thinning of the veils between the physical and spiritual has occurred around us. This happens in meditation, in prayer, in magical ceremony, in fun and creative activities we are involved in. If you have ever been so involved in an activity that you lost track of time, then you experienced a magical Tween Time.

Tween Places are also neither one place nor another and natural intersections are places where the veils are usually thin. For example, a creek bed is a Tween Place. It is not part of the creek and it is not part of the main land. It is in-between. Intersections of roads or paths through the woods are common places where this thinning of the veils occurs. Creek beds, seashores and the edges of ponds and pools are powerful Tween Places. They are intersections between two natural elements (water and earth) making them powerful doorways.

Spirit is more often encountered in Tween Places. When people first actually see spirit, it is often in doorways, windows and hallways. The spirit is neither in nor out. It is in-between. Staircases are neither up nor down. It's amazing how many people experience spirit phenomena on staircases.

Regardless of where or when this thinning of veils occurs, there are a number of tangible indicators that can alert us to their presence. The most common indicators are visual and tactile. Shimmering lights or glimmers in the air – like small waves or crinkles – can indicate the presence of a thin veil. Shifting shadows or shadows where there should not be are also indicators of veils that have thinned or opened. Sudden, unexplained chills or goosebumps can indicate a brush against thin veils that separate our everyday world from others. Dizziness, lightheadedness and even a sense of disorientation can indicate movement through a veil. A change in the air temperature or pressure can also indicate the presence of an open or thin veil. Unexplainable losses of time also indicate a crossing of the veils.

Benefits of Recognizing Veils

Thin and open veils can assist us in many areas of life. They stimulate our own innate magical abilities. We become more sensitive to the subtle nuances of change around us. Thin or open veils awaken us to the presence and reality of spirit and beings of other dimensions – including the Faerie Realm. They expand our perception of reality. They facilitate exploring other dimensions of time and space. They create a dynamic flow of energy that can be used for healing and assist the shapeshifting process. Even the briefest contact or brush with the veils enhances creativity, psychic perception and the awakening of inner magic. In fact, brushes with thin and open veils are often catalysts for creating periods of good fortune.

It changes our perspective of the world. When we experience the reality of other dimensions, it changes our beliefs and the paradigm of our life. We begin to view the world around us more differently than ever before. We begin to see through the illusions of our life and of our own essence. For many, this shift in perspective is the most difficult part of shapeshifting, but it will help develop an individuality that is tremendously strong.

When we learn to see and use the thin veils to enhance shapeshifting, the natural world becomes a gateway to other realms and dimensions, and through shapeshifting, we learn to open and close these veils at will. We connect with animals on a more dynamic level than ever before. We become more connected to life in all its forms. Shamans around the world have done this for ages. Even while shamans maintain a true sense of connectedness to all life, they are able to part and move through thin veils to visit both the heavens and the underworld. They are able to learn from all life forms – plant and animals – by communicating with their spirits. This is much of what we are learning throughout this book. This ability to recognize, shift and use the veils is also what helps create the magic of shapeshifting.

How do we know?

How do we know that these veils exist? How do we know they are not just an illusion? As humans, we need confirmation. We need to strengthen our beliefs, and I have found that the easiest way to confirm the reality of veils and strengthen people's belief in them is to help people part those that separate the everyday world from the spirit world.

Of all the ways in which spirit can be experienced, most people still want to *see* them. They want and need the actual visual experience of the spirit world. Seeing spirit is is the ability to shift consciousness to see through the veils. There are two forms of spirit vision, internal and external.

Internal spirit vision or spirit intuition is when we see or perceive spirit beings inside our mind. Sometimes it is like a photograph. Sometimes it is just a face. Sometimes the image of the spirit is animated – almost like a movie sequence. Sometimes it is just a thought that passes through or nudges at us. The spirit being is softly nudging us to recognize that he or she is present. Dreams and meditation visions are also part of our internal vision. We often dream of spirit guides and loved ones who have messages for us.

External spirit vision is when we see spiritual beings with our physical eyes. We see faces of spirit behind us when we look into a mirror. We walk into a room and we see shadows that should not be in the room. We see people out of the corner of our eyes, but when we turn to look, no one is there. We may see figures looking at us. We see milky forms that appear and disappear. We see different colored lights dancing about. With external vision, we see the spiritual and normally hidden aspects of life and sometimes just as clearly as we see everything else in our world.

The spirit world is separated from the physical world by a veil and rightly so. Our focus in life should be on things in the physical because this is where we are growing and developing. We do not want to be seeing spirit all of the time because it distracts us from our regular life. There are things though that can be done to assist us in being able to physically see spirit through the veils - to confirm the reality of the spirit world. Candles, fragrances and even crystals can stimulate shifts in our nervous system and consciousness, facilitating the seeing of spirit.

When I teach classes on seeing and reading the aura (the energy field around the human body), I teach those attending about specific acupressure points that will gently stimulate the optic nerve. This enables the eyes to take in and register more light and color. These points also stimulate a shift in consciousness. When this happens, we not only see the human aura, but we also begin to see spirit more clearly. On the following pages are some guidelines for using acupressure to stimulate spirit vision.

Acupressure for

In Chinese medicine, acupuncture and acupressure are ways of working with the energy pathways in the body. Stimulation of specific points on the body can alleviate pain, restore balance and result in many health benefits. Some points will stimulate the optic nerve, helping us to physically see the human aura (the energy field around the human body) and spirits more clearly.

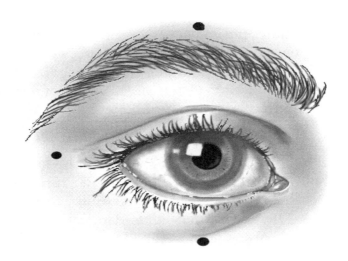

NEVER press hard on any of these points. It requires only the softest touch to stimulate them. Pressing too hard, too long, or too often will result in headaches and will numb the points. Only gentle pressure will help with the spirit vision.

1. Place your index or middle finger and very gently touch each of the three points around both eyes. At each point there is a very slight indentation when you feel around that area. Apply gentle pressure for about 15 seconds and then release for about 30 seconds.

2. Now using your thumb and two fingers touch all of the points for both eyes at the same time. Hold for ten seconds and then release.

Seeing Spirit

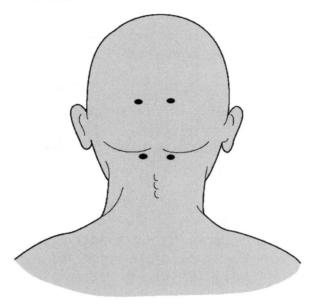

3. Now apply soft pressure to all four points at the back of the head at the same time. At each of these points, there is also a slight indentation. If you are unsure that you found the right points, make slow gentle circles in that area with your fingertips. If you are close, the circular motion will stimulate the correct points. Do this for about 30 seconds and then release.

4. Rub the palms of your hands together briskly to warm them up and then place the palms over your eyes while they are closed. This will soothe them and help prevent headaches.

5. Do this once a day before performing your spirit meditations, while in the dim light of your Tween Time and Place, and within a month you will begin to see some spirit phenomena. Light may seem to shift around you. Shadows may change. Forms will appear and disappear. This is especially effective to use when working with the exercise "Spirit Contact and Astral Travel" in chapter 8.

A Quick Parting of the Spirit Veils

To open doorways safely to the spirit world and help confirm the reality of veils, we need to create a sacred space – an artificial Tween Time and Place. It is an actual place in the outer world that can connects you to the inner world of magic and spirit – just as a door connects one space to another. Sacred spaces – Tween Times and Places - can be anywhere and any time. The marking off of sacred space has been done throughout the ages as a means of tapping the more subtle forces surrounding us. It creates a safe place to shift the veils.

In my home, I have a place away from the rest of the house. It is quiet and peaceful, and when I meditate and pray there, I can get a handle on troubles. I can get a better perspective of things coming my way. I can open the doorways to spirits and ask for their help as well. It is my sacred space.

Creating a sacred space is not a complicated process. There are some guidelines that will help you create a sacred space for parting the veils. First of all, you do not need a large space. A corner of a room where you can spend a half hour or so undisturbed and quiet is all that is necessary. You should have space enough though to sit, and you should be able to close out distractions.

Create an altar or sacred center. This can be a desktop that is cleared or a fold out table. It does not need to be large. On it you will be able to set special items that help you shift your consciousness from the outer to the inner. Have aids to help you. Candles, incense, and whatever is comfortable and special for you are wonderful aids to create sacred space. They set a mood. The lighting and dowsing of the candles also signals the doors opening and closing of doors. Certain crystals will also help stimulate a shift in consciousness. Some people will tell you that you need to mark the space more magically, but for our purposes, nothing more is needed than what is given here.

When you have set up your sacred space, light your candle(s) and take a seated position. Breathe deeply, relaxing. Stimulate the acupressure points and just focus on being as comfortable and as relaxed as possible. Send warm soothing thoughts and energy to every part of your body. As you begin to relax, notice how the atmosphere of the room changes. It will become softer, calmer, and more peaceful. This is the shift. The veils are thinning. Allow your eyes to half-close or use a day-dreamy focus – like you are staring off into space for approximately 10 minutes. Throughout this time, calmly make note of what you experience.

It may take a few minutes before the spirit phenomena manifests, but it rarely takes more than three times of doing this before spirit appears.

It can happen in a variety of ways. We may catch shadows and movements out of the corners of our eyes. We may see flickering lights of different colors and sizes. We may see symbols floating in the air around you. We may see shimmers in the air around us. We may even see an animal appear. If we persist and practice, we will begin to actually see spirit physically. Faces and forms will appear in mirrors, doorways, windows and around your sacred space.

Crystals for Spirit Contact

Quartz crystals contain a form of electrical energy that can help stimulate our higher perceptions and shifts in consciousness. Some crystals are very helpful for working with spirit guides. It is beneficial to have some of these as part of your shapeshifting tools. Use them when contacting your spirit guides. You may set them in front of you, hold them in your hand while meditating, wear them or just rest them on your lap.

Quartz Crystal
Aids in all spirit contact; heightens your overall psychic ability.

Double terminated Quartz
The points on both ends reflects its ability to open doors between worlds; helps with physical vision of spirit. It helps shift you into the Tween Times and Places.

Amethyst
Awakens our intuition and helps us in understanding the messages from spirit.

Moonstone
Gently stimulates our sensitivities, especially when crossing and exploring new thresholds in the psychic and spiritual realm.

Rose quartz
Invites healing spirits and loved ones who have passed on.

Shapeshifting
Exercise
(developmental)

Magical Spirit Cloth

Skills & Benefits:

- **creating a tool for shifting consciousness**
- **teaches the power of magical imprinting**
- **develops ability to make magical tools**

Wouldn't it be great to have a magic carpet that could transport you to other worlds and times? What about a special blanket or shawl that would heal you when you wrapped it around you? Or would soothe you and awaken your magical self? Imagine a cloth that when pulled up over your head would open the veils between worlds for you. Impossible?

Not as impossible as you might believe.

Magical spirit cloths have been used throughout the world. They are blankets and shawls, pieces of cloth, and magical garments. In traditional religions, a meditation shawl is worn and pulled up over the head like a hood during prayers. This creates a private, sacred space – a very personal Tween Place. And because it is only used for special occasions, the shawl or cloth is imprinted with a prayerful energy that makes the experience more powerful each time it is used. Prayers are more effective and answers are clearer.

One of the most powerful magical tools for shapeshifting and moving through veils is the magical spirit cloth. It is a special cloth, charged with energy to do any number of magical things for you. It can be a towel, a blanket, an actual shawl or even a small rug. It can even be a special shirt, robe or garment that is imbued with magical and healing energies. One of my magical cloths is a hooded sweatshirt that I have decorated and only used in meditation. When I pull the hood up over my head, I immediately slip into a Tween Time and Place. (I may look like Kenny from South Park, but it is one of my most effective and powerful magical tools.)

What we will learn here is how to take something ordinary and make it extraordinary and magical. It is accomplished through aura imprinting.

Aura Imprints

The human body is absolutely magnificent. It gives off heat, light, sound, electricity, and even magnetic frequencies. It is in every sense of the words an energy system. These energies surround the human body to form what is called the aura.

This aura is predominantly electromagnetic energy. We are constantly giving off (electrical) and absorbing (magnetic) energy through our auras. This energy exchange occurs between people, plants, animals, objects and places—with just about anything. It is like a kind of energy static cling. This picking up and giving off of energy residue is called **imprinting**.

We leave traces of our energy everywhere. We leave traces in places we visit and on things we touch, especially in our personal spaces and on our personal items - like on our books, on our jewelry, on our desks at school, and even in our rooms. Think about how your room feels different from that of a sibling or your parents. We each imprint or leave traces of our energy that is unique to us. The longer we have an object or inhabit a particular space, the stronger the imprint we leave on it. This is why it takes time for the new place to feel comfortable when we move. It takes time to imprint it.

Types of Imprints

Many places and objects are accidentally imprinted. Places where there have been strong emotional events or objects associated with intense or emotional events become accidentally charged. Most haunted homes are not truly haunted by ghosts, but by intense imprints left by previous residents. That feeling of discomfort in the home may be nothing more than an emotional imprint left behind by someone who once lived there. It is not often an actual spirit.

Imprints can be intentional though. Churches, temples and meditation rooms are places where efforts are made to create an atmosphere of reverence or peace that we experience upon entering. They are imprinted with a sense of the sacred. So every time someone enters that space, they feel the peace and sacredness of it. The creation of your own sacred space – your own Tween Time and Place - is an example of a purposeful imprint.

An object that is used only during times of prayer or meditation becomes imprinted with a prayerful energy. An article of clothing that is only used during times of healing becomes imprinted – charged with healing energy. The Bible tells of a man who touched the robe of Jesus and was healed. The robe was charged or imprinted with healing energy.

I have a small rug that I have used in my meditations for years. It is so charged with energy that all I have to do is unfold it and sit upon it and I move into the Tween Times. I relax immediately, the veils between the worlds slip away and my magical self comes forward.

Your Magical Spirit Cloth

The aura's natural ability to imprint is what makes creating a sacred magical cloth so easy and so effective. You can have your own magical cloths, and you can imprint them with any energy purpose you wish. You can have one that is general and all-purpose, one for healing, one for spirit work, one for shapeshifting and one for all of your psychic work. You can even have one that will help you to astral project or spirit travel - to leave your physical body and travel around. I sometimes use my meditation rug as a magic carpet to help with this. We are only limited by our imagination and focus.

Each time you use this cloth in your magical practices or have it with you, you charge it with purposeful, magical energy. Your aura is imprinting it. Eventually all you will have to do is wrap it around you, pull it up over the head or even just sit on it, and it begins to shift you from normal everyday type of thinking to your creative, psychic and magical part.

1. Find your magical cloth.

It can be a small blanket, a shawl, a beach towel or even a small throw rug to start with. Preferably, choose one that has never been used for anything before by anyone else or it may be one that is your favorite.

·   Choose a cloth whose color or design you like. (One of my healing cloths is a beach towel, which is multicolored. The colors and the imprinting together make it very suitable for color healing work.)

·   If it is a blanket, towel or shawl, it should be large enough to wrap comfortably around your body.

·   If it is a rug, it should be large enough to sit or lie upon. Two foot by three foot is usually adequate.

·   Some people will use a special shirt, robe, or other garment to imprint for this purpose. Do not be afraid to experiment.

·   Do not try and imprint a lot of things too soon. Focus on one to begin with.

-    In time, you will find ways to make and use your own meditation cloths that are unique to you.

2. Wash it if it is washable.

Some throw rugs are not and neither are some shawls too. Washing it will clean the garment of any previous imprints. Even if the item is new, it is a good idea to wash it initially. We want to start with a fresh cloth.

Do not wash it after this for at least six months. And only wash it then if it is horribly dirty. I am pretty careful with my cloths, and if they are cared for, you may not ever have to wash it more than once or twice. If you do wash it, wash it by hand and never wash it with anything else. Washing removes a lot of the energy reservoirs imprinted into it. When they are not in use, keep them folded away.

3. Make your preparations.

Follow the guidelines in the section "Preparing for Shapeshifting Exercises". As you relax in your sacred meditation space, have your magical cloth with you, resting on your lap.

4. Focus on the purpose for this magical cloth.

As you relax, focus upon what purpose this magical cloth should serve. In our case, we want to use it to help shift consciousness to move through veils and assist us in shapeshifting. Imagine this cloth helping you. Picture it wrapped around you, helping you. Imagine and visualize it in as much detail as possible.

5. Now begin imprinting.

Create a sacred space and wrap the cloth around you, pulling it up and over your head, like a hood. If it is a rug, roll it out and be sitting upon it. With your eyes closed, begin rhythmic breathing. Inhale for a count of four, hold for a count of four and exhale for a count of four. As you inhale, see and feel yourself drawing spiritual energy from the other side of the veils into you. As you exhale, see and feel it pouring out of you, making your aura strong and bright. Visualize it imprinting and charging your cloth with strong, vibrant energy. Continue this for five to ten minutes.

6. Perform your grounding exercise.

Part of this should be the folding up and putting away of your special cloth.. Remember that this cloth should not be used for anything other than your own magical shapeshifting practice. As you put it away, remember too that each time you use it, it's energy will grow stronger. It will become a reservoir of magical energy that you can use to boost your own at times when needed. It will make all of your meditations increasingly better and clearer.

7. Strengthen the imprint.

With new magical cloths it is a good idea to imprint it more strongly, so that it has a strong foundation of your energy in it. One of the easiest ways of doing this is by sleeping with it for a week. Place it under your pillow inside your pillowcase. You can even sleep upon it or use it as a blanket. By doing this for a week, you lay a solid foundation of energy into it. Your aura will imprint it strongly. It becomes your magical cloth.

Another way of strengthening the imprint is to have it on you or around you when you perform the Sun and Moon Breath Exercise. It will help infuse your spirit cloth with great energy.

The Elm Spirit

One day while playing in the woods with my brothers and our friends, I scrambled behind a bush at an elm tree's base, trying to hide. The bush was sparse but I didn't have time to move because I could hear the others drawing close.

It was then that I heard my name whispered. I jumped, startled at first, and then heard a gentle laugh. I turned my head to the elm behind me, following the sound of the laughter. I saw a soft face appear in the bark.

"Just lean back against me," the trees whispered, "and imagine that you are part of my bark."

I was stunned, but I leaned back, making myself comfortable. I could hear the others talking; I was the only one still not found. As they drew closer, I relaxed more. I felt like I was sinking into the tree, peering out from the bark - just like the face that I had seen in it. They searched all around me; several of them even stood not more than 2 feet away. I knew that I was invisible to them. When they moved off, I felt myself sitting outside the bark again.

I stood and faced the tree, unsure what to say or do. The face within it was very distinct, and it smiled and again laughed softly. Then the face faded back into the bark. I would go back to that tree many times to hide, and never was I ever caught there. From this elm, I learned how to see spirits in trees and plants and I didn't know it then, but I was also receiving my first lessons in shapeshifting. And my love of being in and around trees continues to this day.

Shapeshifting
Exercise
(developmental & experiential)

The Tibetan Walk to Nowhere

Skills & Benefits:

- **develops ability to move in and out of altered states**
- **stimulates intuition**
- **facilitates moving between veils and into other dimensions**

The *Tibetan Walk to Nowhere* is a series of steps that will induce an altered state of consciousness. It can help shift your consciousness away from the daily hassles, and it will help activate your higher intuition and clairvoyance. It can even help you move between the veils of this world and that of spirit.

This dance stimulates our inner vision and creativity. Use it with visualization and creative imagination to move past obstacles that you encounter in any path of your life. It can be adapted to walk you into higher perceptions along any avenue of life you choose. It can even be used to walk into the energy of an animal totem.

1. Decide what kind of perception you wish to walk into.
In the beginning, I suggest you just walk to awaken your perceptions, your intuition and your own clairvoyant ability.

2. Make preparations.
Choose an incense that is conducive to your purpose. Use a white candle initially, but you will find that other color candles will facilitate different kinds of walks.

3. Mark off your sacred space.

4. Perform one or more of the balancing exercises, to stabilize yourself and your energy system.

5. Now begin the *Tibetan Walk to Nowhere.*

This walk involves a repetition of a pattern of steps. It involves four steps forward and four steps back. Four steps forward and four steps back. Forward, back. Inner. Outer.

The steps should be taken in a sure, slow, and deliberate manner with full attention upon them. Place the heel down first and then the toes with each step. This serves as a reminder to maintain sure footing in all of your spiritual journeys and especially upon the path you are now treading.

Your hands can be folded in a prayer position at the chest, or crossed at the heart with a hand upon each shoulder. Visualize yourself in your magickal body as you perform it. In time, you can visualize yourself walking upon a path of a particular color, a color appropriate to your purpose. For example, use a red path for strength or a green path for growth. Perform this walk for at least five minutes. See and feel yourself growing stronger in the energy of your purpose with each step. After five to ten minutes, pause and either continue standing or sit down, whichever is most comfortable for you.

Take time to feel and experience the energy around you. What do you sense? What do you see physically and in your mind's eye? There may be shimmers around you. You may experience shadows shifting and glimmers in the air. These often indicate a movement through veils. You may experience some dizziness and lightheadedness. There may even be a sense of disorientation. Remember that these are signs that you have parted and may have even moved through veils. Allow the energy from the other side of the veil to be absorbed back into you. When the phenomena stops and the physiological responses calm, the energy has been absorbed. Know that it will grow stronger each time, empowering your own creativity.

6. Perform your balancing movements.

This will stabilize this energy so you can express it more effectively in the outer world. Offer a prayer of thanksgiving or do an affirmation.

Special Note

As you perform this exercise, within several weeks time, you will notice specific differences. Your energy levels will increase. Your mood will be more positive. Do not be surprised when others comment on these positive changes. Your poise in all life situations will improve. You will also notice yourself handling outside, everyday activities with greater ease, grace, and strength. This is the magic of shapeshifting and one of the gifts of learning to moving between veils.

Shapeshifting
Exercise
(developmental & experiential)

Metamorphosis

Skills and Benefits:

- **flexibility and control of energy**
- **healing and transformation**
- **awakens creative imagination**
- **develops concentration and visualization**
- **helps develop shapeshifting abilities**
- **colorful dream activity**
- **weaving of glamour.**

This is a wonderful exercise for stretching our magical muscles. It helps us develop the ability to shapeshift and weave glamour. This very enjoyable exercise is also beneficial for anyone who is having trouble with nightmares. It can be used powerfully in conjunction with the dream techniques explored in Part II. Choose a time when you will not be interrupted. Early evenings before going to bed and before you are too sleepy can be a good time.

1. Make the preparations.

2. Perform the Dancer's Pose, followed by the Tibetan Walk to Nowhere.
As you perform the Tibetan Walk, imagine yourself slowly parting and moving between the veils of your outer life to those more magical.

3. Take a seated position and allow yourself to relax.
Perform your progressive relaxation, using your candles or fragrances to help set the mood. Using slow, rhythmic breathing, imagine and feel warm

soothing energy flowing to every part of your body. As you relax, allow your attention to be focused entirely upon yourself. This is your special time, and you are alone and safe, warm and comfortable. Your eyes are closed and nothing can distract or harm you. The darkness that surrounds you feels as if someone has placed an old comfortable quilt about your head and shoulders.

4. Then allow the following scenario to unfold for you:

You begin to notice that you are not in total darkness. It is more of a gray. In your mind's eye you see that you are sitting within a small spherical enclosure. It is formed of millions of thin threads, spiraling and winding around you, giving you just enough room to stretch if you need to. It appears as if these threads have frozen into a silvery form. What light there is shines through them and casts a grayish-silver shimmer within the dome.

This is your cocoon. It is a cocoon from which you emerge each night. It is the cocoon of your life. Its only colors are grays and silvers. It is comfortable, but it is also limiting.

The threads that form the sides of the cocoon are all of the threads that you have sewn in your life. The threads of your life have created a cocoon in which you can feel comfortable, safe, protected and closed off. And yet through some of the threads come slivers of light from an outside world, causing the threads to dance with new life. It makes you wonder what other beauties the outer world might hold.

You stand and move to a spot in the cocoon where a sliver of light from the outside sneaks through. You place your eye to it, squinting through the tiny opening. For an instant, a rainbow of colors flashes in your eye. It is almost blinding in its intensity. The brilliance of the color is greater than you have ever imagined and it takes your breath away.

You step back, filled with awe. You must see this other world as it truly is. You know that only within its light will you be able to see who you truly are.

You gently feel along the sides of the cocoon, searching for an opening. There are no doors and no windows. The sides do feel a bit rubbery, and as you push and feel, they give with your touch. With your hands you slowly and gently separate the threads, stretching them like soft bands of elastic. You extend your hands and arms through the walls. The outer light touches them, and a sense of freedom and power begins to fill you. Moving your arms, you stretch and wiggle, making the opening wider so that you can squeeze your head and shoulders out as well. The sight is breathtaking and you freeze with wonder – half in and half out.

Before you is every color upon the planet and some you have never seen. There are shimmering emerald grasses, juxtaposed against a vibrant blue sky. The earth is speckled with flowers and plants of every variety. There is a soft sound as if the plants and the air are singing in harmony to greet you.

Before you stretches an expanse of earth and sky so great that you wonder is you will ever be able to know it all. You pull yourself through and you lightly touch the earth. It sings as your feet brush its surface, and the sweet sound sends shivers of joy through your body.

You spin quickly about, trying to take in all of the sights at once. The spinning motion lifts you off your feet. You feel light and free, unbound to the earth. It is then that you notice that you have wing – wings of rainbow light! Emerging from your cocoon has given you the opportunity to fly.

The wings move with your thoughts, lifting you, lowering you. You begin to understand how magical a butterfly truly is. You fly slowly over the landscape, hovering about flowers and trees. Occasionally you light upon the flowers and plants, so that your touch sends forth their songs into the air about you.

There is so much to see and learn. There is so much nectar to be savored, nectar that has always been present but usually ignored. You are filled with a desire to share this nectar – this world – with others. Will they believe? Will others be able to see that there is a magical butterfly within each of us, waiting to emerge?

You know that you must take some of that nectar of light and creativity back with you. As your own life becomes filled with more color, others will notice and ask. But each of us must seek it out for ourselves. To simply tell others will never do. It is only when they are able to see the effects within your own life will their desire to add color to their lives grow. Then it can be shared. When the desire is great enough – when there is the beginning of belief in new possibilities – the butterfly will emerge from the cocoon.

You look about the field of flowers. You choose one in the center of the field. It is a flower that has a special radiance for you at this time. Each flower is special. Each flower has its own unique qualities, energies and messages. Each flower has its own unique energy and gift. You float softly above it and then settle gently on the outer edges of its petals. It sings to you at your touch. The sound carries through your ears and into every cell within your body, caressing them with joy.

In the heart of the flower is its sweet nectar. You cup your hands and sample its fragrant elixir. Your head spins with a dizzying effect. You are filled with great joy. The flower has now become a part of you and you have become a part of it. You share its energy. It is a gift to take back with you. It may inspire creativity, intuition, prosperity, healing or any number of possibilities. Each flower is different. Each is a gift, and there are thousands and thousands of flowers to sample.

You bow softly to the flower in gratitude. You rise up and float gently back to the cocoon. The sunlight shimmers, a rainbow prism reflecting off its surface. You spread the threads and enter, going back into the cocoon. You notice that it is a little brighter inside now. The light shines and penetrates a little more strongly.

You know that as you allow the magical butterfly within you to emerge more and more, the outer you and the inner, magical you will blend more and more. With time, the rainbows of one realm will become the rainbows of the other. Every rainbow has two ends, bridging and linking the two worlds together.

You settle into the center of the cocoon. The nectar is still sweet within your mouth. You know that in the days ahead that it will affect your life, sweetening it in wonderful ways. You breathe deeply and allow the cocoon to fade from around you. Your own room and your physical surroundings begin to return.

You stretch a bit, feeling lighter and more blessed. You remember all that you experienced, and for a moment you can see your wings shimmering lightly around you.

5. Repeat the Tibetan Walk to Nowhere, visualizing yourself moving back out from the other side of the veils.

6. Perform your grounding postures.

It is a good idea to stretch a little after this exercise. Maybe eat something light – a cracker or two. To ground the energy and make the magic of the exercise stronger, do some work with your Shapeshifting Journalt. Research the flower that you touched. Make a drawing of it. Explore its magical, herbal and other aspects. This will help you to understand how the flower's energy will touch your life in the days ahead. It is also a way of honoring the magical process that you have activated through the symbols and images of this exercise.

*Shapeshifting
Exercise
(developmental & experiential)*

A Touch of Invisibility

Skills and Benefits:

- **stillness of the mind**
- **weaving of glamour**
- **patience**
- **invisibility**

The idea of being invisible teases most people. There are so many things we could do. So much fun we could have. Everyone at some point has imagined what it would be like to be invisible.

There are many levels to it and most of us have experienced some form of invisibility. Remember the last time no one seemed to notice you? That's a form of invisibility. Remember the last time someone tripped over you, saying, "I'm sorry, I didn't see you there." That is a form of invisibility.

As a child, I was a bit sickly with very bad asthma, so I was often propped up in a chair in a corner of the room with the adults when there were gatherings and parties. I would become relatively invisible to them. In time, I began to enjoy those occasions because I would find out things about those present that I would never have found out otherwise. When you are "not really there", people don't watch what they say.

When we can walk around without being seen and without anyone taking notice – whether we are physically visible or not, we are experiencing invisibility. When we do it at will, we are weaving the glamour of invisibility about ourselves. We are veiled.

There is a lot of confusion about the practice of invisibility. It is an aspect of the shapeshifting and the weaving of glamour. It is a skill that takes much practice. With the following exercise, you will lay a foundation for the developing of this ability.

1. The key to this exercise is stillness and concentration.
Learning to keep the mind still takes practice. Concentration is the art of holding a thought or image that you have created without the mind wandering. Try counting slowly to ten, focusing only on one number at a time. If you find your mind wandering, bring it back to the number.

2. Practice being still, not moving and only focusing on one thought or image (preferably yourself as being invisible) while in a group situation.
Parties, libraries, and other places people gather can be good places to practice this. Do this for longer and longer periods of time. Start with 30 seconds and then extend it. Visualize yourself as just part of the surroundings, like a piece of furniture.

Much of this ability is learning to control the aura, the energy surrounding the human body. You can learn to adjust its intensity so that you "blend in". Practice standing against a wall and see yourself and your aura becoming part of the wall, just as if you were fading or melting into it.

3. Call upon fox medicine.
One of the best ways of developing invisibility is by working with "fox medicine" in Native American traditions. This is an animal that can be three feet from you in the wild and you not know it is there. It knows how to be still and camouflaged.

Working to blend in with your surroundings, to come and go unnoticed is part of what fox medicine teaches. Working to move silently without revealing your intentions is part of the art of invisibility.

The fox uses its ability at quiet and stillness for its invisibility. The next time you go to a party, take a seat on the couch or chair, and visualize yourself as a fox that blends in perfectly to the environment. Imagine yourself taking on the pattern and colors of the couch or chair. Then sit quietly and watch how many people accidentally bump into you or even try to sit down on you because they did not "see you". You will be amazed.

4. Practice variations.
A variation of #3 is to practice imagining yourself as a fox when you enter or leave a gathering. See yourself as blending into the gathering, melting into it. Do not be surprised as the night goes on that others will make such comments as, "When did you get here?" "How long have you been here?" "I didn't see you come in," or "When did you leave?" The more you work with fox, the easier it becomes.

Part II

Becoming the Dreamwalker

The polar bear is the embodiment of the spirit of the North. It is Nanook and is believed to have great supernatural powers. The polar bear is a shaman, a liason with the spirit world, keeper of the wisdom of ages. It walks between the physical and spiritual - the waking and the dreaming - unrestricted and without fear. It awakens our greatest abilities in all extremes - while awake or asleep.

Tien Hou

Long before there was a long ago, there was a young girl by the name of Tien Hou. She lived on a small island with her four brothers and her parents, and as with most island dwellers, the family made its living by fishing.

While Tien Hou's father and brothers spent their days fishing, she spent her days with her mother. They would walk the shores of their island, and her mother would delight her with wondrous tales of the sea. At night she would dream of exciting adventures of her own while at sea. Once she dreamt of riding on a turtle's back under the water. When she awoke, her sheets were damp and smelled of the sea. It wouldn't be the only time that the sleeping and the waking blended.

As she grew older, her dreams became ever more vivid and many times she awoke – sure that she had experienced what she had dreamt. She dreamed of flying and swimming and seeing people she knew and many she did not. Her dreams became more real and she would know things from them – things that were happening in the waking world around her. In the dreams, she could see into the homes and hearts of those on her island. Sometimes these things frightened her, but even in the fear there was always the wonder.

Tien Hou became more and more aware that the veils that separated the sleep and the waking were very thin – that the waking and sleeping worlds played upon and influenced each other in subtle but very real ways. While she once shared her dreamtime adventures openly with family and friends, she now began to be more silent about what she saw. As a child, it was cute to see the young child excited about her dreams, but now she was older. The once amused smiles from others were now becoming uneasy and suspicious when she spoke of her dreams and what she saw.

One night while her father and brothers were away on a long fishing trip, Tien Hou lay on her mat sleeping and her breath became irregular. She seemed to gasp in her sleep and began to moan and cry out. Her mother awoke at Tien Hou's cries, and when she saw the tears and pain on her daughter's sleeping face, she tried to awaken her.

She bathed Tien Hou's brow with cool water. She stroked her head and spoke softly to her, urging her to awaken. The mother cried softly, desperate to save her daughter from what was claiming her in her dreams.

Tien Hou felt her mother's tears and kisses upon her face and brow, and she slowly awakened in response to them. As she opened her eyes, she repeatedly whispered, crying as she awoke, "I should have stayed longer. I should have stayed longer."

Her mother hugged her tightly to her breast and Tien Hou sobbed, eventually slipping into a dreamless sleep. The next day and for days after, nothing was said of the incident by either Tien Hou or her mother.

Another week passed and the father and brothers returned from the sea. They rushed from their boat running to their home. But one of the sons was missing.

The father told of the violent storm that arose while they were at sea. He spoke of how the winds roared and the lightning flashed. The waves grew larger and more thunderous, battering the boat about. They fought to control the boat in the storm, but a mighty wave washed them all from the deck.

The brothers began to speak. Each in turn told of how Tien Hou had pulled them from the raging waters, descending from the heavens like a great bird. But before the fourth son was saved, Tien Hou had disappeared and the boy succumbed to the sea.

"I should have stayed longer," Tien Hou whispered, her voice cracking with great sorrow. Tears ran freely down her face.

Her mother paled, realizing what had happened and what her role had been. So confusing and astounding were the stories that little more was spoken of it as the family mourned the loss of a son and brother.

Then one night it happened again. Tien Hou cried out in her sleep. Her body twisted with pain. The family awoke at her cries, and her mother, remembering the last time, prevented anyone from awakening her. She watched over Tien Hou and cared for her, making sure she would not be disturbed.

Asleep but not asleep, Tien Hou lay upon her mat, tenderly cared for by her mother until the cries stopped and the body relaxed. Breathing became regular and a look of peace settled over Tien Hou through the rest of the night and into the morning.

As time passed, those who fished the islands began to tell stories of a young woman who flew from the skies and saved them from raging waters or other dangers of the sea. Always they corresponded to times when Tien Hou had one of her dreamtime adventures, and over the years shrines began to arise to honor this child who walked the dreamtime as courageously and honorably as she lived the waking life...

Chapter Six

Shapeshifting
&
The Dreamtime

In more ancient societies, the shamans were the keepers of the sacred knowledge. They were held in high esteem and recognized as the true shapeshifters and dreamwalkers. They were able to use their dreamtime as effectively as they used the time they were awake. They were tied to the rhythms and forces of nature. Two things which they all held in common were an awareness of the power of myth and strong work with dreamtime. They recognized that there is a power behind the images of their tales and dreams, and they knew that myths could be used as a bridge between the realm of sleep and the world of the awake.

True shamans and shapeshifters are capable of living between the physical and the spiritual. They can adapt themselves and change their energies according to their life circumstances. They can shape and mold the life environment, creating whatever they desire and becoming whatever they dream. They can live the dreamtime while awake or asleep.

Shamanism is an experiential growth process. It involves becoming the master of your own initiation. In shamanism, the individual ultimately answers to no human or totem and is alone with the supernatural. Yet, he or she maintains a true sense of belonging and connectedness to all life. This individual is able to visit the heavens and the underworld. This individual can direct and use the dreamtime for finding answers and for changing and influencing the waking time. They learn to control the mind stuff, what in traditional yoga is called the "citta." By stilling the mind, they become aware of the inner realms and develop conscious interaction with them – often through techniques of shapeshifting.

Shapeshifting Tales from around the World

Africa
Nana Mirian

The Snake Chief

China
Lady White

The Crane Maiden

Story of Lady Ren

Finland
The Forest Bride

France
The Doctor and the Pupil

Cat Woman

Germany
The Frog Prince

Iceland
The Seal's Skin

Native American
The Owl Husband

White Buffalo Woman

When Grizzlies Walked Upright

The Girl Who Married Rattlesnake

Bear and His Indian Wife

Norway
East of the Sun, West of the Moon

Peru
The Snake Lover

Scotland
The Blacksmith's Wife

Spain
The Serpent Woman

Sweden
The Swan-Maiden

Learning to shift the dream to reality and the reality into dream - to walk the thread of life between the worlds - is to become the dreamwalker. Much of the ancient knowledge for doing this has been lost, but it has not been destroyed. It can be found again by those willing to put forth the effort and follow the journey. There are guides, reflections, and ways to unfold this knowledge within ourselves.

It begins with realizing that every tradition taught that the dream world was just as real and just as important as the waking world. Learning to stimulate and control the dreamtime does two things for us when developing shapeshifting. First, it enables us to see connections between the physical and the spiritual. What we do on one level, always affects us on other levels. What we do in our waking life, affects our dream life. And what we do in our dream life, affects our waking life. If we create changes in the dreamtime, it will shift things in the waking time and do so more effectively. And second, it enhances our ability to shift energies on more than just the physical level, while also developing our awareness of the subtle and often unconscious aspects of us. It strengthens our magical essence. When we can shapeshift our essence in the dreamtime, we will be more effective and powerful in shapeshifting it in the waking time.

We've all had dreams from which we wish we could awaken. We've all had dreams we wished we could step back into. We've all had dreams that bewildered us. Imagine though if we could change our dreams. Imagine if we could change our awareness while in the dream. Imagine if we could program our dreams for clarity, insight, inspiration, or manifestation. Imagine if we could control and shape the dreamtime. Imagine if we could become lucid (conscious) in the dream. Imagine if we could travel freely through our dreams to other places and times. We could stop our nightmares. We could get answers to waking time questions. We could empower ourselves night after night. We could change the scenario or leave it entirely. We could go anywhere we desired. We could even take that next step beyond lucid dreaming to a fully conscious-out-of-body experience. When we learn to shapeshift our dreams, we become the dreamwalker. Just imagine the possibilities!

The Dreamwalker

Nothing is as universally fascinating as dreams. Dreams shift and dance. They mold themselves into scenarios of wonder and terror. They delight and amaze, amuse and frighten. They are never the same and yet always the same in the way they manifest themselves within our lives. We can dream about anything, no matter how preposterous or unnatural it may seem to be.

Learning to employ ancient and modern techniques to facilitate this process in all areas of our life is the purpose of Part II. We can learn to shift the energies of consciousness, to shift the past and present circumstances of our lives. We can learn to do this in a controlled, gentle manner. We can learn to shift into higher awareness when reviewing past experiences. And we can reshape energies to eliminate karma or to manifest new opportunities. It all lies within our bounds.

We all have the potential to become a dreamwalker, one who can stimulate and shift the dreamtime for greater insight, fulfillment, love and abundance. The dream life is essential to our growth. It is not a replacement for our waking life, but we can use it to strengthen and illuminate our waking life.

Our nocturnal life puts us in touch with realities and energies that can open us to greater productivity during our waking hours. We can become as useful and active within our sleep as we are when awake. We each have the potential of becoming our own invisible helper.

When we learn to shapeshift and control the energies of the dream state, our lives are rewarded. There are many ways to use our formally dormant, sleep time. We can use the hours of sleep to help those who suffer or sorrow. We can learn to extend help and encouragement to both the living and the dead. We can give and receive higher instruction. We can assist, inspire and advise those who would be unlikely to listen to us while awake. We can open ourselves to creative inspiration. We can visit all spots upon the planet. We can even visit others in their dreams. All art and music is at our disposal. We can work with time to correct the karma of the past and set new patterns for the future. We can re-manifest situations that were handled improperly so they may be straightened out. The potentials are unlimited.

Dream alchemy is the process of learning to control and shapeshift the dream state and all of its energies so that we can better come to know ourselves on all levels. It is using dream energy to initiate the process of transformation. Earlier, we discussed some of the principles essential to shapeshifting on any level. One of these applies strongly to becoming the dreamwalker: "As above, so below; as below, so above." This principle teaches us that all things are connected. Everything upon the Earth is reflected in the Heavens, and everything in the Heavens is reflected upon the Earth. What we do on one level will affect us on all levels. Nothing is disconnected. Thus our sleeping life and our waking life are linked. They reflect and influence each other.

Working with this principle is what enables us to uncover the hidden side of things. It enables us to make correlations. These may be the correlations of hidden phenomena to the natural world or it may be the hidden motives, emotions or mental and spiritual energies influencing our physical lives. Stimulating greater dream activity and awareness, and then learning to control and mold those energies according to certain patterns, opens us to the hidden side of things.

As we learn to work with and control our dreamtime energies, we also initiate control over our waking life situations as well. The dreams do not eliminate the obstacles, but they can be used to reveal our obstacles as a means to a higher end. What we do on one level affects us on all others. What we do in the dream time will reflect and affect what we do in the waking time. Commitment to shapeshifting is a commitment to becoming the modem dreamwalker. We are learning to alter, control and shapeshift our waking and sleeping energies for growth.

A Different Look at Dream Processes

Dreams are a part of our life, and as with all life functions, they serve a purpose. Dreams play a vital role in our day to day life. They are more than a stress-release mechanism. Dreams put us in touch with other realities and planes of life not consciously acknowledged.

We are more than just physical beings. We are comprised of other, more subtle bands of energy - sometimes called the subtle bodies of our emotional, mental and spiritual selves. Sometimes, they are just referred to as our astral bodies. What you choose to call them does not really matter, but we must realize that we operate on more than just the purely physical level. These more subtle aspects of ourselves interpenetrate other planes and dimensions that can influence us while we are in the physical. They serve to filter out undue influences, even while they help bridge our ordinary consciousness and awarenesss to those other dimensions and planes. In that bridging, they give us mobility and control within those other dimensions - more than what we usually believe is possible.

Learning to recognize and shift these subtle interplays is part of what shapeshifting is all about. And since dreamtime is a reflection of one of those other dimensions, it helps explain why control of the dreamtime is so important to understanding and developing our shapeshifting skills. (For purposes of simplicity, I will generally refer to these subtle aspects of us as our spirit essence throughout this part of the book.)

Occultism teaches us that control of the environment begins with control of the self, and yet there is an aspect of all of our lives that we do not try to control because we believe it can't be controlled. That aspect is our dreams. People often tell me of their dreams, confounded by them and yet always expressing the same desire: "If only I could control the dreams." While there is a great desire to control and direct dream activity, there also seems to be an unconscious acceptance that the dreamtime is not real and thus cannot be controlled.

Even with all that we know about the human potential in the modern world, we believe we can't change what we are dreaming. We believe we can't change our awareness while in the dream. We believe we can't program dreams for insight, inspiration or manifestation. We believe it is simply a phenomenon of the night that operates according to some strange, unknown laws. Anything which plays a vital function in our lives can be controlled. Dreams play a vital function, but we have come to accept them as part of an autonomic process that we cannot control. We believe that we are simply at the mercy of whatever that process wishes to present to us each night.

Nothing could be further from the truth.

You can influence your dreams to empower yourself. This part of the book is designed to help you do that in four simple steps. When used somewhat regularly (once or twice a week) within one year you will be amazed at how much you can control and shapeshift your dreamtime. These four steps are:

1. **understanding what happens during sleep and dreamtime.**
2. **learning how to influence and alter our sleep conditions through such as herbs, fragrances, flower elixirs and crystals**
3. **developing the use of dream tantra to stimulate more colorful and lucid dream activity**
4. **using dream tantra with mythic dream work techniques to shapeshift and create your own dream scenarios.**

So What Are Dreams?

Dreams are a reality separate from our waking consciousness. The images shift and change, scenarios altering in seemingly disconnected manners. They are farcical and they are terrifying. They are ridiculous and serious. They are emotional and they are spiritual. They are to most people incomprehensible.

Dreams have been defined in many ways by many people. They have been called manifestations of images and sounds. They have been likened to a mirror of our life-conscious and unconscious. They have been called creations of the night. They mystify and perplex, but they unite us all, for it is the one experience we all share - whether rich or poor, mighty or weak, male or female, earthy or spiritual. We all dream. If for no other reason than its universality, dream work should be a part of our overall educational process.

Every night when we fall asleep, certain processes take place. It is important to understand them, so we can more easily control and direct them. The subtle bodies work with the physical functions and energies. We are multi-dimensional – more than just a physical being. When we lie down to sleep, our spirit essence exteriorizes from the physical. (See page 142.) This separation from the physical body serves several purposes. It enables the energy debris and tension accumulated by us throughout the day to be shaken free of our essence. It enables our physical body to relax and re-energize itself. It provides opportunities to connect with teachings and activities on other dimensions. Without the encumbrance of the physical body, our spiritual self can draw energy directly from the universe. Then upon awakening, when the spiritual essence reintegrates with the physical, the physical body is re- energized.

Exercises in meditation and visualization help develop the ability to extend the consciousness beyond physical life dimensions, but exercises in dreamwalking will develop the ability to become lucid in the dreamstate. It does not happen over night though. It is like learning to do anything. There are always preparatory exercises. These exercises stretch and strengthen our muscles to prevent injuries and imbalances. We do not attempt intricate gymnastic moves without learning the basics or without loosening and stretching the muscles before performance. It is the same with dream alchemy. There are exercises to loosen and stretch our energies and develop the ability to extend the consciousness to those more subtle realms with greater control and awareness.

When we attempt to shape our dreams, we do so for a variety of reasons. It is a dynamic prelude to conscious astral projection, the use of our spirit essence as a separate vehicle of consciousness to explore the more

Leaving the Physical Body During Sleep

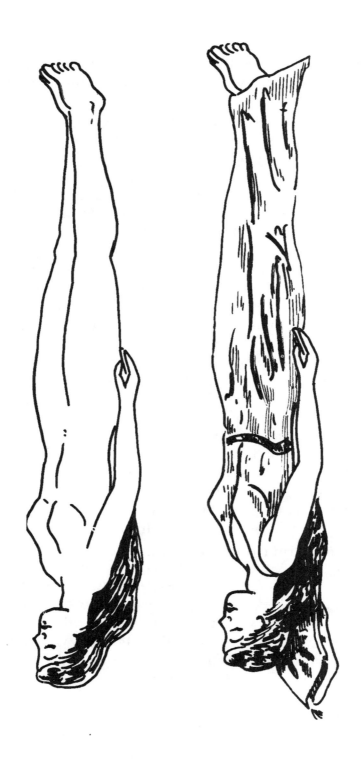

Each night during sleep our spirit essence (subtle body) exteriorizes from the physical body to shake off debris of emotional and mental energies accumulated throughout the day. THis facilitates rest and recuperation of the physical body. Some of this is reflected in our dreams, but this also allows for the exploration of other dimensions.

subtle dimensions surrounding us. Dream alchemy - especially mythic dream work as outlined later - is a powerful means of strengthening these energies.

As we work with the process outlined within this book, we are asserting control over a previously uncontrolled aspect of our lives. This will affect other areas of our lives. What we do on one level affects us on all levels. As we learn to shape and control our sleep and dream processes, we initiate opportunity to shape and change our waking life processes as well. "As above, so below; as below, so above."

Alarm Clocks

 One of the problems of modern society involves the use of alarm clocks. The alarm clock may sound before the spirit essence has reintegrated in a fully balanced manner. It jars this integration of energies. As a result, we may feel out of sunc or even a bit lopsided. We may spend the entire morning drinking cups of coffee and trying to get our "act together." It may take until mid-morning or longer before the spiritual essence shuffles itself into proper alignment. Through the techniques within this book, this can eventually be avoided. As you learn to control the dream state, you will also be learning to control the awakening as well.

Increasing and Influencing Dream Activity

Stimulating greater dream activity is the prelude to shaping and controlling the dream state. One of the most powerful means of stimulating greater dream activity is simply by paying more attention to it. If we give our dreams no relevance or if we look upon them as silly and frivolous, it becomes increasingly difficult to remember them and work with them. The purpose of increasing dream activity is so we can remember them and utilize them more effectively in enhancing our lives.

There's an old saying "a dream unexplained is like a letter unopened." Dreams are communications to us, for us and about us. We would not let a letter from a distant friend set on our table, unopened and unread. Dreams are gift communications.

Many complain that they just cannot remember their dreams, or they believe they don't dream at all. What we must realize is that we have to put forth some conscious effort in the dream process. If someone speaks to us and we never acknowledge that person's presence or that what is being said is worth listening to, eventually that person will quit speaking to you except in extreme cases. Our dreams are the same way. If we do not pay attention to them, eventually the communications cease, except in extreme situations - which are our nightmares. When we work with the techniques and tools that follow, we are passing on a message to other levels of our consciousness. We are sending the message that we wish to reopen communication.

Initially, the results may not be as dramatic as you would like, but this can be a testing of your willingness to re-establish the subtle communication lines. The more you do while awake to prepare for sleep, the stronger the message becomes. Likewise, the more you work with your dreams while awake, the stronger your waking intuition will become. If you work with the techniques in this chapter alone, within one month a tremendous difference will be experienced. Your dreams will become more colorful, vibrant, informative and memorable.

All Purpose Dream Herbs and Plants

One of the most ancient and effective techniques for increasing and influencing dream activity is through the use of herbs. Dream pillows and sachets can be made by choosing herbs and fragrances that affect sleep and dreaming and then wrapping them in a square of cotton muslin. Placing these sachets under or inside the bed pillow (or next to the bed) enables them to work effectively and gently while you sleep. The use of herbs in dream baths, as described in the exercise atthe end of the chapter, is also effective. Drinking certain herbal teas also enhances dream states.

At this point, we are working primarily with physical things to stimulate greater dream activity. Through these outer activities, we work to restore communication with those levels of consciousness which speak to us through dreams. The more physical activities we use to prepare for sleep, the stronger the message is sent to the subconscious that we are open to communication again. Using herbs is one way to open to that communication.

Here's a list of herbs to help influence dreams:

Agrimony
This is an excellent herb to use when there is an inability to fall asleep due to emotional problems. It is calming. It is also effective as a flower essence.

Anise
This herb elicits a protective energy, particularly against disturbing dreams. It has a unique ability to keep one safe in dreams. It is stabilizing to the astral body. When we are asleep we often travel in our astral body, so this protective herb is particularly beneficial.

Ash Leaves
The ash is a tree that wands are often made from. The leaves of the ash tree, when included in dream pillows, stimulate prophetic dreams.

Bay Leaves
This is a stimulating herb and fragrance. It is soothing to the respiration and to the heart chakra of the body. It can be used to stimulate dreams of inspiration. It can be used to stimulate dreams that reveal what is blocking the manifestation of love within our lives. Many times negative past events create a closing down of the full expression of love. This herb and fragrance stimulates dreams that can reveal those blockages, bringing out the events and emotions that are congesting your full and true expression of love.

Celandine (lesser)
This herb makes a good wash, bath or drink in conjunction with dream alchemy. It is beneficial to use in the ritual dream bath described in the "Rite of Dream Passage". It is a very psychic herb. It enhances and stimulates dream activity, restoring a delight in opening and working with dreams.

Cinquefoil
This herb can be used in dream rituals and baths to open to greater awareness of our perfect partner in life. If male, it can stimulate dreams involving a female or the qualities of a female most beneficial to you. If you are a female, it may stimulate dreams involving the ideal male or the ideal male qualities for you.

Dragon's Blood

Dragon's blood as an herb has a long tradition associated with the art of shapeshifting. According to the tradition, this herb enables one to assume various shapes and guises, and facilitates traveling both astrally and physically. It can be an excellent aid in mythic dream work, but the herb must be infused (through meditation) with the purpose of the individual.

Ferns

This plant has a tradition of invisibility associated with it. The seeds, as part of a dream pillow, enable the individual to go about the business of dream alchemy undisturbed by physical and non- physical energies.

Hops

Hops are effective in herbal sachets and pillows for dreams. They are also effective when prepared as a drink prior to sleep. Calming and soothing, they help to restore or instill a peaceful sleep.

Mugwort

Mugwort is a powerful herb for use in dream alchemy. It is also effective as a flower essence. It is known as a visionary herb, and opens one to dreams of the future, and thus it is effective to use with experiments in mythic dream work. It can stimulate dreams which open you to mystical experiences and inner enlightenment.

Peppermint

All herbs of the mint family are known as the friends of life. They have beneficial effects. While spearmint may have the physical effect of being more calming than peppermint, peppermint is more effective with dream alchemy. When taken as a tea in the evening before sleep, it stimulates more interesting dreams with a leaning toward the prophetic. The leaves make a powerful addition to sleep sachets and dream pillows.

Vervain

Vervain, along with mugwort, is one of the best herbs for the mythic dream work techniques described later. It is a visionary herb and it is especially effective when utilized in dream quests or as a prelude to dream quest processes.

Herbs to Influence Nightmares and Fears

Everyone has nightmares on occasion. In most cases, we force ourselves to wake up out of them. This is so we do not have to confront what is in them. Most adults need to recognize that nightmares are important messages. The more frightening they are, the more urgent and important the message is. Nightmares show us our greatest fears.

There are herbal remedies to ease nightmares and to facilitate our exploring them. It is never easy to face some aspects of our life, but unless we do so, we may be forcing our psyche to get in touch with us in other ways, such as through crisis or illness.

In the case of children, nightmares can be a problem. Children are very sensitive to the environment of their homes. There is an unrecognized psychic link to the energies of both parents. Even in cases where effort is made to hide any disharmony from the children, it will still be sensed on some level. Often this is reflected through the dreams of children. Being open to talk about your dreams and those of your children is beneficial to all. A child's nightmares may also reflect fears that the child has brought with him or her into this incarnation from previous ones. In cases such as these, it is important to take measures to ease the nightmares and help the child to understand them as much as possible. If they are not dealt with, the child can develop a fear of sleep. This will create even more problems.

Sleep sachets, dream pillows and dream fragrances are extremely effective with children. They ease the emotions and help them to enjoy peaceful sleep. They also enable the children to speak more openly about their dream experiences. This creates opportunities to correct the cause of the nightmares. The following is a list of herbs known to be helpful when dealing with nightmares:

Anise
A sachet of anise will help prevent nightmares. It helps the individual to feel safe and secure. It is calming to emotions.

Cedar
Cedar has a fragrance that is cleansing to the environment. It purifies and stabilizes the aura of the individual. It balances emotional and mental energies. It is a strong remedy for bad dreams.

Huckleberry
When used as an incense before going to sleep, it calms and balances the aura. It also assists in having dreams which can come true, especially those which are precognitive.

Mistletoe

This is an herb which helps restore peaceful sleep and transmutes nightmares into beautiful dream experiences. It can be included in dream and sleep sachets, or it can be used separately by placing it within the pillow or over the headboard.

Morning Glory

This is a powerful herb for correcting and stopping all nightmare activity, especially in children. Simply place it under the pillow of the child, and it will restore peaceful sleep.

Purslane

This is another herb which can be burned as incense prior to going to sleep. It can also be used in a dream pillow. It provides protection against bad dreams.

Rose

Rose is a powerful fragrance and flower for use in restoring refreshing sleep, especially after a series of nightmares. It balances the heart and the emotions. It stimulates refreshing dreams to heal and soothe the causes and conditions of disturbed sleep.

Rosemary

Rosemary is an ancient English herb, and it is still associated with elves, fairies and other friendly spirits. When used for sleep and dream purposes, it is effective as an oil or as part of a dream sachet. You can also place a sprig under the pillow itself. It stimulates inner peace, driving away nightmares and restoring good sleep. It can be placed beneath the bed to protect one from frightening and evil dreams from deep within the subconscious. It draws those of the fairy kingdom to watch over children and guard them at night.

Thyme

This herb is balancing to the emotional state of the individual. It enables you to sleep more peacefully. It can also be used to help children whose nightmares may be the result of fears brought over from their previous lives. It also has benefits in working with mythic dream techniques.

Dream Fragrances

Fragrance is one of the most effective means of altering sleep states and dream consciousness. Aromatherapy is growing in acceptance and popularity in all of its forms: herbal scents, essential oils, incense, potpourri, etc. Every fragrance alters the vibrational rate of the environment and the individual according to its properties. Fragrances most strongly affect the etheric, astral and mental bands of energy. This is why they are so effective in dream alchemy. They penetrate the consciousness during sleep.

Essential oils have most often been used for two purposes: therapeutic, as an aid in restoring health; and metaphysical, for spiritual upliftment and perception. In dream alchemy, fragrances aid the normal sleep and dream processes by assisting in freeing the body from lower influences and in opening to higher influences.

There are a number of ways of using the oils and fragrances. They can be used in a bath, prior to retiring for the night. One half capful (or less) of essential oil per bath is all that is required. This will be explored later in this chapter with the "Rite of Dream Passage." You can also anoint yourself with essential oils before retiring. The oils can be used in vaporizers, or you can place a drop or two within a bowl of water, setting it next to the bed as you go to sleep. With incense and potpourris, you can burn them as you go to sleep, allowing the fragrance to carry you off into dream time. The best part of working with the oils and fragrances is that it enables you to experiment and play with the process to find what works for you. Use the following list to help you discover more:

Apple Blossom

This is extremely effective in the mythic dream work techniques described in the next chapter. The fragrance of apple blossom has an ancient mythology surrounding it. It helps connect you with the energies and symbols within myths. It is good for promoting energies of love and for connecting into the nature kingdoms. It has ties to the energies of the unicorn which lives beneath the apple tree.

Chamomile

This is a powerfully effective fragrance for children who have difficulty sleeping or who are colicky at night. It stabilizes the aura, and it awakens a sense of security while sleeping. (It is a member of the ragweed family, and those with allergies should be cautious of its use.)

Eucalyptus

This is one of the most versatile and powerful oils for dreamwork activity. It balances the emotions and calms disturbed states of mind. It facilitates the healing and easing of grief and hostility through sleep. It was used in the ancient mystery schools to balance the awakened siddhis (psychic energies) of the students while they slept. It eliminates nightmares and can be used to facilitate consciousness while dreaming.

Frankincense

This fragrance is cleansing and protective. It eliminates negativity within the sleep environment and restores peace to dream states. It can open the individual to high inspiration and spiritual insight through the dreams.

Jasmine

This fragrance is calming to the heart and to the emotions. It can be used to stimulate prophetic dream sequences. It is an excellent fragrance for learning to transform our energies in a variety of ways.

Lavender

This is a very powerful sleep fragrance. Lavender was always considered a magical herb. It eliminates emotional and mental stress, and it can be used to treat insomnia. It can also open you to visionary states while dreaming. It is excellent when used in a bath prior to retiring or as part of any ritual of dream passage.

Myrrh

Myrrh is a powerful healing and cleansing oil. It soothes the emotions and the astral body, making for more peaceful rest. It can stimulate dreams of emotions that are creating blocks within your life. It may stimulate dream activity in which past events are replayed, events whose repercussions are still impacting you.

Rose

(Refer to the previous section on nightmares.)

Rosemary

(Refer to the previous section on nightmares.)

Sage

Sage is a fragrance that can open you to spiritual illumination in the dream state. It stimulates awareness of inner tension and helps to release it through the sleep process. This is one of those herbs which can open us to all times in mythic dream work. It helps us to integrate and synthesize all times and experiences and all symbols into our present life awareness. It can awaken through dream alchemy a true sense of our immortality.

Tuberose

This fragrance has been referred to as the "Mistress of the Night." It brings serenity and peace of mind. It can be used to increase dream sensitivity - especially in areas of relationships. It helps turn our daily dreams toward the spiritual light.

Wisteria

This fragrance has been used by occultists, metaphysicians and healers to attract high vibrations in all situations. It is activating of more colorful dreams. It is also known as the "poet's ecstasy" as it stimulates creative expression and inspiration, especially when used with dream alchemy. It can be used effectively with the mythic dream work techniques. It assists the individual in developing lucid dreaming that leads to conscious astral projections.

Flower Elixirs and Dreams

Flower essences are elixirs made from the flowers of various plants, herbs and trees. They contain the etheric energy pattern of the flower. Each flower and each essence has its own unique vibrational characteristic. They can be used before sleep to stimulate dreams that will reveal information about characteristics we may need to change or those we may need to enhance. There are a number of resources available for those wishing to explore these elixirs more fully. Those listed below are specifically effective in altering and shaping sleep and dream states.

Amaranthus
This essence is excellent for excessively radical dreams and nightmares. It calms disruptive dreams that stem from biological sources. It also can activate visionary dreams as well.

Aspen
This is an excellent remedy for sleep-walking due to anxieties. This is a good flower remedy for children who have developed a fear of dreams and the dark. It assists them in moving past the fear level of the astral to connect with higher energies. This is usually symptomized by such activities as needing a door open or a light on.

Blackberry
This is a remedy for the fear of going to sleep. If used in conjunction with meditation and creative visualization, it can stimulate problem-solving through the dreams. Higher teachings will be revealed through the dreams, and creativity will be more easily transferred and manifested within the physical.

Celandine (lesser)
This flower remedy has many of its herbal qualities. It stimulates dreams which transfer information, and it facilitates the activation of lucid dreaming, along with instructions from spiritual guides while dreaming.

Chaparral
This remedy stimulates deeper states of consciousness, and it helps us in understanding the archetypal symbols within our dreams. This is very effective in the mythic dream work techniques to follow. It facilitates using dreams to uncover information from our past, and it will stimulate an emotional cleansing of the subconscious during the dreams.

Clematis

This remedy is for the "day dreamy" kind of person. It is a good remedy for when there is a loss of sleep. It awakens the creative potential and facilitates greater control of the fertile imagination.

Comfrey

Comfrey balances the nervous system so that sleep is more restful. It balances the right and left hemisphere functions during sleep, and it is an excellent remedy to take prior to retiring and upon awakening, as it assists in remembering dream content.

Corn

Corn is another remedy for when we become overly "day dreamy." It helps prevent us from becoming lost in our dreams. While you are asleep, it works to cleanse the astral body so that upon awakening the astral body will reintegrate more easily with the physical body.

Forget-Me-Not

This is an excellent remedy for times of disturbed sleep. It stimulates the pineal gland and facilitates the release of tensions through dreams. It stimulates visions and helps us to use the dream state to connect with spiritual guides or those who are living beyond the physical.

Honeysuckle

This is a remedy for when we are troubled by thoughts, emotions and dreams of the past. It enables us to put them into perspective, so we can move beyond them.

Iris

Iris essence will stimulate creative inspiration in dreams, expanding avenues for artistic expression. It facilitates attracting ideas from higher realms into our dreams and putting them into waking consciousness for greater expression.

Live Forever

Live Forever acts upon the dream state in a manner that helps coordinate our spirit guides and their information so that the illumination can pass through the dreams into our conscious mind. It helps align the dream consciousness with waking consciousness.

Marigold

This is a remedy that generally heightens psychic sensitivities and clairaudience through the dream state. It opens the inner ears in sleep, so that they function more strongly when awake.

Morning Glory

This remedy helps one who is having difficulty with disturbed and restless sleep. Refer to the herbal qualities listed in the technique on correcting nightmares.

Mugwort

Mugwort is powerfully for dream work of any kind. It increases awareness during dreams, especially of spiritual thresholds we may be encountering within our life. It stimulates lucid dreaming, increases psychic sensitivity. It initiates clarity of the dream experience and its purpose to our waking life.

Pennyroyal

Pennyroyal essence is cleansing to the auric field and to the astral body. It helps provide psychic protection during sleep and while awake. It strengthens our spirit essence so that we can get beyond negative awareness to positive and enlightening experiences. It helps prevent the energies and thought forms of the day from intruding upon the dream state.

Saint John's Wort

This is one of the most beneficial dream essences. It releases hidden fears into our dreams so that we can confront them and eliminate them on that level, rather than in the physical. It helps in developing lucid dreaming that can lead to conscious astral projection, especially beyond the lower astral plane. It eases cluttered dream states and nightmares. It helps eliminate fear of out-of- body experiences. It strengthens the inner light as we expand our perceptions beyond the physical.

Spruce

Spruce is an essence that helps to detoxify the body during sleep. It is beneficial in overcoming disorientation and lack of direction. It stimulates dreams that give greater focus.

Star Tulip

Star Tulip is a remedy for greater dream recall. It stimulates greater awareness of the more subtle realms to which we have access during sleep. It strengthens our spiritual sensitivity while asleep, so that it can be more easily transferred into our waking consciousness.

Dream Crystals

The use of crystals, gems and stones has come into great prominence in recent years. They are natural sources of a form of electrical energy, called piezoelectrical energy. "piezo" comes from the Greek word "piezein" meaning to squeeze. Any stress upon the crystal releases its particular frequency of energy into our auric field.

It takes very little to release a crystal's energy. Even brain waves, generated by thought and focused in the direction of the crystal, will activate its release. Because of this, it is quite simple to program crystals and gems to work in a directed manner for us. Some crystals and stones work naturally with the process of dream alchemy. Others may need some programming for them to be effective.

When using crystals and stones for dream work, it is recommended that they be cleansed once per week. Setting the stone or crystal in sea salt, placing it in the earth, putting it in a running stream, or even running it through fire are effective means of clearing the crystals of negative energy and programming. There are many books available on crystals and their many uses and cleaning procedures.

You must also charge the crystals and stones you intend to use for dream work. This simply means that you want to bring their energy levels to the highest before you start to use them. In many ways, they are like batteries. They become depleted with use, and they must be recharged. There are a number of effective ways of doing this. Placing the crystal or stone in sunlight and moonlight for 4 to 8 hours is one of the best. Place them outside during storms or changes of weather. Small stones can be charged by placing them in clusters of larger stones.

It is always good to have several that you use for dreams. While one is being cleansed, you still have others to assist you in your dream work processes. It is also better to have several crystals that you use solely for dream work. You may wish to use some of these s general boosters to your bedroom environment, while others you lay wish to program for specific dream functions. These can all be part of the "Rite of Dream Passage" at the end of this chapter.

The simplest manner of programming your dream crystals is to hold it in both hands while gazing into it. You may wish to put it on your lap and hold your hands over it. It is at this point that we employ the Universal Axiom of Energy: "All energy follows thought." Wherever we put our thought that is where energy will go. Thus, at this point, clear your mind of everything other than what you wish to have programmed within your crystal. Concentrate on what you wish this crystal or stone to do for you in your dream work. See it, imagine it, feel it stimulating your dreams and your dream memory in dynamic ways. As you become filled with the visualization of it working for you exactly as you wish, project it out of your mind and into the crystal. See it in your mind's eye as if a beam of light is extending from your head and emptying into the crystal. Feel your hands pulsing out the energy, infusing the crystal with this thought.

Continue this process until you feel satisfied that the crystal is vibrating with this intention. Then repeat the process with your next dream crystal. This usually takes five minutes or so of uninterrupted focus and projection. This programming will stay with the crystal until you clean and clear it for some other use.

This method is especially effective in the upcoming mythic dream work process. You can infuse the crystal with the energy of a myth, legend or tale. You choose a myth according to your individual purpose, and you read the tale to the crystal, seeing its energies become a part of the energy pattern of the crystal itself. This infuses the crystal with the archetypal energy patterns of the myth, which in turn will stimulate dream correspondences.

Working with dream crystals requires some patience and practice. Just as with the herbs, fragrances, and flower essences, we are using a physical substance to assist us in shaping the more ethereal energies of the dream state.

In the beginning, double-terminated crystals (points at both ends) or Herkimer diamonds are the most effective for acting as a bridge between the dream state and waking consciousness. Herkimer diamonds are stimulating to the astral body and serve to energize it. This gives our spirit essence greater mobility and consciousness while sleeping and dreaming. Double-terminated crystals are symbolic of linking one state of consciousness with the next.

Regardless of the crystal or stone you use, cleanse it first, program it and then only use it for one particular task. Give your crystal a singular purpose, and it will work more effectively. Don't use the same crystal for dreams that you are also using for healing and divination. You will confuse its programming and scatter its energies. After programming the stone, place it under your pillow, on your headboard, or on a table next to your bed, close to the head. Before you turn off the lights to sleep, touch it, hold it and remember the programming you placed into it. Affirm that you will dream and remember the dream according to that program.

When you are consistently remembering your dreams, try re-programming your crystal to dream the same dream again to elicit greater information. With practice, you can program the crystal for a location in the dream state other than a physical one. This may be an ashram upon another realm, another planet, or another dimension entirely. The crystal can also be programmed to open doorways to the past and to the future. Here is a list of some stones and their properties.

Amethyst

This is an excellent stone for transmuting consciousness while in the dream state. It is good for bridging levels of consciousness. Its violet color is a combination of red and blue, symbolizing the dualities of physical and spiritual, waking and sleeping. It helps to balance and align our energies while asleep.

Chrysoprase

These stones are excellent for programming to clarify problems through dreams. They strengthen our inner vision, of which dreams are but one manifestation.

Clear Quartz

Any clear quartz crystal can be an effective dream crystal. They are easily programmable and size does not influence effectiveness. Small quartz points can be programmed and easily slipped into the pillow.

Double-terminated Quartz

As mentioned, this is an excellent stone for bridging waking and sleeping consciousness. It also facilitates memory of dreams.

Herkimer Diamonds

This is one of the best stones for mythic dream work. It stimulates great dream activity and if worked with consistently, it will lead to lucid dreaming. It can also be used to help develop conscious astral projection, of which the lucid dreaming is an excellent prelude. It energizes the etheric and astral energies, making dreams more vibrant and memorable.

Jade

Jade has a tradition of being associated with dreams and it is sometimes referred to as the dream stone. Red jade can stimulate connection with our master teachers in the dreams. Lavender jade stimulates a psychic understanding of our dreams. Jadeite is a stone which facilitates emotional release through dreams, and imperial jade stimulates prophetic dreams.

Onyx

Onyx is good general stone for increasing dream activity. If used properly, in a single night it will stimulate multiple dreams, often with the same theme.

Phantom Crystals

Phantom crystals are very powerful dream crystals. Their full power and significance is still somewhat veiled. They hint of realms and dimensions of true reality. Those which have earth elements within them forming the phantom are actually doorways to the world of dreams from the physical. These are powerful stones for mythic dream work. They open you to the archetypes of myths and tales which lie beyond our physical reality.

Quartz Clusters

I like to refer to these as dream clusters. They have a tremendous potential for stimulating multiple dream scenarios that are tied together. Many times the subconscious gives us many dreams at night, each different in the imagery and yet each the same in its theme. Clusters are excellent tools for relating the elements of a single dream or the elements of a variety of dreams. They assist in dream comprehension and interpretation.

Sapphire

Sapphire is a stone which can be used in dream work to lift the dream state from mundane reflections to higher spiritual imagery. It helps transform and lift the consciousness to higher realms through dream activity.

Tourmaline (black)

Black tourmaline is effective for sleep and all nightmare work. t is a powerfully protective stone which aids our inner search. It helps us in finding the light within the darkness, the significance within our dreams. It is an electrical transformer. While we are asleep, it can alter the energies of our dreams and our consciousness, enabling greater expression of light when awake.

My Shapeshifting Dreams

Animals are one of my most common dream symbols. They appear frequently in my dreams. Back in 1991, I was having a tremendous amount of owl dreams. I was even learning about owl from a medicine woman who was strong in owl.

Several dreams would be the catalyst for eventually writing this book about shapeshifting and the role of dreams in it. Thesy also helped inspire my book *Magickal Dance*.

Shapeshifting Dream Excerpt - August 30, 1991

Met a man who was wealthy and manipulative - who enjoyed destroying other people's lives. He was bent on destroying mine. The man stood at the top of the stairs in a theater type setting, laughing with confidence - as if he knew his power and magic was unstoppable. I smiled back, confident he could do nothing to hurt me.

He said, " You think not? Watch what I do to your mother."

I realized my mother was sitting midway on the left. I went to her and tried to convince her to leave. She said there was nothing to worry about, but I knew that she didn't really understand what was happening.

I presented her with a pair of earrings. They were small owl feathers. I made her promise to put them on and wear them at all times and she did. When I turned around, the man was approaching her. The owl feathers suddenly became owl talons and lunged out at the man. Surprise and fear filled his face. He glared at me and backed away. A great horned owl flew in and rested on my shoulder, its eyes fixed on the man. Both the man and I knew that my magic and medicine would be stronger...

Shapeshifting Dream Excerpt - Autrumn equinox 1991

The same man from the earlier dream was changing shapes, becoming different animals to hurt and kill others. I was not afraid of him, although he tried to intimidate me with his ability. I had faith in my own power. He was trying to kill Kathy (my wife) and I intercepted him, challenging him to turn into a fox. I told him that I knew this was the most difficult animal of all.

He just laughed and I was afraid he knew I was bluffing about the fox. I knew that if he became a fox, he could not hurt Kathy and he would become vulnerable.

Behind a door, I had a wolf waiting to be turned loose on him when he was most vulnerable. Unexpectedly, some people came through the door and almost allowed the wolf to be seen by the man. I moved to block his view and he turned himself into a fox. I stepped aside and turned my wolf loose on him ...

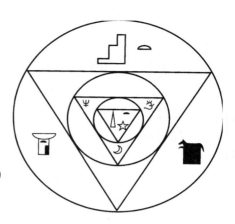

Shapeshifting
Exercise
(developmental & experiential)

Dream Tantra

Skills & Benefits:
- **develops lucid dreaming**
- **nakes dreams more colorful and memorable**

One of the most powerful means of stimulating greater dream activity is the use of dream tantra. The purpose of dream tantra is to develop a continual consciousness, an unbroken continuity through both waking and dreaming states. Although most people associate tantra with forms of sexuality, it corresponds to a wider spectrum of spiritual activities. Tantra comes from the Sanskrit "tanuti," meaning "to weave." It is a spiritual method originating in Hinduism, combining the use of ritual, discipline, and meditation. It draws upon all of the metaphysical sciences to expand awareness in all states of consciousness. It employs the feminine energies of power and creativity to unite and explore the universal and spiritual through the physical. Because of this, it is a term very applicable to mythic dream work. We will use dream tantra (dream rituals, disciplines, and meditations) to direct the "weaving" of our dreams.

When we are working with shapeshifting and dreamwalking, we are developing will and control of will over the dream state. There is an energy center in the body that corresponds to control of the will and it can be stimulated through specific techniques to increase dream activity. It is called the throat chakra. The throat chakra is one of the energy centers in the body controlling our force of will, in conjunction with the unconscious mind. Here's the dream tantra technique to activate the throat chakra:

1. Visualize a ball of red light in the throat area of the body.
Red is stimulating and activating. Using it is like turning on a light switch.

2.   In the middle of this ball of crystalline light, visualize the ancient Sanskrit symbol of the Om in bright scarlet.

The Om in Eastern philosophy is the sound from which all sound came forth in the universe. It is the creative word. This symbol, when used with this visualization, awakens and activates the energies of the unconscious mind.

For this exercise, it is important to lie on the right side of the body, while continuing to visualize the Om symbol in the throat center as you go to sleep. Since our masculine or sun energies are associated with the right side of the body, by lying on the right side, we are telling the subconscious to keep the masculine energies subordinate while we activate the feminine. In this position, the left side, (associated with the feminine or moon energies), becomes dominant. Using this position with this visualization activates the feminine psychic channel. This in turn facilitates creative dreaming.

3.   You can also use the symbol of the trident instead of the symbol of the Om.

In Eastern philosophy, the trident was the symbol of Shiva, the ultimate yogi. It also is symbolic of the junction of nerves found at each psychic center. The trident is also a glyph used to represent the influence of the planet Neptune in the astrological chart. Neptune rules the unconscious and dream states. This symbol or the symbol of the Om helps to stimulate the ability to retain consciousness during dreaming. This lucid dreaming ability is important in dream alchemy, and so many of the techniques in this book are designed to develop lucid dreaming. When we become aware that we are dreaming while we are dreaming, we can change ourselves and the dream.

4.   While lying on the right side of the body and visualizing the symbol in the throat area, just go to sleep.

Your dreams will be more vibrant, colorful and memorable. Even if you have not remembered a dream in years, performing this exercise for three nights in a row will restimulate your dream activity.

Shapeshifting
Exercise
(developments & experiential)

Rite of Dream Passage

Skills & Benefits

- **stimulates dream activity**
- **awakens deeper levels of consciousness**
- **assists in ability to shapeshift while awake or asleep**

The Rite of Dream Passage is a preparatory ritual to mythic dream work, which we will explore in the next chapter. It is a process that can powerfully dedicate a year of dream initiation or a single night's efforts. It can be adjusted to your own dream purposes and goals. It is an excellent prelude to each night's retirement to the sleep and dream realms. It can also be renewed each month at the time of the full moon.

This rite assists in stimulating dream activity. It helps to place your physical energies into synchronization with the more universal energies, which reveal themselves through our dreams. It is important to remember that it is a powerful knock on the doors of the subconscious mind.

Actions are empowered by the amount of significance we attach to them. With this exercise, we are infusing the entire dream work process with greater power, dedication and spiritual significance. We use this ritual to energize, bless and initiate our dream alchemy procedures. All rituals are only as powerful as the significance we imbue them with. Through them we learn to utilize and synthesize body, mind and spirit. They help us to imprint upon the deeper levels of our consciousness the command to integrate and activate energies according to the purpose of the ritual itself. In this case we are imprinting deeper levels of the mind to facilitate our shapeshifting development.

This ritual serves as an aid to crossing that threshold from the physical to the spiritual through our dreams. It inspires dynamic dream activity. A ritual is anything done with strong intention or emphasis. As it relates to our dream work, it takes on powerful dimensions. It utilizes an outer activity to enable us to experience inner realities. It opens the doors of passage to inner realms that operate beyond physical existence.

Preliminary Considerations

For any ritual to be effective, there are preliminary considerations. Know what your purpose is, and hold to it. Know why you want to be involved in it. Make sure that you know what you will need. Understand the significance of what you need and use. The more significance you can attribute to all aspects of the ritual, the more powerful the effect will be. Know when the best time for the ritual is. Gather together all that you will need before you start. Make sure it has a definite beginning and ending. You may wish to use a specific gesture or prayer for it. Approach it with great respect and reverence, for you are working with a method of invoking dynamic plays of energy into your life.

Preparation is the key to an effective ritual. This includes preparation of your self and your surroundings. Work out the specific details and significances prior to the actual working. This prevents energy being dissipated needlessly. Have any herbs, fragrances, crystals and stones that you intend to use present for this ritual. Prepare any sleep and dream sachets that you intend to use ahead of time. Also have your shapeshifting journal available. You may also wish to have on hand any books on mythology that you may use in your future dream work activities.

Gather these items together, refreshing your memory on their significance. You may wish to perform this ritual for the first time on the night of the full moon. If you choose not to wait, that is fine as well. Regardless of when you choose to perform the ritual, make sure that you will not be disturbed once you start. Take the phone off of the hook, and inform others that there are to be no interruptions.

This ritual will take place within your bathroom. Make sure the tub is cleaned before the time of the ritual. You will be running a bath of hot water in which you will be able to soak, meditate and bless the process you are about to initiate.

1. Prepare the bathroom.

Lay the tools for your dream work activity on a pillow beside the tub. In the comers of the bathtub - either resting on the tub or inside it - set your dream crystals and stones that you have programmed but not used yet. Light candles in the bathroom. Do everything by candle light - symbolic of the light of awareness that is reflected within your dreams.

2. As the bathtub fills, add any fragrance or herbs that you also used in making your sleep and dream sachets.

As the fragrance fills the water and the room, know that it is going to permeate you as well. It will vibrate on both physical and spiritual levels, opening you to more memorable, powerful and beneficial dream activity.

3. Step into the bath water, lowering yourself gently, as if easing yourself in full consciousness into the dreamtime.

Imagine you are entering into the watery astral realm that exists between waking and sleeping.

4. This next step is optional, but it is very effective.

There are many water soluble crayons on the market for children to use while bathing. Many are made of soap. You may wish to purchase a set of these for this part of the exercise. With a red crayon, draw a circle on the bathroom tiles in front of you and behind you. Make the circle about a foot to a foot and a half in diameter. Draw it so that it will be easily visible when you lie back within the water. In the center of the circle, draw the Sanskrit symbol of the Om or the symbol of the trident, as discussed in the previous exercise.

5. Now lie back in the water.

Take a few moments and close your eyes. You may wish to perform some rhythmic breathing or a progressive relaxation. Inhale the fragrance of the bath and feel it permeating every cell and fiber of your being, opening you to greater awareness. If it helps you to relax, you may wish to have a piece of meditation music playing in the background.

As you begin to relax, visualize a ball of red light forming within your throat chakra, and in the center of it see the formation of the Sanskrit Om or the symbol of the trident. When you feel this symbol alive in your throat center, open your eyes slowly and softly focus them upon the symbol on the wall in front of you. Imagine the wall as a mirror, reflecting this same symbol that is glowing within your throat center. And then allow your eyes to close again.

6. This is a good time to offer a prayer of thanks for the shapeshifting and dreamwalking that is about to open to you every night hereafter.

Give thanks for this in advance. Imagine it as if you have just placed an order from a catalogue and now will await its delivery every night.

7. Close your eyes and feel the dreamer in you come alive.
We are all dreamers. When we were children, dream life was as important as waking. We want to reactivate that same kind of childlike wonder. Allow yourself a few moments to let your imagination run free, dreaming of things you still wish to do. Let these imaginings take whatever direction they wish.

After a few minutes of this, begin to direct your imaginings more specifically. Allow your mind to create images of how you wish to shapeshift your life. See your dreams becoming more vibrant. See yourself being able to control them. Imagine all that can open to you when you can control you're your energies and your life – awake or asleep – through shapeshifting. Imagine all of the benefits that will come as a result. Visualize yourself growing stronger, more vibrant and more alive as you work with shapeshifting.

See other people acknowledging this new energy about you. Imagine yourself being able to control, handle and shape your physical life circumstances more fully. Imagine yourself becoming anything and everything that you desire. When you have worked these images up within your mind, allowing them to fill every pore and atom of your being, visualize it all being set in motion with this ritual.

See this energy filling and infusing your crystals, sachets, herbs and fragrances. See your shapeshifting journal becoming a manual of the alchemical arts. See yourself becoming a shapeshifter, able to mold your dream energies and images in any way you desire.

8. Now imagine the symbol on the wall in front of you.
If it helps, softly open your eyes briefly and gaze upon it. Visualize it beginning to grow larger, until it is lifesize. Visualize it as being large enough to walk through. This symbol then becomes a threshold, separating the veils between waking and sleeping. Know that each night hereafter, all you will have to do is visualize this symbol within your throat and then reflect it outward, seeing it as a large passage into the dream state. Visualize yourself crossing over and into it - in complete control.

You have now created the doorway that leads to greater dream passage. With practice and persistence, this doorway will become more real and vibrant. When you are able to see this symbol as a doorway, give thanks for its manifestation and for all that you will experience because of it. Know that with its formation, everything associated with your dream work has become dedicated to greater self-awareness. Know that a new sense of self-empowerment is being stirred and awakened.

9. With a soft cloth, gently erase the symbol upon the wall.
As you do that, visualize it as a closing of the veils. Allow the symbol that

you visualized within your throat center to gently dissipate, until called into activity again. Offer another prayer of thanks and extinguish the candles. As you dry yourself, while the bath water empties from the tub, know that every part of your being is now more alive and sensitive. Know that you are about to start a new adventure, one that will return control of your life back to you.

10. Gather your crystals, pillows, sachets and other dream tools and place them in their designated spots within your bedroom.
See your bedroom as becoming now a dream temple in which you will be able to meet the sacred in your sleep. Going directly from the bath to the bed and sleeping naked will bridge the ritual's energies more effectively the first time. As you turn your lights off to sleep, visualize the veils to the dreamtime opening before you and inviting you through.

Special Note:

Dreams are multidimensional. No matter how much we try to control and direct them, they will always reflect energies that deal with all aspects of ourselves. They will not limit themselves to our singular purposes. They are like gifts within gifts.

We can develop lucid consciousness within dream scenarios, but there will always be free variables. The scenario will always reflect more than what we may have set in motion. Dreaming is such a dynamic and creative process that it can follow the program as we have shaped it, while it still incorporates information and perspectives that we can apply to other aspects of life as well.

Chapter Seven

Dreamwalking

Learning to be a shapeshifter involves destruction and creation, two faculties of imagination. We cannot separate the two. We destroy one image so that another can be born. It reflects the process of birth and death. We die to one form to be born to another. This is reflected each night in our sleep. We die to physical consciousness as we are born into dream consciousness.

In the ancient myths and tales, there were primarily three ways to become a shapeshifter, or one who could metamorphose into another form or image. One way was to be trained as a magician or witch and learn to change at will. A second way was to become enchanted by a magic-maker, perhaps by eating something which caused one to change. A third way was to be born a natural shapeshifter, transforming by using the natural forces.

Through a process that I call **mythic dreamwork**, we take steps to be all three. We are all born shapeshifters, adjusting our behaviors to our surroundings. Each night when we go to sleep, we are transformed into dream images and realities. We are also enchanted by the magic-makers of our environments, which so strongly influence and shape us.

We are learning to transmute energies and forms so that we can shape the energies of dreams and their corresponding waking realities in accordance with our own desires, regardless of external influence. Developing and strengthening shapeshifting ability through the use of dream alchemy involves changing our life from the inside out. We change the inner activity, and it will create repercussions in the outer world. That is the significance of the scriptural phrase, "The kingdom of God is within." The divine works through the inner first and then manifests in an outer expression. It also makes it much easier to perform the outer shapeshifting that we will explore In Part III.

*"Dreamtime is claimed
to be a formative or creative period,
which existed
at the beginning of things.
Mythic beings shaped the land
and brought forth the various species.
The mythic beings no longer exist,
but they did not die.
They were transformed
and
became a part of ourselves."*

- **Stan Gooch**
Guardians of the Ancient Wisdom

Everyday we change. When we work with shapeshifting, we are acknowledging these changes, honoring them and empowering ourselves. When we work with mythic dream techniques, we are learning to direct those changes. We are becoming an active participant in them. We are learning to control and use symbols and images to access and invoke the archetypal energies operating through and around us, so that when we initiate the changes in the outer life, they are easier and more empowered. It balances and aligns the physical, mental, emotional and spiritual together in the shapeshifting process.

The Importance of Myths in Shapeshifting

As we have discussed, a major part in the shapeshifting process is building a bridge between our waking life and the more subtle realms beyond it. This involves unfolding our intuition, creativity, and creative imagination. This bridging process is described through myth in a variety of ways. The individual learns to visit the heavens and the underworld by means of an axis. This axis can be the image of climbing a rope, climbing a tree, being carried or led by an animal, by becoming a bird or an animal, following a cave through a labyrinth, etc. Ancient societies employed mythic imagination to facilitate this step.

The resurgence of the shamanic tradition is breathing new life into the modern mythic imagination. It is awakening that part of our mind which can still feel the archetypal forces behind the mythic imagery. Working with the mythic imagination exercises our more subtle and undeveloped levels of consciousness.

We must move beyond the orthodox treatment of mythic imagery as found in modern religions. These images and their associations to outer reality are held to a fixed, unchangeable dogma. They have grown stale. They have lost their ability to touch each of us uniquely. We must restore the experiential aspect to the mythic images of our life. Only then can we imbue the imagination with the energies of transformation and renewal.

One of the best ways of furthering the educational process with shapeshifting is through the study and use of myths, tales and legends. Like dreams, they reveal images and scenarios which show uncommon relationships. They reflect aspects of our lives - conscious and unconscious. They put us in touch with realities and dimensions of life that we do not consciously acknowledge. Myths touch the core of humanity. They touch those aspects of us that are ultimate and universal. They are timeless, reflecting a flow of the past, present and future simultaneously. They are replete with symbolism linking universal archetypes to our everyday consciousness. They remind us of our greatest possibilities.

The fables, myths and tales of the past are replete with esoteric teachings. Many of the ancient masters used them to teach and open the minds of their students. In the Western world, this is most recognized in the parables of Jesus. The student has the responsibility of working with the tale, myth, or parable to find all of the hidden significance within it. Then they would be able to release the archetypal energies, operating through the story images into their lives.

Work with myths and tales develop a form of thinking and relating that facilitates all shapeshifting work (as well as other forms of initiation). It helps bring us in contact with our higher consciousness. In ancient societies, fables and myths were often recited prior to major initiation rites, releasing even greater power into the ritual. In fact, in many of the ancient mystery traditions, students were not allowed to recite historical, religious or real events, except under strict conditions. This prevented the powers and energies connected with the events from being invoked unnecessarily.

The myths and tales were used to stimulate and enhance initiation rites and exercises of higher consciousness. The initiates would meditate upon the myths and use them in a very ritualistic, empowering manner. It was the students' responsibility to practice working with the symbolic material of the myths and tales. They had to learn to internalize them first and then translate them into specific actions. They learned in this process to use the mythic imagery to stimulate visions while awake and dreams while asleep.

It is for this reason that myths and tales are so effective in dreamwalking. They stir the creative imagination and stretch our image making ability. It is the image which then becomes a matrix for a dream scenario. One method of doing this mythic dream work will be explored through most of the rest of this chapter. We will learn to combine the methods discussed in chapter six with techniques that use myths and tales to stimulate greater dream activity and higher dream consciousness. We will learn to shape the energies of the dreams to bring greater revelations and resolutions.

Mythic Dreamwork

In the previous chapter, we learned how to influence sleep and stimulate dream activity. The next step is learning how to shapeshift the dream scenarios we have at night. This can be done through the technique of mythic dreamwork.

In mythic dream work, we stimulate dream activity in a manner that elicits specific kinds of information. We manipulate the symbology and imagery of myths and tales to impact upon our subconscious mind, which in turn responds with a dream that is most appropriate for us in relation to the archetypal energies operating through the myth. In this manner, we can elaborate upon dream emotions, attitudes, and perspectives. We can clarify what we may not have understood.

Remember that the symbols and images of our dreams are attempts by the subconscious to convey information and directions to the conscious mind. The symbols and images of our myths are also a means by which the conscious mind can convey directions to the subconscious, so that it will respond according to those directions. Dream communication becomes two-way. (See the diagrams on the following pages.)

We will use myths and tales in a ritual manner at night to trigger responses within our psyche. The ensuing dream response will reveal where those same mythic energies are currently playing important roles in our life circumstances. The myth and tale thus become the catalyst for greater dream realizations. And as we become more lucid in those dreams, we can shapeshift them even more to our specific needs.

Symbols and images are very chameleonlike., but they are also very powerful. They assume forms according to the moods and attitudes of the individual. They shape themselves in scenarios that express and impress the individual. Our myths and tales are replete with a symbolism that we can use in a ritual/meditational manner to access deeper levels of mind and awaken an awareness of potentials that are translated to us through our dreams.

Our dreams come to us through the subconscious mind. It is the bridge between the conscious mind and the archetypal energies playing within our life. The subconscious mind serves as a translator of those energies to conscious awareness through dreams. Through a directed form of meditation and guided imagery, we can consciously send messages to the subconscious, so that it will access, elaborate and clarify the archetypal energies in our life. Through mythic dream work we learn to work consciously in the subconscious. This ultimately opens us to dream magically, and with an awareness of our true nature of existence.

Sending Messages Through Myths

Archetypal Energies of the Universe

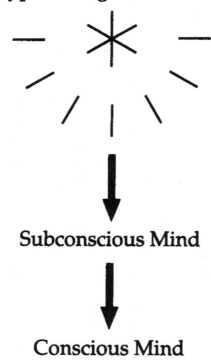

Subconscious Mind

Conscious Mind

We can use mythic symbols and imagery to consciously send specific mesages to the subconscious mind. The subconscious mind in turn accesses the appropriate archetypal forces to which the image is connected which is operating around us in life (usually without our awareness). This creates a greater release of that archetypal force uniquely within our own life circumstances. This energy release is in turn re-translated by the subconscious mind into a meditation or dream scenario that the conscious mind can more easily understand.

Communicating
with
Deeper Levels of the Mind

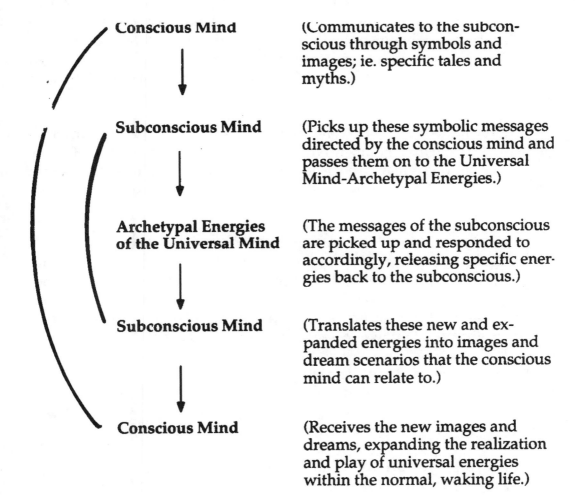

Conscious Mind (Communicates to the subconscious through symbols and images; ie. specific tales and myths.)

Subconscious Mind (Picks up these symbolic messages directed by the conscious mind and passes them on to the Universal Mind-Archetypal Energies.)

Archetypal Energies of the Universal Mind (The messages of the subconscious are picked up and responded to accordingly, releasing specific energies back to the subconscious.)

Subconscious Mind (Translates these new and expanded energies into images and dream scenarios that the conscious mind can relate to.)

Conscious Mind (Receives the new images and dreams, expanding the realization and play of universal energies within the normal, waking life.)

When we understand how the mind works in response to archetypal imagery and movement to enhance it, we begin to realize how easily we can influence dreamtime and even tap inner potentials that will enable us to shapeshift our dreams and ourselves.

How to do

Part of the mythic dream work process involves using symbols to create an dream doorway. We began this process in the previous chapter through visualizing the Om symbol or trident image in a ball of red light within the throat chakra. The next step is to visualize the red light emanating out from the throat to form a second ball of red light, large enough for you to walk through. See it as a door through which you can enter into dreamland. This visualization is an important facet of dream control and direction.

Repeat this process for three nights in a row, using the same myth or tale. Three is a creative number. When things are done in a rhythm of three, it activates our own creative energies more dynamically. In this case, we are releasing our creative energies to stimulate dreams along specific lines.

1.   Make preparations about an hour before you go to sleep.
Once you become familiar with the process, it will not take as long to prepare. As a part of the preparation, you may wish to do any of the following, singularly or in combination. Prepare a ritual dream bath with appropriate fragrances as we did in the previous chapter: program a crystal to assist you or use an appropriate flower essence to amplify and assist the process.

2.   Make sure you will not be disturbed.
Relax yourself, using guided visualization, progressive relaxation, etc. Alternately tensing and relaxing each muscle group is effective.

3.   Close your eyes briefly, visualizing the symbol of the Om or trident in the ball of red light within the throat center of your body.
This is the same exercise you learned in the previous chapter. Visualize, imagine and feel the light emanating outward from this center to create a circular doorway through which you will visualize stepping.

Mythic Dreamwork

4. **Gently open your eyes, and softly read aloud to yourself the myth or tale you have selected.**

5. **Having read the story aloud, close your eyes and once more visualize this doorway. Make it more vibrant.**

6. **As you create this mythic dream doorway, visualize, imagine and feel the leading character of your tale, standing within it.**

Have this character extend his or her hand, to lead you across the threshold. See yourself stepping through the doorway and into the scenery of the tale itself. As you do, allow the lead character (or the one to whom you most strongly relate) to melt into you. Visualize yourself now as this character, going through the activities and events of the tale. Try and feel what the character felt. Experience it as strongly in your mind as you can.

7. **As the tale comes to an end, imagine yourself back at the dream doorway.**

As you stand there, allow the character to separate from you. Offer your thanks, and step back through the doorway.

8. **Allow the doorway to shrink back, fusing itself once more within the throat center.**

This serves two purposes. It develops the ability to mold and create energies on the more subtle levels, and it develops control of the will force.

9. **You may wish to re-read the tale once more, aloud.**

Reading aloud grounds the mental energies into physical expression. It is a way of affirming that the archetypal energies behind the images and symbols will play themselves out within the physical more clearly. The messages you send and receive will be more clearly heard.

10. **Now you have arrived at the end of the process.**

Just roll over and go to sleep, reminding yourself to remember your dreams. Do not be concerned if you fall asleep during the process. Having read the story and prepared the energy at the beginning will enable it to carry itself through even if not consciously finished.

Benefits of Mythic Dreamwork

Using myths as catalysts for dream activities serves a variety of purposes - predominant among them is the elaboration of the content of previous dreams or even specific situations in life. I have often heard individuals say, "I wish I could go back into that dream and find out more about what it meant." Through mythic dream work, you can stimulate a dream or whole series of dreams that express the content of the original scenario, giving you more to work with and facilitating understanding.

You can use mythic dream work processes to stimulate revelations about specific aspects or qualities operating in your life. For example, using the mythic dream work technique, you could use the tale of "King Midas and His Golden Touch" to elicit dreams that reveal where greed or carelessness might be operating in your life. It may even reveal around whom or what this greed is centered. As we will demonstrate in the next chapter, we can use mythic dreamwork to connect with our animal totems and even shapeshift into them. The dream will not be a replication of the tale, but it will be translated into a scenario appropriate to you and your own individual life circumstances.

Dreams stimulated through mythic dream work can reveal opportunities to correct situations in your life or reveal where such opportunities exist. Choosing a myth that is tied to the symbologies and energies of new and unusual opportunities will trigger inspirational dreams around activities, people or events that are applicable to your life.

You can also use myths and tales to reveal where your energies are blocked. Choosing myths and tales that involve the symbols and images of overcoming restrictions and bonds will resonate with the subconscious. This will trigger dreams that reveal the restrictions in your own life that must be overcome or help clarify those restricting situations.

Mythic dream work awakens inspiration and creativity. Poets, writers, and artists from all times have told how inspiration was drawn from dreams. Coleridge, Goethe and Jung are but three. Mythic dream work stimulates the unconscious intuition so that inspiration can manifest through dream energies. It also awakens higher teachings through the dream imagery. Dream work can be a probationary path for the spiritual disciple, providing great symbolic instruction and eventual contact with masters.

Working with the mythic dream work process will increase dream activity in general. They will become more vivid and colorful, and it will lead to the development of lucid dreaming. This is the realization of being in a dream while you are dreaming. Remember that we are attempting to infuse conscious control over a state that we have allowed to occur unconsciously. Initially in dream scenarios, the setting is involuntary, but in lucid dreaming, more and more volitional elements enter into it. As we become more aware of our role in the dream and the dream's purpose, we car change the outcome. We begin the ability to shape the course of the dream while in it. (Lucid dreaming is a dynamic prelude to consciously controlled out-of-body experiences.)

As we work with this, many opportunities for growth in our outer life will occur. This is part of what we are invoking through the dream alchemy process. Creativity will increase. Opportunities to face personality issues and fears will arise. There will be an increased awareness of karma and the path of correction. We will have greater opportunity to clear the subconscious of limitations and restriction, self-imposed or otherwise. We open ourselves to greater healing opportunities on all levels. We begin to harmonize the inner and outer worlds of our life. We also gain greater control, or opportunities for control, over our life circumstances.

"There is some myth
for every man,
which if we but knew,
it would make us understand
all he did and thought."

-William Butler Yeats

Metamorphosis

The effect of mythic dream work is much deeper than you may initially realize. The energies of the myths will influence the dream state, but they also will bring a new kind of energy into your waking life as well. Through mythic dream work, you are learning to manipulate symbols and images to alter the energy circumstances of your waking life.

If you stimulate dreams through mythic dream work to provide information and opportunity to overcome anger, you may find that it affects your physical life. You may find yourself having to overcome anger in specific real life situations. It has been said that you should never pray for patience unless you wants to encounter situations that will try your patience. This can be a side benefit of mythic dream work. You may stimulate dreams for greater revelation of weaknesses to be overcome, but you may also release energies that manifest similar situations in real life, testing your ability to overcome them. When this does occur, you can use the dream scenario to help you know how to handle the situation.

The following exercise opens doors to the psyche. It is an example of mythic dreamwork and it builds flexibility in your subtle energy fields. It stretches the creative imagination, developing concentration and visualization. It will send messages to the subconscious, messages that will become more active as you get deeper into the alchemical and shapeshifting process.

This exercise is not just cute and fun. It serves specific purposes and functions that assist in developing our ability to awaken full consciousness within the dream state, and ultimately, it will facilitate all of our shapeshifting abilities. It strengthens the spirit essence so that it can become a dynamic vehicle for our consciousness while we are asleep. The more we infuse ourselves with thoughts of shapeshifting and alchemy, the greater the results. This exercise stimulates more creative versatility. It helps establish a mindset that enables us to discover new options within our life situations. We are working with basic universal principles. What we do on one level carries over and affects us on all others.

Initially, perform this exercises three nights in a row and then repeat periodically. It will quickly develop the ability to shift your attention and energy. Feel free to adapt it to your own needs. Performing this shapeshifting meditation stimulates more vibrant dream activity. Also, as you become familiar with them, they will take little time to perform.

Be aware that when we are working to control the subconscious mind, we will encounter resistance. For most people the subconscious mind is used to following whatever whim it encounters. When we use meditation, ritual and other methods of accessing and controlling it, it will resist. This resistance can take many forms to distract us from our purpose: an itch, a worry over a work or family matter, a thought that you don't have enough time to do it, etc. The mind may wander in fifty different directions.

When this occurs, do not get upset. Simply persist, and eventually the resistance will diminish. Resistance is actually a positive sign. We only encounter resistance when we have tapped into the subconscious. Recognize it as such, bring your attention back to the point of focus and continue with the exercise. You are training the subconscious to work along the lines you consciously decide - whether awake or asleep! For all three of these exercises in metamorphosis, take care to prepare:

1. Choose a time in which you can perform them uninterrupted.

2. You may wish to use soft, meditation music that is soothing to you. The more relaxed you are, the greater the benefits.

3. Perform slow rhythmic breathing or a progressive relaxation. Feel and imagine warm, relaxing energy melting over and through every part of your body-from your toes to your head. Take your time in doing this. With practice, you will find yourself shifting into a relaxed state the moment you start your rhythmic breathing.

Special Note:

There are many ways to work on developing a consciousness of shapeshifting and alchemy. Many myths and tales involve these transformative energies: The prince who turned into the frog, the story of Beauty and the Beast, etc. Read as many of these tales as you can. In the previous chapter is a small list of some of these to help get you started. Remember that we are exercising our mental energies to create and expand consciousness while awake and asleep. Creativity works at all times; with these exercises we are accelerating its manifestation by working from the inner to the outer.

Most importantly, have fun with the exercises. It is infused with images and symbols to elicit dynamic effects, effects which prove themselves out in our physical life. Development and unfoldment do require energy and effort and a certain amount of time. There is no "fast-food" remedy. However, we can enjoy that effort. What is most essential and beneficial from these exercises is that they bring back to life the dreamer within us, the dreamer that lives while we are awake or asleep.

Shapeshifting
Exercise
(developmental & experiential

The Tale of the Master and Pupil

Skills & Benefits:
- **stimulates dreamwalking**
- **awakens the unconsicous to enhance shapeshifting**

The tale which follows is an old tale, adapted from several sources. It is a tale of shapeshifting. More specifically, it is about a contest of shapeshifting. It has been told in many ways in most areas of the world. It has been called the "Wizard Battle" and "The Doctor and his Pupil." Although its origin is often given as France, versions of it appear everywhere. When it comes to folktales, it is often difficult to discern the origins.

This is an excellent exercise to do as part of the mythic dream work process, by creating the doorway and stepping through into his tale. It can also be used as a separate meditation, for a kind of waking dream. It is a means of activating the mythic energies through meditation, reflection, visualization and contemplation.

You use your creative imagination to empower altered states such as dream activity. It is comparable to the exercises used by Ignatius Loyola to bring a particular scene to life within the mind. It is comparable to what Carl Jung referred to as the active imagination, a "turning willfully to the unconscious while awake." This is an excellent exercise with which to practice placing our self in the different roles found in tales and myths, as described in the last chapter. Even though we may prefer to see ourselves as he hero or protagonist, we usually have qualities similar to the antagonist or other characters. This exercise can help you develop the power to visualize yourself as one of the characters.

This exercise has definite effects. It can be used prior to sleep to stimulate dreams for self-awareness, prophecy and initiation. It can also be used to create opportunities for their development in our life circumstances. It creates opportunities to develop versatility and flexibility of our creative energies.

1. Make preparations before performing this exercise.
You may wish to use a favorite fragrance – essential oil or incense. Make sure you will not be disturbed. Perform a progressive relaxation, sending each part of the body warm and relaxed thoughts and feelings. The more relaxed you are, the better it will work. If you are performing this before bedtime, read through the tale several times so that it is firmly implanted in the mind. This way if you fall asleep during the process, it will still work for you through the dream state.

2. Visualize a ball of red light in the throat area of the body.
Red is stimulating and activating. Using it is like turning on a light switch.

3. In the middle of this ball of crystalline light, visualize the ancient Sanskrit symbol of the Om or the trident in bright scarlet.

4. Visualize, imagine and feel the red light emanating outward from this center to create a doorway as we learned in the last chapter.

5. Visualize, imagine and feel you're the main character of the tale standing in the doorway.
As you step through the doorway, the character greets you and then melts into you. Imagine, see and feel yourself as the main character…

Once there was a poor boy that was looking for work. In his travels, he heard of a great wizard, a teacher who needed a servant. The boy sought out this man. He came to a large castle and banged loudly upon its door.

Before long, a man appeared at a window and called down to the boy, "What do you want?" he said. The boy replied "I am looking for work, kind sir, and I heard you were in need of a servant."

"Do you know how to read?" asked the wizard.

The boy hesitated. He was not sure how to answer, as the question sounded a bit like a test of a sort. "No," he lied, "But I am a quick learner if you are worried about being able to teach me."

The wizard replied "I do not want anyone who can read, so I will hire you."

The boy entered the castle. The man greeted him at a tall stairwell and motioned for the boy to follow him up. They ascended the stairs in silence. At the top they entered a room which seemed a mix between a laboratory and a library. In the center of the room was a pedestal upon which sat a large book. "While I travel, I expect you to dust this room and to protect its belongings, particularly this one book," he said. The boy nodded, looking at the book with curiosity.

Before long the Master left on a long trip. He was no sooner out the door when the boy opened the large volume on the pedestal and began reading. It was a book of the magic and wonders of the universe. The boy studied voraciously and was always careful never to let the Master know what he was doing while he had been gone.

After three years, the boy had learned the entire book by heart. When the Master returned from his next trip, the boy said he must be on his way, and he left the castle. The boy returned home to his poor parents, anxious to tryout his new knowledge.

On the eve of the village fair, the boy spoke to his father. "Tomorrow, you will find a magnificent steer in the stable. Take it to the fair and sell it, but make sure you return with its rope." The next day the father found this magnificent steer, took it to the fair and sold it for a good price. On his way home, he heard footsteps behind him. He turned and saw his son. The boy had turned himself into a steer and when he had been sold, at first opportunity he turned himself back.

Both he and his father were delighted with the deal they had made. Whenever money ran low, the boy would transform himself into a steer or a horse or whatever could be sold. After the sale, at the first opportune time, he would transform himself back.

What the boy did not know was that to a Master of Magic, any magic in the land would be recognized. It was only a matter of time before the Master for whom the boy worked would discern that something was amiss in the land. It did not take him long to find the boy. Then it was just a matter of waiting for the right opportunity.

The next time the father brought his transformed son into the village to sell, the Master recognized him and bought the horse from his father. He then took the father to a pub and made him drink so much that he forgot the rope by which he led the animal and which enabled the boy to return to his normal form.

While the father was passed out from too much drink, the Master took the horse to blacksmith. "Give my horse a good shoeing," he said, and then he left for a time. Before the blacksmith got a chance to do so, a young child came along and the horse spoke to her. "Untie me!" he ordered.

The child was so startled, that she did as told. No sooner was the horse untied, then he transformed himself into a rabbit and ran off. The Master saw this and transformed himself into a hunting dog, giving chase. The rabbit came to a river and turned into a fish. The Master bought the river and ordered that all the fish be cleaned. As the fish that was the boy was about to be cleaned, it turned into a lark and flew away.

The Master then transformed himself into a hawk and gave chase. Weary from flight, the lark dived down a chimney and turned itself into a gain of wheat which rolled under the table. The hawk followed, seeing the change. He immediately turned into a rooster, pecking at the loose grains upon the floor. The boy waited until just about to be eaten and then transformed himself once more. This time he turned into a fox, which immediately ate the rooster.

And the boy lived out his days in wealth and prosperity in the castle of the old Master.

If you make it through the complete visualization before you fall asleep, visualize yourself back at the dream doorway. The main character separates from you. You offer your thanks, and step back through the doorway. Allow the doorway to shrink back, fusing itself once more within the throat center. This serves two purposes. It develops the ability to mold and create energies on the more subtle levels, and it helps you develop control of the will force. Then roll over and go to sleep.

*In dreams,
we can encounter
any kind of
animal.*

*We are not limited
by geographical
boundaries.*

*Thus,
the entire world becomes
a realm of possible totems.
To Dream of an animal
is always of equal importance
to encounters
in the waking life...*

and just as real.

Chapter Eight

Dream Totems

Through the years, I have taught thousands of people about animal guides and guardians. And in almost every workshop or seminar, two common questions arise:

"What does it mean when you dream you are an animal?"

"What does it mean when you dream you are part animal and part human?"

They are very common experiences, and when we are working to connect with our animal totems and guides, we will very likely dream of being an animal or being part animal at some time. On one level, this often indicates how strongly that animal is becoming a part of you and your life. It is an indicator of how that animal's medicine or power is beginning to manifest in you.

These dreams are wonderful reflections of the shapeshifting that is already manifesting in you in your work with that totem. You are learning to integrate and express that animal's power, medicine and spirit in and through you. And that is always when that animal truly becomes an ally for you in your life.

Connection with an animal in the dreamtime is a dynamic way of reinforcing the connection being established during the waking time. Later, when you begin to work with the actual shapeshifting dances (Part III), this type of dream experience will become more common. We do not have to wait for that though. We can begin the connection through the dreamtime to reinforce the actual physical work and connections we are employing.

All animals, wild and domestic, have their own unique abilities. They have varying degrees of intelligence. They have a great ability to show love, fear, anger and other emotions. They have spirits that are strong and although

The Paradox of Opposites

Shapeshifting leads to initiations into greater mysteries of life. This requires that the shapeshifter develop an individuality that isgreater - that is master of opposites:

- Keeping silent and talking

- Receptivity and resistance to influence

- Obeying and ruling

- Humility and self-confidence

- Lightning-like speed of thought and circumspection

- To accept all and yet retain the ability to discriminate

- Ability to fight and the ability to establish peace

- Caution and courage

- To possess nothing and to command everything

- To have no ties and to be loyal

- No fear of death and high regard for life

- Indifference and love

- Be alone without being lonely

some might disagree, they also have souls. And they dream as well, so we should not be surprised that when we work to connect more dynamically with our animal guides that they start showing up in our dreams.

It also should not be a surprise simply because animals have always served a great but often forgotten purpose in our development. We are exposed from the time we are little to myths and tales, books, cartoons and movies involving animals that speak, love, play and even solve problems. When most of us learned our alphabet, it was with the help of animals. "A is for ape, B is for Bat, C is for cat, D is for dog..." We have experienced through media influences what shamans and medicine people have taught for thousands of years. Animals do speak. They deliver messages and they call us to greater awareness.

I am frequently asked in interviews why I believe that my books on animals do so well. I believe that it is partly because everyone has a story about animals. Almost everyone has had some unusual or moving experience involving animals - if only from their dreams. Animals fascinate people – whether wild or domestic. Animals touch people, often without people realizing. Animals provide a spiritual tie to the Earth. I believe there is an unconscious recognition that animals reflect archetypal forces within the world, reminding us of the primal sources from which we came.

Part of the shamanic tradition is connecting to the primal and universal energies of the Earth and to *all* life upon it. Pets and domestic animals are often the first step to this reconnection. Today's world is often one of sensory overload and our pets and other domestic animals provide a link for us to those universal energies without feeling further overwhelmed and overloaded.

Archetypal Energies of Animals

Part of the shamanic tradition is connecting to the energies of the Earth and all life upon it. To assist with this, animal imagery is strongly utilized. In the East, it is often said that the way to heaven is through the feet. By connecting with the energies and rhythms of the earth we give greater impulse to our life.

Animals hold a great purpose in the development of the true shapeshifter and dream alchemist. In many myths and tales, animals speak, deliver messages, and call the hero to awareness. They lead individuals into and out of the wildernesses of life. They are a manifest part of the initiation process. Animal totems and guides can assist us in breaking down barriers and in opening up to the new. Carl Jung tells us that animals are representatives of the unconscious, and all animals belong to Mother Earth. We also belong to Mother Earth, and part of the shamanic tradition in dream work is to re-establish the ties to the Great Mother, which has become temporarily lost.

In some societies, the power of an animal (its "medicine") is obtained by killing it. When we use animal imagery in dream work, we are participating in a symbolic and yet ritual killing. We are killing our orthodox and stagnant view of life and power for one that is primal and alive. We learn to merge with the archetypal energy of the animal. Thus, it is no longer the same and neither are we.

It is not enough to keep our images autistic and undeveloped. We must breathe new life into them. Begin by recognizing that all forms and images - including animals - reflect archetypal energies. We do not have to believe that these animals are beings of great intelligence, but there is an archetypal force behind them, one that oversees them. These archetypes have their own qualities and expressions of energies and these are evident through the behaviors and activities of specific life forms.

When we honor an animal, we are honoring the creative essence behind it. When we open and attune to that essence, we begin to manifest it. The animal then becomes our totem, our power or medicine. It is a symbol of a specific kind of energy we are inviting and manifesting.

Humanity has lost that instinctive tie to the rhythms and patterns of Nature. However, we can develop an intuitive tie to enhance our lives. Each animal reflects specific energy patterns. By aligning yourself with the animal, you align yourself with the energy pattern that works through it. When we use the mythic imagery of animals in meditation or dream work we are asking to be drawn into harmony with the essence behind it. And this will help us tremendously when we work to do so through shapeshifting dances in our waking time.

Our myths and tales are filled with animal-people who teach, guide and protect. From Aesop's fables to Navajo tales of Coyote the Trickster, animals and creatures perform in the same way humans do. Although allegory on one level, they also stimulate the realization that dynamic forces operate through other kingdoms of life. It is this realization, which helped some societies develop an animal mythology that explains everything from creation to how and why dreams operate.

One of the most striking examples is found in African Bushmen tales of the Mantis. The stories of the praying mantis deal with the time when animals and birds were supernatural beings that later became what they are today. The praying mantis is conceived of as a kind of dreaming Bushman. He was endowed with supernatural powers, along with human qualities. He taught the Bushmen that big things come from the small, and thus they paid great attention to everything in their dreams.

The Mantis worked his magic through other person-animals. When disaster was impending, the Mantis would always have a dream that revealed what to do, and the disaster would be averted. Since the Mantis had the ability to bring the dead back to life, there was a strong belief that their dreams could restore their lives as well. If danger threatened the Mantis, it would form wings and fly to water. Water is a symbol of life to the Bushmen, but it is also an archetypal symbol for the astral plane and the dream state.

Animals in myths and in dream work serve as symbols of that which we have not expressed or even acknowledged. If we can discover our dream animals, they can serve to lead us into dream time, using the mythic dream work techniques already explored in chapters 6 & 7. And we will learn to adapt those techniques to do this at the end of this chapter.

The Meaning and Importance of Animals

Animals are guides, guards, brothers and sisters. They are very willing to develop a tremendous relationship with humans. When we begin to work with shapeshifting - in our waking life or our dreaming life - this relationship will grow beyond the bounds of our traditional beliefs. No longer will we see animals as subordinates or lowly beasts. We will see them as powerful spirits and we will willingly take on the role of stewardship with them.

Discovering meanings in anything can sometimes be difficult, which is why dream work and animal imagery are so compatible. Dream imagery is natural to everyone, and animal imagery triggers our own primordial faculty of imagination. Together they liberate the mind. We then become aware of what Jean Houston refers to as the lure of becoming. The dreams begin to change the dreamer. They begin to shapeshift us.

There was a time when humanity saw itself as part of Nature and Nature as part of it. Dreaming and waking were inseparable, the natural and the supernatural merged and blended. Shamans used the symbols of nature to express this unity and to instill that transpersonal kind of experience. These totems help individuals to see themselves as part of the universe.

A totem is any natural object, being, or animal with which we feel closely associated and whose phenomena and energy seem related to us in some way. Some totems reflect energies operative for only a short time in our lives, and some remain with us from birth, through death, and beyond. They are symbols for integration, expression, and transformation.

Animals in particular always play a strong role in symbology. They reflect the emotional life of humanity, often representing qualities of our own nature that must be overcome, controlled, and re-expressed as a tool of power. They are symbols of the archetypal power that we can learn to draw upon when pure reason no longer serves. It's that archetypal power that makes shapeshifting possible.

Adopting the guise of animals and wearing their skins or masks, symbolized the endowing of ourselves with that primordial wisdom and instinct. Terrestrial animals are often symbols of fertility and creativity that must be re-manifested in our evolution. Thus, each species has its own characteristics and powers to remind us of the archetypal power we must learn to manifest more consciously. They help us to build bridges between the natural and the supernatural. They awaken us to the realities of both.

Birds in myths and tales are often symbols of the soul. Their ability to fly reflects our ability to rise to new awareness. It reflects the ability to link the physical realms with those of the sky (heavens). Birds reflect the linking of the waking with the dreaming, and thus are powerful totems for all dream work. We are all given to flights of fancy, a phrase often used to describe our dreaming. As totems, each bird has its own peculiar characteristic, but they all can be used in meditation and dream work for inspiration, hope, and new ideas.

Aquatic life also serves a role as a powerful totem. It can also be very effective in dream work. Water is the symbol of the astral plane experience, much of which reflects itself in our dreams. Water totems return us to our origins. There are many myths of life springing from primordial waters. Water is the creative element, reflecting the feminine archetype of the Mother.

It is the feminine, the intuitive, and the creative that is brought to life each night when we dream. The moon, a symbol of the feminine, controls the tides of water upon the earth. The quality of water in our dreams often reflects the character of our present life events. Journeys in or upon water reflects the journey archetype, the seeking for transformation.

Various fish and other forms of aquatic life make dynamic totems for meditation and dream work. In myths, they often symbolize guidance from our intuitive aspects. One of the most dynamic totems is the shell, reflecting the powers of water and the feminine force. It is often a symbol of the journey across the sea to new life and the sounding forth of that new life, like the trumpeting upon a conch shell.

Insects are also a part of Nature, and they can make powerful totems. They have ancient mythological histories. From the bee of fertility in Egyptian tales to the Mantis of the African Bushmen to the many tales of the Spider Woman who created the universe, they are as much a part of the mythic power of life as any animal form. Most people look upon insects as pests, but they serve a powerful purpose in the chain of life. They each have unique qualities, reflecting archetypal influences with which we can align. One of the most common tales is that of the "Ant and the Grasshopper." The ant is industrious and works to survive the upcoming winter, while the grasshopper relaxes and enjoys the summer.

Shamanism teaches us that all forms of life can teach us. By studying and reading about animals, birds, fish, and insects, we can learn much about the qualities they can reflect in our lives. By connecting with them while awake and in the dreamtime, their teachings become more powerful. The more we learn of our totems, the more we honor the archetypal energies that affect us through them. Remember that each species has its own unique qualities. An ant may not seem as glamorous as a bear, but an ant is industrious and has a strength that far exceeds its size.

Part of working with Nature and our dreams is to break down the outworn preconceptions. Our individual totems in meditation and dream work assist us in this.

Types of Totems

There are five main types of totems we are all likely to have. There is some variation depending upon the particular tradition, and some of the roles overlap. For example, a power animal may also be a protector and a message bringer. We can also have several animals in each of these categories.

Message Bringers

These are often animals whose appearance provides guidance in our life. They bring direction to us about situations, choices, decisions and activities we are involved in. Their presence is often temporary. A study of their characteristics and behaviors provide clues and insight as to what our behaviors and actions should be in situations around us. When we have a problem, learning to ask for guidance and then taking a nature walk to get the message is one of the best ways of finding answers.

Personal Power Animals

Power totems are animals that are with us throughout our life or through major periods within our life. They are message bringers, protectors, teachers and healers. Different traditions disagree about how many power animals we have. It can vary, each animal working and helping us in different areas of our life. For example, one of my totems is the red-tailed hawk. I have worked hands on with hawks and other birds of prey for many years, but I have also worked spiritually with them for many years. Hawk has helped me to develop and focus my spiritual / psychic vision. It has taught me patience and it serves as a messenger to warn me of the ease or difficulty of the path ahead of me. But it is not my only power animal.

Protectors

Protectors are often power animals, but these are animals that give us extra strength and energy, often without our realizing it at the moment. They alert us to trouble. They often appear in dreams of conflict to let us know what qualities to draw on to handle the conflicts in our life. Many people wrongly assume that protectors are always big and ferocious animals. They can be, but every animal has its own unique defense strategies and abilities. While dragons are powerful protectors for many aspects of my life, the opossum also serves as a protector for me. When it appears in my life, it warns me that things and people around me are not what they seem to be. Opossum warns me to be careful of my own words and actions, that I may need to "play possum" in some situations.

Teacher

All animals that come to us are teachers. They teach us about our own potentials, about energies at play within our life and about our spiritual path in this life. We can learn something from every animal, but those who appear regularly have something special to teach us, something we need to learn. They also serve as spiritual guides for us, leading us and helping us in sacred quests and journeys. Often animals that appear regularly in our dreams are teaching totems. They are guides into and out of the dream world and the underworld. Take a look at the animals that are living in the same environment in which you are living. These animals are usually doing so quite successfully. They can teach us to live more successfully within that same environment – whether it is the home, work, school or some other kind of environment.

Healing

These are animals that provide us with energy and guidance in regards to healing others or ourselves. Many animals have unique resistance to certain diseases and drawing upon that animal's energy helps us be more resistant to it as well. Some animals are archetypal symbols of healing. The snake is one such animal. It sheds the old skin and moves into the new. It is a symbol of leaving the old behind for the new. As a symbol of transformation, meditating and focusing on the snake during times of illness will help accelerate the healing process. Animals that appear to us at times of illness, provide clues as to the best way to focus our healing energies.

*Shapeshifting
Exercise
(experiential)*

Riding through Time

Skills & Benefits:

- **develops psychic vision**
- **expands perceptions**
- **helps past life exploration**
- **stimulates dreams of past animals**

Time travel takes great care, practice and effort. It is best to practice accessing other times and places, such as those described in myths and tales, through meditation first. When we can control them in meditation, it becomes easier to control time and locality in dreams.

We are learning through dream alchemy to work with the astral plane. This is a realm of great fluidity. Everything that has ever been felt or experienced has left its imprint upon this dimension, including mythical times and places. This is the realm of imagination, and we must not make the mistake of equating imagination with unreality. Images, and the energy behind them, are real and take form in other dimensions. It is only upon the physical that they are more ethereal and intangible. One of the reasons for dream work is to open this realm, to learn the laws within it and how it impacts upon the physical life.

There are many kinds of astral operations and processes that can connect us more fully with that dimension and its energies. Daydreaming, meditation and nocturnal dreaming are but a few. We are learning to connect with it in a directed manner. Meditation techniques and mythic dream work facilitate a more conscious awareness of its interaction with our life on a daily basis.

We are not our bodies. They are simply tools for the physical life, tools which we can set aside at night for more essential work. Part of this work involves learning how these subtle dimensions help shape the physical.

It can take time to control the time element and the locality of your dream experiences. To assist in this, you can use the symbology found within myths and tales. This next exercise is a meditation that can strengthen your energies to access ancient times and localities- real and mythical. As you learn to control them through meditation, you can learn to control the dream state. Persistence is the key.

As you learn to access other times, you may manifest dreams which reflect those energies as they are currently influencing you. Ultimately, you can develop the ability to access the past and correct the mistakes (and thus the karmic repercussions).

Initially, this exercise should not be performed too frequently. It is very powerful and may trigger a replay of situations from the past. This does not mean the same instances with the same parties will re-occur. More likely, similar kinds of situations will arise, infused with the same emotions and attitudes of the past, providing opportunity to handle them differently. In essence, you create an opportunity to tell the divine universe that you have learned that particular lesson. This eliminates the karma. Karma is a Sanskrit word which means "to do." Anything we do is a learning opportunity. If we do not learn the lesson the first time, it arises later to give us another opportunity. With this exercise and with application of it to mythic dream work, you are learning to manipulate symbols to accelerate your learning, while awake and asleep.

Preparations

Horses are amazing and magical creatures. They have great intelligence and great power. They have always stirred the imagination of humans and because of this they are powerful allies in taking sacred journeys.

Horses were critical to the spread of civilization. Without them, travel and expansion was relatively limited. The horse allowed for new lands to open. This exercise employs the magic of the horse to open us to the past and the future. We will learn to ride the horse through time. It is a sacred journey.

This meditation exercise will help you explore the past and the future. We can return to the past to resolve issues, and we can open to the future to see how the past and present are affecting what will unfold within our life. Its mythic imagery will stimulate dream activity, especially when performed sometime in the evening or before going to sleep. Even if you fall asleep during this exercise, it will often stimulate dreams of the past when performed for three days in a row. It can also stimulate prophetic dreams of the future. The people and places within the dream scenario provide clues.

As in all meditations, music and fragrances can enhance the effects. One of the most effective aids for this exercise is the drum. Drums are connected to the heartbeat of the earth and are very important to incorporate in this shaman-type journey for the best results. Drumming helps the shaman to enter tan expanded state of consciousness. It is a tool for sacred journeying into the dreamtime and other realms.

The drumbeat should be slow and steady, and the participants should allow the drumbeat to lead them. Riding the drumbeat to the dream world is part of all shaman experiences. With practice it is easy to allow the drumbeat to escort you to the inner realms. As children many of us tapped out the clippety-clop rhythm of horses on our thighs. This same rhythmic beat of the horses' hoofs is a powerful aid to this journey. Practice drumming the rhythm of hoof beats, slowing to the rhythm of our heartbeat.

Individuals sometimes wonder if they are experiencing a true shaman journey. The difference between a meditation and a true journey is the depth of the experience. In the journey, we are actually in it, feeling it and experiencing it first hand. It also will not always follow a prescribed pattern. On the other hand, in meditation exercises, we often observe ourselves experiencing the situation or imagine how it should be experienced. Imaging practices and meditation exercises lead to an ability to immerse ourselves fully into the midst of the experience. We become part, rather than just playing a part. The meditation aspects lead us to the control and experience of true shaman journeys.

1. Make preparations before performing this exercise.

You may wish to use a favorite fragrance – essential oil or incense. Make sure you will not be disturbed. Perform a progressive relaxation, sending each part of the body warm and relaxed thoughts and feelings. The more relaxed you are, the better it will work. If you are performing this before bedtime, read through the scenario several times so that it is firmly implanted in the mind. This way if you fall asleep during the process, it will still work for you through the dream state.

2. If you have a drum, use it throughout this exercise.

You may wish to use a recording of a slow drumbeat. Ideally it will be the slow, steady, rhythmic drumbeat of horses hooves on the drum for about five minutes. Then gradually slow it down to the rhythm of the heart. Make sure it is slow and steady.

3. Visualize a ball of red light in the throat area of the body.

Red is stimulating and activating. Using it is like turning on a light switch.

4. In the middle of this ball of crystalline light, visualize the ancient Sanskrit symbol of the Om or the trident in bright scarlet.

5. Visualize, imagine and feel the red light emanating outward from this center to create a doorway as we learned in the last chapter.

6. Visualize, imagine and feel your animal guardian/totem standing in the doorway.

If you do not know what your animal totem is, visualize your favorite animal standing there or a beautiful horse. This totem will lead you through the doorway.

7. Imagine yourself stepping through this doorway and follow that animal guide into a green meadow beyond. Then imagine the following scenario, as you go off to sleep.

You are standing in a green meadow. The sun is warm upon the body. In the distance is a great river. Then there is movement at the far end of the meadow. You hear the whinnying of a horse and you watch as a beautiful horse trots into view, head held high and its mane flowing. It looks at you, tosses its head and trots toward you.

It stops in front of you and the sunlight seems to shimmer off its strong body. Its eyes fix you and you realize that you know this horse. You are not sure from where, but you do know it. Its head bobs as if acknowledging your recognition and it moves over to a large boulder and stands next to it. It looks back at you and waits.

You realize that you are being invited for a ride. You slowly walk over and you stroke the horse gently. It is comforting and familiar. As you walk around, you are not sure if you should. But with each touch of the horse, your confidence grows. You stand up on the boulder and holding the horse's mane, you slide your leg over the side of the horse. It stands steady and strong. You are tense, afraid that the horse will bolt and you gently lower yourself onto its back. The horse stands steady.

You wrap your hands in the mane and as you settle onto the horse, it steps slowly away from the boulder. It's as if it knows your nervousness and is going out of its way to ease it. Soon you relax as the steady walk begins to relax you.

You let the horse take you and you soon realize that it is moving toward the river. As it approaches the river, you can see that it seems to flow forever. You cannot see the beginning or the end – just bends and turns.

The horse stands at the edge of the water and you look out into the eddies and current. As you do the sun flashes upon the surface and you see images of things going on in your life at the present. You see your home, your place of work, your school, your family and your friends. Images of projects, goals and even difficulties shimmer and flow by you in the current. You are filled with wonder at the sight.

You look upstream, and you see images of the past week, glimpses of the recent past on the surface of the water. Further upstream you see flashes of the more distant past, events that have affected your life and what you now are.

You begin to realize that this is the river of your life. It is the flow of what you have done and been throughout time. You realize that even further up stream, beyond what you can see are probably past lives that have flowed down into what you now are.

Then you look downstream, and you see things that will unfold in the next day or so. You see current projects being completed, problems being solved and even some possible difficulties. You know that if you follow the river downstream you will discover what is yet to be.

Your heart is filled with wonder. Then the horse shifts under you. You realize that it is waiting to be told which way to go – upstream or downstream. You realize that part of the horse's magic is to ride you into the past or the future – if you desire. The horse can take you along the river so that you can see in the water the flow of events in your life.

You are amazed. Such possibilities! You realize this will take some thought but what adventures there can be. You decide that you will explore some other time. For now it is enough to know that the past and future are open.

The horse seems to read your mind and turns. It heads back to the meadow and stands next to that boulder. Holding onto the mane, you slide off its back and onto the boulder. You step around to look at him, stroking his cheeks and rubbing his neck. You thank the horse for this gift and step back. The horse lifts its head and lopes off to the far end of the meadow. There it turns and whinnies at you and disappears until the next time.

The images begin to fade and you find yourself back where you first began this journey. You understand that in time you can ride this horse into the past or into the future, It is your guide for sacred journeys through the veils of time.

If you make it through the complete visualization before you fall asleep, visualize yourself back at the dream doorway. Your animal guide is there waiting. You offer your thanks, and step back through the doorway. Allow the doorway to shrink back, fusing itself once more within the throat center. This serves two purposes. It develops the ability to mold and create energies on the more subtle levels, and it helps you develop control of the will force. Then roll over and go to sleep.

An Important Explanation about Shamanic Journeys

With these exercises, individuals sometimes wonder if they are experiencing a true shamanic journey. The difference between a meditation and a true journey is the depth of experience. In the journey you are actually in it, feeling it and experiencing it first hand. It also will not always follow a predescribed pattern.

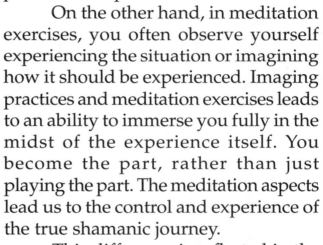

On the other hand, in meditation exercises, you often observe yourself experiencing the situation or imagining how it should be experienced. Imaging practices and meditation exercises leads to an ability to immerse you fully in the midst of the experience itself. You become the part, rather than just playing the part. The meditation aspects lead us to the control and experience of the true shamanic journey.

This difference is reflected in the contrast between mediumistic trance experiences and shamanic trance experiences. In the former, the individual leaves the body and allows another entity or being to work through the physical vehicle. It involves achieving a passive and receptive condition. In shamanic trance, the individual leaves the physical body (leaving it protected), goes out upon the inner planes, experiences them firsthand and brings back the knowledge for themselves. It is an active form of trance.

Shapeshifting
Exercise
(developmental & experiential)

Spirit Contact & Astral travel

Skills & Benefits

- **increases spirit contact in and out of dreams**
- **improves sending and receiving messages**
- **assists in dream travel**
- **stimulates flying dreams**

Traditionally there are two kinds of trance – mediumistic and shamanic. In mediumistic, the individual learns to withdraw consciousness from the physical body, allowing a spirit to communicate through it or overshadow the personality of the individual. In shamanic trance, the individual learns to withdraw the consciousness from the body, leaving the body protected, and then goes out to communicate with the spirits directly, later consciously returning to the protected body. The soul, while outside of the body explores other dimensions, communicates first hand with spirits of various sorts and returns with full memory.

It requires much more development and skill for the second form. It is active, while mediumistic trance is passive. We live in a fast food society. People like their psychic stuff quick and easy and so people do not apply the time and energy needed for shamanic journeys and spirit contact.

It is always more beneficial to develop and control our faculties than to simply sit, waiting to be used as an instrument. Consciously controlled spirit work involves taking our development directly in hand.

Bird energy and feathers are wonderful aids to developing this ability.

1. Make preparations.
Make sure you will not be disturbed. You may wish to light a candle or use some unobtrusive incense. The incense should be light and airy, nothing musky or heavy because we are dealing with birds. I have found flute music to be helpful.

2. You will need two feathers.
The feathers should be of the same species of bird. I often use flight feathers for this, but any type of feather will do, particularly if there will be astral journeys involved.

3. Hold a feather in each hand and begin to relax.
The more relaxed you are the better the exercise works. Allow your eyes to close and breathe deeply.

4. Imagine yourself growing lighter.
Imagine that with each breath the heaviness of the physical world begins to fade. Take your time with this. See and feel your aura extending out from you, expanding throughout the room, making your body density less. As you do, imagine the veils separating the physical from the spiritual becoming thinner and thinner.

5. Visualize a ball of red light in the throat area of the body.
Red is stimulating and activating. Using it is like turning on a light switch.

6. In the middle of this ball of crystalline light, visualize the ancient Sanskrit symbol of the Om or the trident in bright scarlet.

7. Visualize, imagine and feel the red light emanating outward from this center to create a doorway as we learned in the last chapter.

8. Visualize, imagine and feel yourself moving through that doorway.
As you move through it imagine yourself flying across the landscape. You realize that as long as you are holding the feathers you can fly anywhere. See and feel yourself riding the wind. Do not be surprised if you see yourself as a bird or your arms as wings. Just enjoy the freedom of flight as you go off to sleep.

   As you perform this exercise, the energy around you will change. It will require less effort. You will feel lighter. You may feel like your arms are helium filled and want to float. You may feel as if you are barely resting upon the chair. You may have the sensation of going over that dip in the road while riding in the car. You may begin to feel like you do in one of your flying dreams. There may even be an occasional jerking sensation, such as when you start to fall asleep and you feel as if you are about to fall out of bed.

If you make it through the complete visualization before you fall asleep, visualize yourself back at the dream doorway. Step back through the doorway. Allow the doorway to shrink back, fusing itself once more within the throat center. This serves two purposes. It develops the ability to mold and create energies on the more subtle levels, and it helps you develop control of the will force. Then roll over and go to sleep.

9. If you perform this exercise at a time other than as you go to sleep, return from your flight to the doorway.

You step through and allow the doorway to shrink back, fusing itself once more within the throat center. This serves two purposes. It develops the ability to mold and create energies on the more subtle levels, and it helps you develop control of the will force.

10.   Slowly open your eyes.

It is not unusual to experience spirit after this exercise. The veils will still be initially thin and spirit will let you know of their presence in subtle but very real ways. You may feel a soft brush of air. You may see shadows shift around you. There may be colored, flickering lights, you may see forms and shapes appear and fade.

Breathe deeply, feeling your aura beginning to draw back closer around you. Feel yourself growing heavier and denser - returning to your normal weight. Feel the body solidly beneath you. See and feel the veils between the physical and the spiritual thickening and closing.

This type of exercise can draw the consciousness away from the body and there is a need to ground us. Slowly stretch, moving all parts of the body. Set the feathers down and feel your feet firmly upon the ground. Breathe deeply and open the eyes wide. Perform your grounding postures. It is a good thing to eat a little after this type of exercise - nothing heavy but something to trigger the body's digestive processes. Digestion takes the most energy of any body process, and even if only digesting a few crackers it will help ground you.

Initially do not repeat this exercise too often. Once or twice a week is sufficient. If you find yourself rushing home everyday to perform it, then you are getting out of balance and should cease it all for a while. Over the next few months you will find that it becomes easier and the confirmations become stronger. You will find that your dreams will become more lucid and astral projection / out of body experiences will occur. You will become more aware of the presence of spirit around you.

What animal
sleeps inside you,
waiting for you
to dream it awake?

Part III

The Art
of
Shapeshifting

Sometimes we think of shapeshifting as being just humans transforming themselves into animals. But folklore and myth is filled with circumstances in which animals shapeshift to become human – if only for a short time. Bears walk around as humans. Seals shed their skin and dance on the shore. Swan maidens remove their coat of feathers and explore the human world. And always it is done to learn more of others.

The Lady in White

Long before there was a long ago, a young man lived on the shores of a most beautiful lake in China. One spring during the Festival of the Dead, Shushuan visited a temple on the far side of the lake.

Quite suddenly, it began to rain and he looked for a ferry boat to carry him back across. As the boat pulled away from the shore, someone shouted to be ferried across. The ferryman returned to the shore, and a beautiful young woman dressed in white with her maid in blue, seated themselves on the ferry.

As the ferry crossed the lake, the young woman spoke to Shushuan.

"My name is White," she said. "I was recently widowed and since today is the Festival of the Dead, I have been to tend to the grave of my husband. I left in such a hurry this morning that I forgot to bring any money with me. I do not have enough to pay the ferryman. Would you be kind enough, sir, to pay him on my behalf? When you have time, you could come to my house near the Arrow Bridge and I will repay you."

Shushuan was willing and when they reached the other side, he paid the ferryman for them all. It was still raining and since Shushuan had an umbrella, he offered to walk part of the way home with her. In the end, he gave it to her, saying that he would be happy to come to her house the next day and fetch it.

He could not sleep all night, his thoughts returning to the beautiful woman and early the next morning he set out for her house. He asked around, but none of the people at the Arrow Bridge seemed to know whom he was speaking of. It was then that he met the maid and she directed him to a small house nearby.

The lady received him in a beautiful decorated room and offered him wine and food. She spoke to him softly but directly, and after awhile she told him that she felt a great affection for him.

"I believe our meeting on the ferry was destined to happen," she said. "I hope you too have some affection for me and that you will be able to marry me."

Shushuan was overwhelmed with delight, but he remained silent because he did not have any property of his own and did not see how he would be able to marry her. When he explained this to her, she smiled with understanding. She then gave him 50 pieces of silver and said that she had more than enough money for them to live in comfort till the end of their days.

"Think about it this evening, and then return to me in the morning with your answer," she said.

On his way home, he stopped to purchase food and gifts for his family and when he told them his story, his brother-in-law examined the coins carefully.

"This is terrible," he exclaimed. "We shall all be ruined. These coins have the mark of the official treasury. They must be stolen!"

Shushuan was terrified and told the magistrate how he came by the silver, but when the police went to the house at Arrow Bridge, it was locked and empty.

That night, as he walked the street, the Lady White came from out of the shadows. She smiled gently at him and although he was cautious, she explained.

"It was all a terrible mistake. I am not a thief. The silver was left to me by my husband and I have absolutely no idea where he got it. I was terrified when I heard that you might get into trouble and when my maid saw the police coming, we just ran away."

She was so convincing that Shushuan believed her and before long they fell greatly in love and were married. And for a year they were extremely happy.

A year later, Shushuan's family invited him to a religious festival. His wife refused to go and was reluctant to let him and only did so - on three conditions. He must not speak to any priest. He must not enter the temple itself and he must not stay out late.

While at the festival though, the family convinced him to go into the temple, and when he did, a much-respected priest noticed him and kept looking at him strangely. Finally the priest called to him, but Shushuan did not hear and left the temple to go home.

When he walked into the house, he found his wife sitting and staring at him in a way she had never done.

"Although I treated you with all my love and consideration and although we were happy together, you could not do three things for me." And then her voice took on a threatening tone. "One disobedient word from you ever again, and I will turn your family into a blood bath."

Shushuan paled and backed out the door. His wife stood, following, her eyes flashing great anger. As he backed out, he brushed against the priest from the temple who had followed him home. As his wife stepped out the door, the priest took a bowl from under his robe and clapped it on her head. He began pressing down, feeling her shrink beneath him.

Shushuan stood, wide-eyes, unable to move. And then he heard her voice, low and pleading from beneath the bowl.

"Husband, husband, do not allow him to do this to me. Remember our love. Remember our life together."

The priest kept pressing down until the bowl touched the ground and then he commanded: "Show your true form. Who are you?"

A voice softly answered from beneath the bowl, "I am a white python, many centuries old. The movement of tides and wind brought me to live here at the lake, where I made friends with an ancient blue fish who became my faithful maid."

The priest spoke some ancient words - a powerful spell - and then turned the bowl over. There inside was a tiny white snake and a small blue fish. The priest covered them and nodding to the shocked Shushuan, he carried them back to his temple.

Chapter Nine

The Power of Imitation

O ne of the most common forms of sacred and magickal dance was the imitation of Nature and the life within it. Individuals would perform the dances of various animals to align themselves with the animal's power and awaken this power within his or her life. In more ancient times, shamans were the keepers of sacred knowledge. They were held in high esteem and recognized as true shapeshifters. They would employ dance to tie themselves to specific rhythms and forces of Nature.

A prevalent symbol for shamanism, the Masked Sorcerer, is shown throughout this book. The image is taken from a prehistoric cave painting. Early humans, surrounded by mysterious forces, responded to them through imitation. They tried to bring the divine into accord with humanity. Priests and priestesses used totems and images to assist them in coming face to face with this mystery. Through dance, costume, and ritual, the priest or priestess would share the deity's identity and its powers.

Part of the shamanic tradition involves re-connecting to the energies of the Earth and the life upon it. Animal imagery and sacred dance are used to assist with this re-connection. All forms and images, including animals, reflect a manifestation of archetypal energies. We do not have to believe that these animals possess creative intelligence, but there is a power, an archetype, that resides behind and oversees these life forms. These archetypes have their own qualities and characteristics which are reflected through and symbolized by the behaviors and activities of the animal.

When we honor the animal through sacred dance, we are honoring and invoking the essence that lies behind it. This essence is both creative

The Masked Sorcerer

This is a symbol of the prophet, the medicine person and the manifestation of the powers of Nature. Images such as this invoke a presence which helps us to transcend the physical. Wearing the skins of an animal was a means of appeasing its spirit and honoring its power.

and dynamic, and it can enhance our own life circumstances. When we open a sacred space and then attune to that essence through dance, movement, and posture, we share in its energy and manifest it within our own lives.

The animal becomes our totem - our power or medicine. It is a symbol of a specific kind of energy that we are invoking and using in our life. When we take on the image of the animal and dance its movements, we release the archetypal energies behind and through the animal into our lives.

Each species of animal has its own characteristics and the ability to remind us of the infinite power we can manifest in our own lives. By aligning and dancing to them, we are awakened to the realities of the natural and what we now call the supernatural.

Through dance, we learn to shapeshift our energy into a pattern similar to the energy of our totem animal. Developing this shapeshifting ability teaches us that we can re-create our lives. It shows us how to walk in harmony with all environs and in all worlds visible and invisible. It illustrates to us that we are not truly separate from anything upon the Earth and that we can bridge the natural and supernatural realms.

A totem is any natural being or animal to whose energy we feel closely associated and can relate to within our life. The most powerful are those of the animal kingdom. Some totems reflect energies operating for only short periods in our life, and some are with us from birth to death and beyond. They are symbols for the expression and transformation of energies, stimulating our creative forces.

There was a time when humanity recognized it was a part of Nature and that humanity and Nature were inseparable realities. The natural and supernatural merged and blended. People used Nature symbols to express and strengthen this unity. These symbols were often employed in sacred dance to reinstill a transpersonal kind of experience. This involved the use of fetishes - carrying or wearing of certain feathers or animal skins, creating a headdress of deer antlers, or holding flowers and crystals throughout the dance. A fetish is an object regarded as being the embodiment or the habitation of a potent spirit. It is the object that ties us to the specific archetypal totem force we are trying to awaken and invoke through the dance. They are symbols of the natural forces of Nature. They are anything that helps to tie you to the energies of your totem.

Fetish use is most recognizable in the Kachinas of the Southwest. All Pueblo Indian tribes had Kachinas, but the Hopis and the Zunis have the largest number. They are not gods themselves, but they are representations in human form of the spirits of plants, animals, and birds. The Kachina dancer is believed to receive a spirit when the mask with its fetishes is worn. The dancer then becomes a mediator between the prayers of the village and the deity or natural force.

Adopting the movements and guise of Nature in dance is a way of re-awakening primordial wisdom in us. The fetishes we employ in the dance represent the totem force we wish to invoke. They, along with the dance movements, are symbols of the energy and creativity we wish to manifest. They help us to shapeshift our normal consciousness to a stronger alignment, perception, and consciousness of that particular force of nature. The alignment is invoked through the dance so it may fulfill a particular purpose for a dancer.

First Some Science

The human body is a magnificent mechanism. It is a bio-chemical, electro-magnetic energy system. The human body gives off light, sound, thermal energies, electricity and magnetics. The field of these energies surrounding our body is traditionally known as the human aura. It serves as a protective field and it reflects physical, emotional, mental and spiritual aspects of us.

One of the most powerful and beneficial forms of shapeshifting is auric shapeshifting – changing the shape and intensity of that energy field. Our auras (the energy field surrounding us) can be changed to take the form of an animal or creature. In such changes, it becomes easier to express the qualities of that animal or creature. Thus, if we need to be more bearlike in a situation, we make our aura more bearlike. And sometimes this auric change can become visible, manifesting like a mask over the person. Have you ever seen someone take on a birdlike appearance or see their face shift briefly to that of a cat or some other animal? Many have experienced this auric shift when calling upon the medicine and energies of a particular animal.

One of the things we know about both human and animal bodies is that every time there is a muscular contraction, an electrical stimulus is also elicited in the body. If we apply this to shapeshifting, we begin to understand the power of imitation. If we move, posture, gesture and dance like a particular animal, we create an electrical change within our body. It becomes similar to that of the animal. We create resonance with that animal.

This is important for very powerful reasons:
1. **It makes it easier to express the qualities of that animal and use them for our benefit.**
2. **It becomes easier to communicate with that animal(pet or wild). It helps establish a physical, psychic & spiritual link.**
3. **Because some animals do not have certain health problems that humans do, by creating a link that resonates with a particular animal, we can alleviate and even heal some human conditions.**

We can also perform simple and even ecstatic dances and rituals that create such a powerful change in consciousness through changes in our electrical system that we feel as if we are actually changing and becoming the animal or creature. In such cases, even though we may not physically change to observers, internally we may have a profound transformation that can be accompanied by dramatic physical responses and releases. These kinds of experiences awaken hidden abilities and are empowering. These inner can even stimulate tremendous healing, higher consciousness, out-of-body experiences, spiritual and creative illumination, heightened spirit contact - along with many other benefits.

Healing with Shapeshifting

Techniques of shapeshifting may be the key to healing certain human imbalances or at least stimulating a turn-around in a disease. It could assist in restoring homeostasis to imbalances – especially since some animals do not have problems with many of the dis-eases that afflict humans. When we create resonance with an animal, we create changes in our entire bio-chemical system and its conditions.

In music and sound theory, forced resonance occurs when two energy systems have different frequencies and the stronger vibration is forces the weaker into alignment or resonance with it. Forced resonance can overcome imbalanced health condition, restoring homeostasis.

We know that long exposure to certain drum rhythms will create fluctuations in our own heart rhythms. Using specific drum rhythms in shapeshifting dances that imitate the heart rhythms of an animal could theoretically shift our own heart rhythms to a rhythm, which is similar to that animal. This may result in a shift in the dis-ease.

Another aspect of this theory to further heal through shapeshifting is by imitating the animal's breathing rhythms. This creates changes in the human body so that it is more similar to the animal. That resonance may trigger a turn-around in certain health problems.

Where to Begin

The first step is to determine what your animal totem might be. Some meditation techniques can help us identify them, but one of the easiest is to simply begin with the animal or animals that have interested you the most.

Which animal or bird has always fascinated you? What animal or animals do you see most frequently when you are out in nature? Of all the animals in the world, which are you most interested in? Do you often dream about a specific kind of animal? Are there animal dreams that you have never forgotten? Answering these kinds of questions provides strong clues to which animals are likely to be totems for you.

Go to your library and examine books and films about this animal. Notice the way it moves, the way it stands. How does it hold its head? How does it place its feet when it walks? Then pantomime those same postures and movements. Most of the ancient sacred animal dances were developed by simply mimicking and imitating animal forms and postures, Study some of the Eastern sciences such as yoga or Kung Fu. There are many books which depict these postures. This can give you a starting point in which to build your own dance.

The Next Steps

Dancing and movement for shapeshifting involves more than transforming oneself into a beast. This is not going to happen, at least not in the physical realm. As we learn to use dance, we can change the form in which we appear on other planes, this in turn will affect us on the physical plane. Shapeshifting dances, as we will learn, will help you align and manifest the power of the totem animal more strongly within your present physical form and life. The following steps can be used as a guide to shapeshift through magickal dance.

1. Begin by determining and researching your totem. Find pictures, make collages, and look for things that can represent it to you. Develop a mask and costume that will assist you in attuning and synchronizing with the energy of your totem.

2. Next decide on three to four basic moves which reflect the energy of this totem you wish to incorporate within your own life. Practice mimicking and pantomiming its movements and postures.

3. Take time to meditate upon this animal. Visualize and imagine it as a spiritual companion wherever you go. Visualize and imagine its energy coming alive within you and enabling you to accomplish specific goals.

4. In the center of your dance area, place any fetishes, pictures, costumes, or other items that will serve to align you with your totem. In the next chapter, we will explore the use of costumes, body art and masks in the shapeshifting process. If you wish, you may already be dressed and prepared. Do what works best for you.

5. Begin your shapeshifting dance by marking off the sacred space. Encircle your dance area three times. Then take three steps toward the center and perform the balancing postures. Pause and allow yourself to feel and experience the energies of the physical and the spiritual worlds blending and merging. Feel this new influx of energy.

6. Put on your costume slowly and deliberately. Imagine that this new energy is transforming you into your totem. See, feel, and imagine your totem appearing in the circle with you.

7. Perform the balancing exercises to stabilize yourself with these new energies. Use the Tibetan Walk to Nowhere to help open the veils to align yourself with the animal.

8. Now, begin the movements and postures associated with your totem. As you take the stances and make your steps around the circle pantomiming and imitating this power animal, feel it coming alive within you. You may even wish to act out how you will use this power successfully in your daily life. See yourself manifesting it creatively and productively. Know that you have aligned yourself with its essence.

9. Now assume one of the physical attitudes described in Part I - sitting, kneeling, prostrate, or standing. Hold the position like you know your totem would. If your totem is a bird, stand like that bird. If it is an animal, you may wish to lay prostrate as that animal would. Be creative. Absorb the energies of the circle while holding this pose. Perform the Tibetan Walk to move back acrossthe veils to your everyday life and then perform the balancing exercises again.

10. Remove the costume, knowing that the outer form and the energies it represents are now alive within you.

11. Take three steps back from the center, and perform the balancing postures again.

12. Encircle the area in a counterclockwise motion three times to dissipate the energy of the sacred space and to return the area back to normal.

Important Reminders for Shapeshifting Dances

Be flexible in these steps. Experiment with them and adapt them to find what works best for you. Dance and shapeshifting are creative processes. We can give you the basic formulas and ideas, but for them to become truly magickal you must apply your own creative imagination and intuition.

Of course, there are precautions necessary in any kind of shapeshifting work, especially when done through dance. The effects of dance rituals are powerful. The dancer should be prepared for dramatic physical responses and releases. Initially, it is best that the taking on of totem aspects be done under the supervision of a knowledgeable and responsible priest or priestess.

Even though the dancer may not change physically to other observers, internally he or she may have a profound transformation and believe it has occurred physically. This should not be treated casually or lightly dismissed. Time and care must be used in assimilating and balancing the energies released through dance.

For the beginner, it is best to work with simple movements and postures before attempting ecstatic dance states. If you are not sure of your own ability to control and handle the energy activated through the dance, do not use it. No dancer should ever be allowed to continue dancing until they are exhausted. This is unhealthy and very damaging to the energy field of the individual.

Many shamanic techniques involve using the drum to induce the altered state and facilitate the shapeshifting. The drum can also be used to draw the individual back into reality. One drum technique involves using a slow, heartbeat-like rhythm and then building in intensity to release the consciousness and facilitate the transition. Reversing this and moving from the frenzied rhythm back to the heartbeat-like rhythm will draw the consciousness back to normal. This is especially effective because the individual does not then move from the deeply altered state to normal consciousness too abruptly.

Taking the hands of the individual and performing joint deep breathing assists in grounding the individual back into reality. Massaging the feet to open and activate the chakras that connect us to the earth and its reality will also assist. Sitting or laying prone on the floor while accompanied by the removal of any fetishes or costumes used in the transformation will facilitate this grounding process.

It is also beneficial to stroke the spine downward from the crown of the head. This stabilizes the chakras and draws the consciousness back into present reality. Remember that part of the goal is to develop conscious control and awareness through movement.

Simple Animal Shapeshifting Rites

The Butterfly

Empowering Aids:
- **Paint your face with the image of a butterfly as shown in Chapter 10.**
- **Paint or draw caterpillars on your arm**
- **Make yourself a pair of butterfly wings**

These movements reflect the emergence of the butterfly from the cocoon. The butterfly is a powerful symbol for metamorphosis and resurrection – of coming into new life. It brings beauty and light into this new life. If we wish to shapeshift our lives into one that is magickal, we must learn to emerge from the cocoon of old perceptions. The totem and dance movements will assist you in attaining new perceptions.

In the first position, bend over and hold onto your feet. This is symbolic of being wrapped in a cocoon of physical life and perception. While holding this position, begin to squirm slowly and deliberately. See yourself as a caterpillar that is beginning its metamorphosis into a butterfly.

In the second posture, you become the butterfly. Raise your head and draw your arms back from your feet slowly. See and feel your arms as radiant wings.

At this point, you can rise from the floor into your new life. Spin about and see this spinning as lifting you lightly from your feet. Feel yourself as light and free. Notice the wings of rainbow light. Notice how your wings move with your thoughts. Allow yourself to fly about, hovering over flowers, trees and people.

See and feel yourself as the magickal butterfly that flies out to enjoy the nectar of life. Let this nectar represent a goal, purpose, or desire within your own life circumstances. Taste it and savor it!

The Cobra

Empowering Aids:
- **Paint snakes on your arms**
- **Paint the image of a snake swallowing its own tail on your forehead**
- **Incorporate the white snake hand gesture, described in the next section**

Snake dances are universal. They were performed to activate the kundalini - the creative life force, to stimulate a shedding of the old and to initiate resurrection and rebirth. The serpent is the serpent of higher knowledge and wisdom.

The posture depicted below is the *Cobra Posture* of Eastern Yoga. To perform it, lie flat upon the ground, face down. See yourself as a snake. Slowly lift your head to see more clearly, to raise yourself higher. Place your elbows under you, pushing yourself up even higher. Finally, with your head back, looking up as high as possible, stretch your arms out straight and hold the position of the cobra. See and feel yourself as the great serpent of knowledge. See yourself opening to new sight and new birth with this movement.

Take a few minutes and see yourself shedding what is no longer beneficial for you. Feel yourself emerging bigger, stronger and more beautiful than ever.

The Cat Stance

Empowering Aids:
- **Paint your face like a cat**
- **Buy or make a cat mask and costume. Body suits work well for this.**
- **Incorporate the leopard fist or tiger claw hand gestures, described in the next section of this chapter**

Cats are ancient, powerful symbols of magic and mysticism. They have been dynamic symbols of immortality - nine lives and such. In Egypt, it was associated with the moon and thus the feminine energies of intuition and instinct. Different cats are symbols of different variations of these energies. A study of specific cats will help you identify their unique powers.

This is a position taken from traditional Kung Fu. A cat is light on its feet, often walking on its toes. It is stealthy and silent in its movements. It is assured, steady and strong. The hand positions demonstrated in this chapter for the leopard and the tiger can be used in conjunction with this stance.

Practice prancing sure-footedly and softly within your circle. Know that as you become the cat, you become more sure-footed in life. Know that you will live through anything that you feel is overwhelming you at the moment. In fact, performing cat dancing and postures helps create opportunities that put you back on your feet again.

The Crane

Empowering Aids:
- **Have feathers of any kind on you or in your hand.**
- **Make a crane mask**
- **Keep feet and legs bare from the knees down**
- **Incorporate the crane hand movement, described in the next section**

The crane has been esteemed for its majesty and grace. In Chinese and Mediterranean cultures, it has been a symbol of justice, longevity, and the abiding soul. It has also been considered a messenger of the gods, a mediator between heaven and earth. Its massive wingspan - up to eight feet - gives it great power of flight. It was believed to carry souls to Paradise and to the Underworld.

This martial arts posture activates this same energy. It creates balance and strength. All kicks in Kung Fu involve this stance at some level. Learning to move and hop from one leg to the other gracefully will help you traverse the physical and spiritual realms gracefully. This posture activates intuition and greater discernment in working and walking between worlds and dimensions.

Butterfly Shapeshifting

Snake Posture

Animal Hand Gestures

In Part I, we discussed how powerful and effective hand postures and movements are in shifting energy in the body. When we perform shapeshifting dances, they take on even greater power. Animal hand gestures can be incorporated into dance movements to enhance shapeshifting. Part of what we can learn from the martial arts is the ability to mimic animal gestures with the hands. In the Ninja tradition when held and used properly, the hands are points where the intrinsic forces of Nature can manifest themselves.

The samples given below are by no means the only gestures and positions of hands. They are just a starting point. They are only presented to give you ideas to build on for your own totem dance. Hand gestures and movements are powerful aids to shapeshifting success.

The *crane hand* can be used with the crane stance. It helps activate the dynamic and strong energies of this totem even more. The hand position mimics the long slender beak which can peck and hook fiercely and quickly.

There are two common hand postures found in the martial arts and they can be applied to working with any cat shapeshifting. The *leopard fist*, as shown in the illustration, helps develop strong and fast responses. A leopard uses quick, short movements. It is symbolic of valor and has been associated with Dionysus. The leopard fist is formed by folding the fingers halfway down with the thumb tucked in at the side.

The *tiger's claw* gesture is also powerful and significant. It is known for its ferocity and strength. It has also been associated with the sun and the new moon. In its usual posture, the hand is tensed tightly and the fingers are turned inward. To strengthen and imbue the body with greater energy, the finger tips are pressed together as hard as you can for a count of ten. Most of the major meridians or energy pathways in the body culminate at the fingertips. By pressing the fingertips together, all of them are stimulated, sending energy throughout the body.

The *rams head fist* is a gesture of power. Any fist position activates the energy of strength and power. The ram is strong and sure-footed and has been the symbol of many kings in the past. It is a symbol of masculine fertility and strength and the creative impulse. To form it, the fist is turned slightly so that the first two knuckles are in front of the others. These two knuckles symbolize the horns of the great ram.

The last sample is called the *white snake hand*. In Kung Fu, it is sometimes called the poison hand. It can be used in all serpent dances and with the cobra postures. The snake is fast and accurate when it strikes. The strike of some snakes has been timed at 100 miles per hour. This hand position helps awaken greater energy for speed and accuracy in handling life and for taking advantage of new opportunities. Snake dances, using just the hands, can create quick and sudden opportunities for transformation.

And let's not forget...

In Nature, there are animals - often considered imaginary - but which represent powerful forces in Nature. They are animals such as the dragon, the phoenix, and the unicorn. They represent powerful archetypal forces in the world of Nature. We will explore some of these fantastic creatures and shapeshifting rites to tap into their energies in the last chapter. For now though, there are hand dances and postures associated with two of them, which are very powerful.

Dragons are symbols of great power, strength, healing, and protection. In the orient, dragons have an ancient and tremendous mythology and they were often the symbols of emperors. Even though they are considered mythical, they also can be used as a totem.

The *dragon hand* has two forms. In the first, the knuckle of the middle finger is extended forward just little. It is the powerful head of the dragon. The claw of the dragon is formed by spreading all five fingers, and then bending and tightening the tips.

The *eye of the phoenix* hand can be used in dances for resurrection and for rebirth in times of trauma. It can be used to help create new opportunities from seeming losses through ritual dance. The phoenix rose from the ashes. Shapeshifting into its form activates that same energy in your life. The *eye of the phoenix* hand is formed by extending the knuckle of the index finger forward a little, as depicted in the illustration. Holding your hands in this position imbues the spirit with the ability to try again and again.

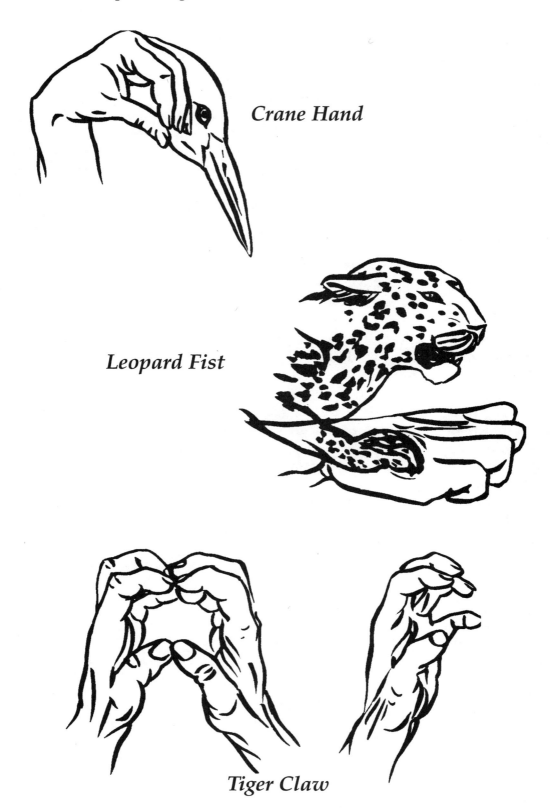

Crane Hand

Leopard Fist

Tiger Claw

Ram's Head Fist

White Snake Hand

Eye of the Phoenix

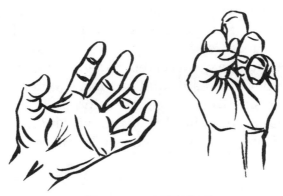

Dragon Hand

Shapeshifting
Exercise
(experiential)

Becoming the Owl

Skills & Benefits

- **heightens senses**
- **increases intuition and hearing**
- **vision of things not readily seen**
- **awareness of spirits increases**

The owl is the silent guide. It has been worshipped and hated throughout the world, but always it intrigues and fascinates. It is the epitome of mystery, magic, vision and guidance. It is often a symbol of vision and guidance

In the natural world, the owl is not the most intelligent of animals, and yet it is a powerful and instinctual creature that can teach us much. Its visual and auditory senses are tremendous, and so its appearance always reflects a heightening of our own senses – especially of the intuition.

The owl is a creature of the night, and night symbolizes the darkness within – the places where great secrets and great treasures are hidden. The night is the place of our dreams and our fears. When owl appears, dream activity will be intensified, bringing perspective and clarity to daily activities. A study of dreams and their hidden wisdom is always beneficial when owl appears. Shapeshifting to connect with owls will make your dreams more vibrant.

The owl's eyes are adapted to see the subtlest of movement with the least amount of light. Because of this, after this shapeshifting you will see subtleties that you may not have noticed before. Trust these impressions, whether they come during the day or at night because owls see very well during both times.

An owl's hearing is just as acute as its sight. Because of this, when you align with owl, you will hear undercurrents in the voices of others. Trust what you do or do not hear in the conversations around you – no matter how strange you may think your impression is. When we learn to trust those instincts, then we see our own wisdom manifesting.

Owls fly silently. The front edges of their wings and feathers have a fringe, which quiets their flight. This facilitates the silent hunt, and thus when owl shows up, it is time to turn to our endeavors with silence. An old adage tells of how there is strength in silence. Never is this more significant than when the owl appears. And when the opportunity presents itself, we must aggressively and quietly go after it.

Owls teach us to trust our instincts, the silent impressions. They provide guidance through heightening our senses. Their appearance always indicates that help and guidance are available to us, but it is still up to us to act upon it.

The owl is a powerful and aggressive hunter, with instincts that are honed for survival. Each species of owls has its own unique qualities, and the individual species must be studied to clarify all of its meaning within our life. Regardless of the species of owl though, if we shapeshift with owl, we will need to pay attention to our inner perceptions.

1. Begin by studying owls.

Study the owl. Learn how it moves. Go to the library and get some owl recordings. Prior to any shapeshifting with owls, I will listen to their recordings. If I do an owl shapeshifting in the spring, I will try and do it outside at night. Nighttime is their time and the spring is a time when their hooting is strongest. I have a very large population of owls surrounding my farm and it negates the need for recording sounds – especially in the spring when their hooting is the greatest.

Owls fly silently, and so all movements should be slow and as silent as possible. The wing movements are slow, deep and powerful They can not turn their heads completely around but they can go three quarters of the way. And they turn their heads smoothly to see peripherally.. Their eyes are fixed, so in order to see, they must be able to turn their heads.

Owls are often thought to look human because they blink like we do. They will blink singly or with both eyes – usually much slower than humans blink. I have found in working with owls in rescue and rehab that mimicking their blinking is a way of helping them calm. It is even believed that they may communicate with each other through blinking.

3. Make preparations

Make sure you will not be disturbed. If possible have a feather to hold in each hand. It does not have to be an owl feather. It is illegal to possess the feathers of birds of prey without federal and state permits. Many believe that you have to have the feather of the bird to connect with that species. *This is wrong.* Any feather can help connect you to any member of the bird kingdom.

4. If you have recorded owl sounds, play them now.
Perform your balancing postures as the sounds play - holding a feather in each hand. Then perform the Tibetan Walk to Nowhere to open the veils.

5. Perform the movements and postures for the owl that you have chosen.
Perform them slowly and deliberately. Visualize yourself as an owl, making those movements. Repeat them three times. And then take a seat.

6. Relax and imagine yourself growing lighter.
Imagine that with each breath the heaviness of the physical world begins to fade. The more relaxed you are the better the exercise works. Allow your eyes to close and breathe deeply. Take your time with this. See and feel your aura extending out from you, expanding throughout the room, making your body density less. As you do, imagine the veils separating the physical from the spiritual becoming thinner and thinner.

5. Invite the owl spirit to make itself known.
Mentally invite the spirit of the owl to guide you and bless you with this shapeshifting.

6. Pay attention to body sensations.
As you perform this exercise, the energy around you will change. It will require less effort. You will feel lighter. You may feel like your arms are helium filled and want to float. You may feel as if you are barely resting upon the chair. You may have the sensation of going over that dip in the road while riding in the car. You may begin to feel like you do in one of your flying dreams. There may even be an occasional jerking sensation, such as when you start to fall asleep and you feel as if you are about to fall out of bed.

7. Then visualize the following scenario.

You are standing in a large meadow. It is night and the stars sparkle clear above you. The ground is cool upon your bare feet and very soothing. You can hear a few sounds, but for the most part it is quiet. As your eyes adjust to the darkness, you notice a large rock formation in the middle of the meadow. As you approach it, you notice that it is just right for sitting upon it – which you do.

As you take your seat, you realize that you are holding two feathers and you just know that they are owl feathers. And in response to that realization, you hear an owl hooting from the trees surrounding this meadow. As you turn your head in the direction of the hoot, you catch sight of a large owl rising up out of the tree and it is silhouetted against the night sky. It circles the meadow and then disappears.

You are filled with awe and you wonder to yourself what it would be like to be an owl. And in response there is a soft brush of air. You feel it catch the feathers in your hand and it sends a tingling through your hands and up your arms.

You feel yourself relaxing deeply as that tingling grows. You look down to your hand and you see that feather becoming a part of your hand and your fingers stretching becoming feathers themselves. Your eyes widen, but you are not frightened by this at all. You are amazed.

As that tingling spreads up the arms, you see tiny feathers beginning to form over your hands and arms – soft down. Slowly it spreads to yours shoulders and the tingling moves down your back and your front. Where ever the tingling moves, soft down feathers appear. They seem to dance and shimmer with the softest breeze. The tingling moves up your neck and aver your head. Your feel your hair growing lighter, becoming feathery. You laugh at how amazing and wonderful it is, but the laugh is more hollow and short.

You look down to your legs, watching as the tingling continues and your legs and feet are soon covered in soft down feathers. Then from the down larger feathers begin to manifest, covering the down. You feel feathers spreading and with each one, you feel yourself growing lighter and yet somehow much stronger.

As your face begins to tingle, your eyes grow wider and the meadow becomes much clearer. You suddenly realize that you are getting the eyes of an owl and you can see every leaf on every tree surrounding the meadow in perfect detail. Such tremendous vision!

And you feel your ears drawing in underneath the feathers, and although the ears disappear, your hearing seems more acute than you have ever imagined. There is the sound of a mouse moving slowly through the grass – fifty yards away. And even though you cannot see it, you hear exactly where it is. Your hearing is more acute than your eyesight. You laugh in wonder again. But it is not your laugh that comes out, but the hoot of the owl.

You realize that your nose and upper part of your mouth have come together and that instead of a nose, you now have a powerful beak. You clack that beak several times. It is very powerful and you realize that it could tear things very easily. A part of you realizes that it has significance on other levels, and you make a mental note to explore that later.

You look down to your feet and your see your toes slowly becoming powerful talons, covered in soft feathers. You stretch out one of your legs and flex the talons *on that foot. Never have you felt such strength and power. There is no doubt that anything you grab, could not escape.*

You hop up on the rock, your eyes and ears taking in the minutest detail in the meadow. You spread your arms and see that they are now full wings. You move them slowly, feeling them catch the air. You feel them try to lift you and you realize that you probably can fly.

You are light and strong.

You are owl.

Then you jump and begin beating those broad wings. They move silently but they capture the air powerfully. You begin to fly across the meadow. You circle, testing your ability, getting comfortable in your owl skin. Such strength runs through you. Your senses are alive, sharp and alert. And you begin to climb.

Soon you are circling high above the meadow. From hear you can see a path leading down to a distant valley. Your sharp eyesight can pick out the details. You can even hear bits of conversation because your hearing is so sharp.

You soar across the night sky, aware of every movement and every sound around you. You tilt your body and soar down toward that rock and as you approach, you flap your wings and land gently upon it. Your head moves slowly around taking in every sight and sound. Then a soft breeze brushes over you and you breathe deeply. As you do, the tingling begins once more.

You feel it first on the top of your head and in your feet at the same time. You feel feather beginning to withdraw. Hair returns where there were feathers. Talons become toes. And as the feathers slowly disappear, your body begins to return. Feathers fade from the legs and the front and back of you. As the tingling moves down the arms the feathers disappear, until there are only your hands – each holding a feather.

You stand up off the rock and you realize that your senses are still heightened. You can still hear animals that are normally out of sight and sound. You can still see details of trees and brush –in spite of the night.

Then you hear the hooting of an owl and as you look up, you see the owl silhouetted against the sky as it returns to the meadow. You bow and thank it for its guidance and its sharing. And the meadow fades and you feel yourself back where you first started this shifting.

Just sit and be still for a few moments, Stretch a little, allowing your hands and feet to move. Breathe deeply. As you sit there, you may feel a soft brush of air. You may see shadows shift around you. There may be colored, flickering lights, you may see forms and shapes appear and fade. In the beginning it will probably be subtle things that you may wish to attribute to your imagination. Remember though that birds see and hear much better than we do. They can detect the subtlest things. Do not respond to them; simply note them and the sensations. Do this for only a few moments. They are after effects of the exercise. As the veils close entirely, they will fade.

Then slowly stand and repeat the owl movements, again giving thanks for this sharing. Then perform the tibetan Walk to Nowhere to move back across the veils completely. Follow this with the grounding postures. Stretch and begin to move. And know that in the next few days your senses will be a bit more acute. You may see and hear things more clearly. You may hear hidden meanings in others' words. You may start to see auras and even spirit. But throughout, there will be a strong sense of guidance and protection.

Shapeshifting Exercise (developmental & experiential)

Dance of the Unicorn

Skills & Benefits:

- **stronger connections with animals**
- **healing**
- **gentle strength**
- **contact with nature spirits**
- **heightened intuition**

Since the earliest of times, the unicorn has mystified humans. It has been a symbol of gentleness, power and fertility. It is a creature of extraordinary perception, stamina and magic. It has been revered for its ability to heal and feared for its ability to kill. And its appeal has never faded for any great length of time within the minds and hearts of humans. It is one of the major archetypes and protectors of the natural world.

Unicorns fascinate us, for more than any other creature, it seems the most plausible. While most people believe that the dragon is pure myth and fantasy, this same belief does not hold true for the unicorn. It has such close resemblance to so many animals in existence that its reality is a possibility to the average person. Most often depicted and related to the horse, it has been linked to many horned creatures. The most common are the deer and the goat, but it has also been related to the narwhal and the rhinoceros. One hundred and twenty million years ago there was even a dinosaur unicorn, the monoclonius.

They are born without fear and with a great love for play. Running and jumping are joys to them, which is why they are often seen with deer. They have a great love of flowers, the scent and the look. The young love wild blackberries and raspberries. They understand the language of all animals, but they have a special relationship with birds. They protect the animals of their environments. They will often help feed the other animals, going so far as to use the horn to dig nut holes for squirrels or knock fruit and nuts from trees. They have been known to free animals from traps.

From the moment they are born, the senses of the unicorn are much more acute than any other animal. It can detect the softest whisper of a breeze before it enters its territory. It can detect the subtlest of movement, even while it's being thought. It can smell the fragrance of a flower a mile away. It is so fast that it seems to fly and disappear magically. Because its senses are so highly developed, it rarely allows itself to be seen. Casual human contact is virtually non-existent.

Dances for Mythic and Fantastic Animals

Many societies had movements and postures associated with mythic animals. These postures, when used in conjunction with other animal meditations, empowered them. This is especially true in the case of the four sacred beasts in the Chinese tradition – the unicorn, the dragon, the phoenix and the turtle.

When I do workshops on magickal dance, I frequently teach the group simple dance rituals that elicit quick and definite effects. In this way the group experiences and confirms for themselves how much more quickly results are achieved when the proper movement is used in conjunction with meditation or rituals. The group dances that I teach most frequently are connected to the fantastic creatures - the unicorn, the dragon and the phoenix. We will explore some of these more fully in the last chapter, but we will work with the unicorn archetype now.

In Northern Shaolin Long Fist Sword techniques, there are eight fundamental stances. Two of these have great application for shapeshifting with the unicorn. These do not require an actual sword. A knife, athame, a stick or your own creative imagination will more than suffice.

The first is the traditional horse stance. The second is a movement from the horse stance into the unicorn stance. After learning these two, do not be afraid to adapt them. I use these two and several variations of them for certain magickal rituals and exercises that I perform in my personal spiritual work with the unicorn.

The unicorn stance is basic but very powerful. Performing it everyday is a means of aligning ourselves with the unicorn energy, and thus, it can be done as both a morning and evening ritual and meditation by itself. The unicorn energy strengthens our connection to all of Nature. It is one of the most gentle and powerful archetypes of the natural world. It will strengthen your connection to all animals and it will enhance the overall effectiveness of your other work in shapeshifting.

The unicorn stance can also be expanded into an entire dance ritual for groups, involving costumes and all of the other elements of magickal

The Horse Stance
(Ma Bu)

To assume the horse stance, begin with the feet parallel and slightly beyond shoulder width. Then widen the stance further the length of one of your feet on each side. The knees should be bent until an angle of approximately ninety degrees is formed between the back of the calf and the back of the thigh. The back is straight, shoulders relaxed and the buttocks are tucked under.

The Unicorn Stance
(Chi Lin Bu)

This stance originated with the belief that a unicorn had to bend its knee in order to bow or to heal / cleanse water. From this stance the martial artist can move back easily and still have the ability to kick with the rear leg. (Like the unicorn, this posture allows the martial artist to avoid being caught unaware and unprepared.)

From the horse stance, place the right leg behind the left. The knee of the right leg should be ideally one inch above the ground and directly behind the left ankle. (Only go as far as is comfortable for you.) The right leg is on its toes. The left foot is turned out, and the left leg holds 80% of the bodies weight. (Reverse this process for the other leg.)

The Unicorn Dance

Build upon the basic stance. Incorporate costume and creative imagination to create your own unicorn dance and/or ceremony. Imbue your movements with significance. The more you do so, the more powerful the effect. The stronger your focus upon the unicorn and seeing yourself as it, the stronger you will align with it. The unicorn energy will manifest more dynamically as a result strengthening your connection to all animals and empowering all shapeshifting activities.

It is not difficult to use these stances to empower ourselves and our connection to the unicorn:

1. Become familiar with the movements.
Practice them.

2. Take time to meditate upon the unicorn and its correspondences.
Visualize it as a companion wherever you go. Visualize it coming more alive within you each time your focus upon it.

3. Begin by standing straight.
Relax. Close your eyes and take a few moments to breathe slowly.

4. Step into the horse stance.
Keep your weight over your feet. Visualize yourself as a horse or astride a horse. Imagine the strength and energy of the horse coming alive within you. Imagine how you can apply this energy in your daily life. Hold this position for only a few minutes. Five minutes is sufficient, or as long as you are comfortable. Until you get used to this posture, you may feel some discomfort. **STOP IF YOU DO!**

5. Then move into the unicorn posture.
Try to keep the movements smooth. Visualize yourself becoming one with the unicorn. See, feel and imagine its qualities coming alive within you. Imagine and feel your energy coming into attunement with that of the unicorn. Know that as you assume this posture that the unicorn's energy is being invoked and will manifest in your life. Maintain this posture only as long as you are comfortable. No longer than five minutes is necessary. **Stop if you feel any discomfort!**

6. Do not become discouraged if you have difficulty maintaining these   postures.
In time, it will become easier. See it as a signal to how well you are aligning with the unicorn energy. As you become more adept at it, the more aligned and resonant you are to the unicorn and its essence.

7. Performing this exercise at the beginning and end of the other exercises   and meditations will further empower them.
When performed at the beginning, they serve to shift the consciousness and the body's energy to be more in sync with that of the unicorn. When performed at the end, they serve to shift back and ground the unicorn energy. This helps prevent the spaciness that can occur after some meditations.

8. When performed at the conclusion of other unicorn meditation / attunement work, assume the postures in their reverse order.

Begin with the pose of the unicorn. Move from it to the horse stance. Then move from the horse stance to a relaxed standing posture. This further emphasizes the grounding, and shifts the consciousness back to the daily life. In essence, you are moving into the unicorn energy, accessing it through the actual meditation, and then you bring it back out to manifest in your life.

Chapter Ten

Spirit Masks & Shapeshifting

Most traditions around the world had dances that imitated the movement of animals. It was a way of honoring the animal. It was a way of aligning with its energy. It was a way of invoking its energy into one's life. Today the animal dancing has become ignored and yet it is still one of the most effective ways of developing a dynamic connection with the animal.

If you wish to align truly and deeply with an animal totem, study the way it moves. Imitate the way it walks and the gestures it makes. The human body is a bio-chemical, electro-magnetic energy system. Every time there is a muscular contraction and electrical stimulus is elicited within the body. When we imitate how an animal moves we are changing our body's electrical system. We are making it similar to that of the animal.

If we wish to empower that process of linking to the animal's energies and make our shapeshifting more powerful, we can use more ritualistic aspects. These can be formal or informal. The most effective for shapeshifting is the use of some kind of body art. Body art assists in invoking the archetypal energies of the animal and align us with its spirit. As we put on the body art, we immediately begin to align with the animal. Resonance begins to be established. Wearing the body art only in times of shapeshifting rites and exercises, keeps it special and it then serves to initiate a thinning of the veils and a strengthening of connection to the animal's spirit.

There are many kinds of body art that can be used to enhance shapeshifting rituals. These can include tattooing, body paint, costuming, and jewelry. They are all effective in helping us establish a connection with and honoring of the animal that will be the focus of our shapeshifting.

Face Painting and Body Art

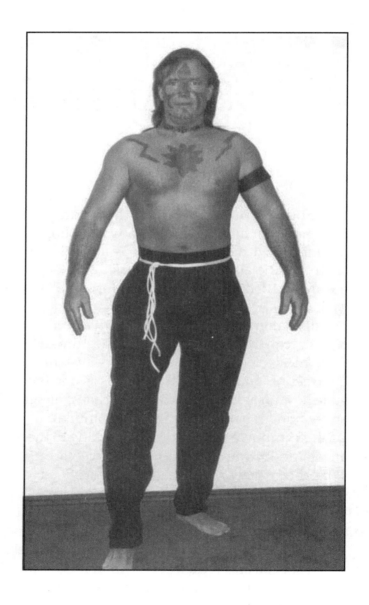

The body does not necessarily need tattooing for shapeshifting – although this is a very ancient ritual. It has become very popular today. If this is what you are drawn to as a way of helping to establish a link with the animal to honor its presence in your life, there are plenty of books out there that can help you explore this further. People often ask me about tattooing their animal totems on their body somewhere, and I never have a straight answer. This is partly because our totems do change and when the tattooing is done, it is permanent. Thus, great care and thought should always be given to that process.

The body can be decorated less permanently though to enhance the significance of the animal and your dance. Many societies incorporated body painting as part of their ritual. The face, hands and other parts of the body can be marked with signs, images and colors that reflect the animal and the purpose of the shapeshifting dance. Henna / Mehndi body art is one of the newest ways and can be very powerful. There are also many face-painting kits on the  market today. Many are hypo-allergenic and are easily washed off with soap and water. In this way, you can adjust more easily the body markings to your purpose.

Costumes and ceremonial dress have often been used in various ritual traditions. Costumes can be made to look like a particular animal. The putting on of the costume initiates the mental shift so that we begin to take on the energy of the animal. Another aspect of costuming that can be used to connect to the animal in your shapeshifting rites is through related jewelry. Rings, necklaces and other jewelry can reflect the energy of the animal and your purpose. And because jewelry can be easily and strongly imprinted with the energy of the ritual and our focus, it is a powerful tool for connecting with and expressing the animal's medicine. The more of these elements that you include in your shapeshifting ritual and exercises, the stronger your alignment and resonance with the animal will be.

The Power of Masks

Masks have always seemed to have a magical power about them. Concealed behind it, we can become something or somebody else. We can become whatever we want to be by wearing a mask. Whether a simple headdress or helmet mask, it helped to enlarge you. To own a mask is to possess a potential power. The wearer magically assumes a new identity. It enables present reality to be suspended.

Masks are invested with mystery. They are tools for transformation. They are equivalent to the process of chrysalis. Metamorphosis usually is and should be hidden, so it is not interrupted. The hidden aspect, the secrecy, leads to transfiguration. It helps us to change what we are to what we want to be, giving us magic.

There is an ambiguity and an equivocation about masks. The ambiguity is the fact that when we wear one, we are no longer whom we thought. The equivocation is that we are making ourselves one with some other force. By wearing a mask, we become part of the mythical "'Tween Times and Places". We move into an intersection between the outer real world and other dimensions. We create a doorway of the mind and in the physical world - a threshold that we can cross to new dimensions and beingness. When working with animal masks, we move into a more intimate realm of animal connections. We are less passive and more active, bringing the energy of the animal alive more strongly within our life.

Mystery of Mask Making

The origin of masks is unclear, although there is very ancient evidence of their use all over the world. This evidence has been found in artifacts and in literature. Mask making is an ancient art employed all over the world for ceremony, celebration and in magical practices. The Tibetans wore masks to represent ghouls and skeletons in devil dances at the seasons of the year. The Chinese used papier-mache masks in religious drama. On Java, people used masks of wood in celebrations and ceremonies, often supplemented with shadow puppet presentations. The Suka males of the Congo during ceremonial dances following circumcision rituals wore helmet masks. The Aztecs used mosaic masks for worship and celebration.

The Greeks in their amphitheater wore large masks so the audience at a distance could see them. They were constructed with a tube to amplify the voice. The miracle and mystery plays of the early church often involved the priest wearing masks to represent metaphorical ideas such as death, the devil and life itself. The Noh plays of Japan - also developed in the 14th century - were highly stylized, each movement and each speech done precisely as it has always been done before. Today about 250 of them still exist. Men play all of the roles, using at least 125 kinds of full face masks made of lacquered wood.

In Italy full face, half-face and masks with beaks became an art form during the Renaissance. Mummers in Great Britain and in colonial America were masked actors who around Christmas time portrayed characters such as Father Christmas.

To the North American native peoples, spirits influence all aspects of life and are found in all things. To the Eskimo (Inuit) of the Bering Sea even gnarled driftwood has an "Inua", a dwelling force that gives it meaning, real existence and life. Such pieces of wood were often carved into masks or made a part of a mask. Different Native American societies had their own mask making techniques and rituals. The Iroquois had their twisted facemasks. The Pueblo have their Kachina masks, and the Eskimos their wooden masks.

Masks have served a variety of purposes:

* Worn ceremonially to appease certain forces
* Worn to communicate with the spirits and the supernatural
* Worn to scare children and give them warnings
* Worn to terrorize the enemy
* Worn to represent mythological being or creature
* Worn as a memorial,
* Worn to connect with animals or some other force in nature
* Worn to make rain or control the elements
* Worn to prevent illness and cure disease
* Worn for drama and theater and storytelling
* Worn to facilitate shapeshifting
* Worn to court a lover, for fertility and sexuality
* Worn for amusement and ornamentation
* Worn for ritual and initiation
* Worn to facilitate change of consciousness
* Worn to represent family and clans

Ceremonial Masks

Traditionally masks were made to frighten away natural enemies, to resist evil spirits, for protection, for success and for fertility. In ritual, they can be used for almost any purpose. The masks can be worn or they can be used to decorate the temple area as well. Masks help us to enter into the imaginative world. They facilitate creating illusions. They facilitate connecting with the supernatural. They help suppress one personality while encouraging the assumption of another. They are a dynamic tool for shapeshifting in they help bring out the persona and energy associated with it - be it a deity or an animal.

There are many types of masks. There is the stick mask, which is difficult to employ in magickal dance. It doesn't leave the both hands free. There is also the domino mask that was first used in 16th century Italy. These masks are the most popular. They cover the upper half of the face - some as far as the lips and some only as far as the nose. There are hat masks, which rest atop the head and generally leave the face uncovered. There are full helmet masks, which encompass the head and face, often resting on the shoulders.

Stick Mask

Domino Mask

Eagle Head Mask

Twisted Face Helmet Mask

Iroquois Masks

Native masks of North America often represented spirits that influence all of life. Rituals and masks were created to both appease and/or invoke. Masks were made of wood, fur, gourds and other materials. The Mandan made masks from the heads of dead animals.

The Iroquois nation is comprised of six major tribes: Mohawk, Oneida, Cyuga, Seneca, Onondaga and Tuscarora. All believed that evil spirits caused disease. At such times they would seek the assistance of someone from the False Face Society. An individual could only become a member of the False Face Society if he or she had been cured by the society. It was comprised mostly of men. The individual also had to have dreamed of it. In the dream, the dream spirit instructs the individual how to make a healing mask and gives the individual a healing song. Usually this dream had to be confirmed by another member of the society.

New members had to learn rituals and the songs of the society. They were required to create an elaborate costume to completely conceal the identity. The making of the mask was very ritualistic. A tree would be picked out, and the bark peeled from a section of it. Then a rough outline of the mask would be carved into the tree. The mask was then to be cut out of the tree without harming the tree. If the tree were chosen in the A.M., it would be predominantly a red color. If in the P.M., it would be predominantly black. Often the masks would have three colors.

Their masks were oval-shaped with twisted and exaggerated features. The nose was large and protruding and often broken. The mouth was its most distinguishing feature, always taking an odd shape. The hair was made of yarn or vines, twisted and attached.

Making a Paper Bag False Face

1. Take a brown paper bag that will fit over your head.
2. Make sure the bottom of the bag rests on the shoulders and the top on the head.
3. Use excess at the open end to make a fringe:
4. Mark the eyes and cut out the eyes.
5. Choose three colors.
6. Make the eyes different sizes. The eye holes may be the same size, but you can paint around them to make them appear different sizes.
7. Give it a crooked nose.
8. Make the mouth twisted and very large.

Northwest Masks

The natives of the Northwest are of many tribes, but their masks were often similar in style. Their masks mixed fear, reverence and acceptance of spirits. They also were often totem related. Totem comes from the word "otoman" meaning "his brother and sister kin". In the Eskimo traditions there were many clans. These clans are related through common ancestry. This ancestry could be human or divine, as gods and supernatural beings were often considered ancestors. The clan crest was often reflected within the totem poles, the masks and the fronts of the house.

Among the Eskimo peoples was the belief that all things and all creatures possessed spirits. Every animal, object, element and place had its spirit. Every mask had its own story and dance to a particular spirit. Their masks were important and no two were alike. They were used for religious, social, healing, fun and ritual purposes. They even had their own secret societies. They also created transformational masks (one or more faces hidden behind an outer face. Unlike the Iroquois, among the Eskimos the right to be a mask carver was most often inherited. Their masks were often imaginative, but they usually resembled humans, animals and/or birds.

Dancing and masks went hand in hand. Every mask had a story, a dance and a song. These were used in various activities. The Messenger's Feast was a masked ceremony in which hunters would seek favor from animals for food. The kazgi was a ceremonial house for festivals in which masks and dances formed a predominant part. Every family and clan had its shaman. This shaman was the healer and a spiritual leader.

The mask of the shamans had some common characteristics. They were always ugly faces. They also had a large tooth sticking out of the mouth. The mask was often splashed in red, dripping blood and they were made in the image of a guardian spirit that had been dreamt of.

The clan or totem mask reflected the protective energy of the guardian animal spirit. It was often carved out of wood or attached to a stick. The eyes were the most distinguishing feature. The eye patterns were oval or round. Sometimes they were crescent shaped, teardrops or just slits - regardless of what the animal's natural eyeshape was. The masks were often left unpainted or only soft colors were used. If it was a spirit mask, it would be given a white face.

Kachina Masks

There were three main tribes among the Pueblo peoples: the Hopi, the Zuni and the Acoma. They communicated with the gods (Mother Earth and Father Sky) through spirits called Kachinas. The Apache and the Navajo also had Kachinas. Every Kachina has a name, an appearance and its own unique power.

One legend tells how Kachinas taught the Pueblo how to hunt, fish and make useful things. Eventually humans began to quarrel with them, so they left, going deep into the earth, leaving their masks behind. When the masks are worn, the Kachina enters into the individual and gives the person power. Each Kachina had its own mask, dance and' ceremony. Each person had to make his/her own mask. The mask had to be in perfect shape to be worn in a ceremony. Throughout the year, the masks are fed by sprinkling them with cornmeal and pollen to renew their powers. Navajo and Apache would simply wear their masks until they were worn out or the magic was gone

Most of the Kachina masks were helmet types, often square or cylindrical in nature. Great care was taken in their construction. The choice of colors, the placement of colors, etc. - every aspect was symbolic. The colors were most often bright:

Yellow	-	north or northwest
Blue-green	-	west or southwest
Red	-	south or southeast
White	-	east or northeast
All together	-	zenith or sky
Black	-	nadir or below

Symbols are painted on the forehead and cheeks. This could be animal and bird tracks, clouds, lightning, sun, moon, stars and vegetation symbols. Vertical lines under the eyes indicated a warrior and phallic symbols were used for fertility.

Real eye openings are slits and have no relation to the visible eyes painted on the mask. Eyeholes are usually small circular holes or narrow slits. The painted eyes may be round, rectangular or half moons. The nose is seldom realistic or seldom seen. It is often left out of the mask. The mouth is often painted in different shapes. Beaks, tubes and snouts are often used. They are often painted on in geometric shapes.

Kachina masks are almost always colorful. The shapes and features are often geometric and the left and right sides do not always match. Above all else, it should suggest a characteristic or force.

African Masks

The first masks were probably animal. Remnants of crocodile and elephant masks are as common in Africa as are the wolf and raven in America. Antelope and leopard masks were also common. Dances were constructed with them. The eland and the antelope were sacred to the Kalihari, and masks and dances were used to honor them. The antelope spirit taught the people how to dig the earth, and thus ritual dances were created with antelope masks to help seeds grow. The Oloko of Africa had masks to represent the leopard warrior. African masks though could also represent spirits or humans. The masks of West Africa are probably the most abundant and colorful. The Senufo people of the Ivory Coast have a rich tradition of masks, dance and music.

West Africa is rich in the variety of masks. They served many functions and often had multiple meanings. Often only the men were allowed to wear the masks, but there were secret societies of both men and women, each society possessing its own masks. Only members of those societies were allowed to wear the masks. The masks were kept in secret places, often hidden away in sacred woods. A juju house is a house where the masks were made and readied for ceremony. The windows were covered so that no one would be able to see inside and observe the sacred preparation and transformation.

Masks were used in initiation ceremonies, especially along the Guinea coast. In the Congo, masks represented demons and spirits. In some parts of Africa, masks were purely ornamental. The Bini of Southern Nigeria made ornamental masks of ivory.

Masks were most often used in conjunction with sacred dances and ceremonies. Drumming was a significant part of these rituals. Drumming and chanting was a means of calling to the spirit of the mask. The drumming and chanting often had a rhythm of three. The balafon is a wooden xylophone common to the Senufo people of the Ivory Coast and was often used in the ceremonies. The stilt dancers of the Dan people would incorporate bell ringing. Their standing upon stilts represented their ability to sit upon air. They would ring their bells and dance about chasing off witches and demons from the village.

The Eyes of the Mask

In most native traditions, the eyes were the most important features, and these should be given extra care in your own mask making. For each of the traditions listed in this chapter, I have provided some of the qualities of the facial features of their masks. In general though, it is a good idea to know how the eyes can be used to express the character of the force that is reflected in the mask.

This character is often determined by the shape of the eyes:

- SURPRISED FACE =

- SAD FACE =

- EVIL FACE =

- COMIC FACE =

- TRAGIC FACE =

- ANGRY FACE =

Making and

Masks have been made from a variety of materials. These include, but are not limited to, fiber, wood, shell, bone, feathers, hides, cloth, bark, leaves and even husks. The materials and the making of the masks were done usually in solitude and with great deliberation and concentration on the force to be awakened by the mask. The mask making was never rushed.

1. Know what force you wish your mask to represent.
Know that the more significance you can find in it, the greater ability it will have to help you make the transformations you wish.

2. Mask making does not need to be a complicated affair.
Begin with simple masks, so that you can experience the enjoyment of the creative process and be freer to feel the energies awakened by the mask. (The simplest masks are those made from paper. A plain paper bag provides many possibilities.) I like to use the plastic mask forms that can be found at most hobby shops. They are easily painted. They easily hold the form for papier mache and even wet plaster.

3. Don't rush the process or compare it to others.
What you do with your mask will be most effective for you. Take your time, and keep in mind that with each part of the process - when done with deliberation - you empower the mask to help you begin to shapeshift to a new expression of energy.

4. Make your mask as comfortable as you can.
Remember that a mask needs air holes to enable you to breathe. Although some traditions have utilized a "bondage" or sensory-deprivation mask for initiation purposes, these were only employed under the strictest conditions because of their ability to augment radical changes in consciousness.

5. Be elaborate with your materials.
Subtlety has its place, but most masks have an exaggerated quality about them. It helps the individual to make the shift in consciousness to that which is greater than the self.

6. In most societies, the eyes were the most important part.
The eyes as the window of the soul have great play in mask making. In the

Using Masks

different types of masks and their construction that you work with later on, be particular about the location and shape of the eyes. The eyes will convey the character of the mask.

7. Use ordinary and simple materials in making and decorating your masks.

Keep in mind though that as you do, you are using the ordinary for extraordinary purposes. It is a reminder that no matter how ordinary or inconsequential we may feel our life to be we can still manifest the extraordinary within it. Use beads, dried flowers, feathers, lace, paints, rhinestones, ribbons and whatever you have available. Be as elaborate with the materials as you wish.

8. When you are not using your masks, keep them covered.

It makes them more powerful. The energies evoked by them are not allowed to leak or dissipate. It is a way of reverencing and honoring the forces of the mask. For temple masks, or those that are hung for decoration, this is not necessary. Temple masks are often reminders to us of the forces within our life. If you choose to make the wall mask more powerful for you, you may wish to have candles next to it. The lighting of the candles can be visualized as the igniting and activating of the forces represented by the mask.

9. Use your imagination in the creation of the mask.

Your designs and the forces you invoke through them are only limited by your own imagination. Remember that masks help us make transitions from our ordinary levels of consciousness to those beyond. As you open and express your imagination through the creation of the masks, you expand the opportunities to connect with greater power and force. You move closer to the primal energy and essence that is you or part of you. Above all, have fun with the process. Creation and imagination are necessary to enjoy ourselves fully.

10. Use ritual to help awaken the power of the mask.

Ritual dances are very effective for this. Later we will learn to use masks to create rituals for whatever purpose we desire. Ritual dances help make lifeless masks animated. Ordinary ceremonies become dynamic spiritual dramas. Masks and movement empower each other. The making of a mask is fun, but the mask to be effective must be secure and comfortable and it should not restrict breathing, speech or sight.

Papier Mache Masks

Papier mache masks are old and very traditional in many parts of the world. They are also very easy and fun to make

Materials Needed:
Newspaper to tear into small strips
White glue
Water
A plastic mask to use as a form - available at hobby & costume shops.
Paper towels
Paint
Spray clear gloss paint

1. Tear the newspaper into small strips about two inches.
2. Mix the white glue with water so it is runny.
3. Cover the working surface and set the plastic form on the surface.
4. Dip a strip of paper into the glue and water and place it on the plastic form.
5. Completely cover the form.
6. Exaggerate some of the features by putting extra layers on parts of the mask face. You can build up parts to add ears, nose, beaks, horns and more.
7. Allow it to dry over night.
8. Separate it from the form and paint and decorate it. Spray it with the gloss at the end to give it a shinier finish and to help seal it.

You can also make your own paste for papier mache masks. Stir three parts water to one part flour until the mixture is smooth and creamy. An inflated balloon can also be used as a form.

Plaster Cast Mask

Plaster cast tape makes a beautiful and strong mask. Plaster cast tape can be purchased from a medical supply house and even some pharmacies. They can used to make a mask that fits your face perfectly. You can work with a partner – each of you applying the tape to each other's face or you can do it for yourself by using a mirror

Materials Needed:
Plaster cast tape
Warm water
Covering for your clothes
Headband for the hair
Scissors
Petroleum jelly
Paper towels

Begin by pulling the hair back, using the headband to keep it off of the face. Then cut the plaster tape into small strips of about 1-4 inches. Smear a coat of petroleum jelly over the face area to be covered by the mask. Put extra on the eyebrows and hairline so that when the tape hardens, it does not pull the hair out at the roots. Ouch!

Dip the strips into the warm water, just long enough for them to get wet and begin applying them to the face. And rub it lightly so that the plaster spreads around. Keep the face still for about ten to fifteen minutes while the plaster hardens.

*Shapeshifting
Exercise
developmental & experiential)*

Simple Raven and Owl Masks

Skills &Benefits:
- **improves ability to connect with totems**
- **improves intuitive and creative abilities**
- **develops strong connections to raven and owl.**

To own a mask is to possess a potential power. The wearer of a mask can magically assume a new identity. Through it reality can be suspended. All ancient societies recognized this. It was most evident among Native Americans and in the shamanic societies of Africa and other countries. Mask making is an ancient craft. Many societies considered it an artform in many instances. Masks were made from a variety of materials - including feathers, stones, jewels and wood.

The basic principle of mask making is to know what force you wish to represent. Gather your materials. Use colors appropriate for your purpose and be creative in this process.

The Raven Mask

1. Take a large piece of paper or cardboard and fold it in half.

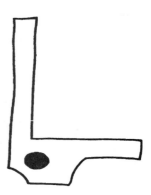

The paper must be large enough so that the vertical bar shown in the diagram will go over the top of the head. The horizontal bar must be long enough to go around the head and overlap in the back. When the horizontal and vertical flaps are fastened, the mask will fit over your head like a hat.

2. Adjust the fit so the mask will rest comfortably on the bridge of the nose.

The basic shape is the foundation upon which you can make a wide variety of mask images – animal and human.

3. Take a second piece of paper and fold it in half.

Sketch the pattern as shown in the illustration. The more curve you put in the bottom part of the drawing the more curve the beak will have.

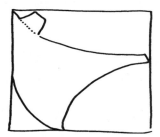

4. Now cut along the lines and fasten it onto the basic shape described in step 3.

The small flaps are fastened to the outside of the basic shape or you can cut two slits and feed them through. They can be glued or fastened on the inside and won't show.

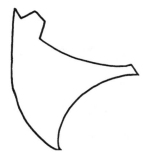

5. At this point, you can paint, color and further decorate your mask.

Attach feathers and streamers. Use colors appropriate for your purpose

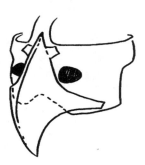

The Owl Mask

1. Draw or photocopy the design and enlarge it so that it will fit over your face. Poster board is heavier and will often work better than just plain paper.

2. Cut out the design and fold the flaps of the beak and attach to the underside of the mask.

3. Select colors and patterns appropriate for the great horned owl, including its beak.

4. Attach small feathers to the face, and especially over the points at the top to reflect the feathery tufts or horns on this owl.

5. Make two small holes on each side of the face at the level of the eyes.

6. Take a piece of ribbon or string and weave in through those slits on each side. This will allow the mask to be tied at the back of the head.

Quick Guide to Awakening Your Animal's Power

Having a mask, costume or simply some body painting can truly help us align with our animal totems. They help us shift into the animal's energy and awaken it within us - especially when we incorporate dance and movement with the masks.

1. Make sure you will not be disturbed.

2. Have your mask available.
If you do not have a mask available, you can use body art, painting the face and body to reflect the animal.

3. Know what your movements will be.

4. Have an opening and grounding posture.
This helps prevent disorientation and that "spacey feeling".

5. Imitate the movements of the animal.
It doesn't need to be elaborate. Perform it slowly. Take about five minutes.

6. Now imagine, see and feel the animal coming to you.
See it before you and greet it. I use the following: "My heart to your heart, your heart to my heart. I am honored by you and I thank you for sharing your life with me."

7. See the animal melt into you.
Feel yourself becoming the animal. Feel its energy and qualities coming alive stronger within you with every breath that you take. Visualize how you will be able to apply its qualities to your life.

8. Offer thanks to the animals for coming into your life.
Visualize the animal moving off to watch and guard from a distance.

9. Perform your grounding posture.
Feel your self grounded and strengthened by the animal's power and medicine.

Dance Imitation and Shapeshifting

Through costume, masks, body paint and other aids - in conjunction with imitating the movment and posture of a tiger - we can align ourselves with tremendous tiger energy. This energy reflects thespirit of the tiger and the archetypal forces of Nature that manifest through it. It is its medicine that we are awakening and invoking into our own life for our own purposes through this shapeshifting ritual.

Chapter Eleven

Sacred Journeys

Dance is one of the most powerful shamanic tools. It awakens and stirs the energies of life. True sacred dance is a means of focusing and directing consciousness through physical behavior. When incorporated with mask making and other shapeshifting practices, it becomes a powerful force for transformation. We can create simple dances of protection, as invitation to spirits, for attunement to animals and for empowering any aspect of life.

Dance and movement is natural to the universe. Plants move in graceful and rhythmic ways. They turn to face the sun; they wave in the breeze; they grow in spiral and other exquisite forms. Birds have their own movements and dances, spreading their wings and plumage in magnificent displays of courtship and strength. All animals have unique dances and movements to show strength, aggression, attraction or just high-spirited fun.

The human body is designed for movement. It is as natural and important to life as breathing. Like breathing, it fills us with energy. It enables us to transcend our usual perceptions and consciousness. Movement balances, heals, awakens, and energizes. It generates psychic energy for strength, for enlightenment, for life and even for death.

Dance and movement links the hemispheres of the brain, joining the intuitive with the rational. Directed physical behavior, like dance, can help us overcome our tendency to over-rationalize and block our own growth process. It aligns our physical responses and energies with our spiritual goals and helps us to maintain contact with the higher forces of life.

Eagle Dancer

Costumes and movements are employed to awaken archetypal forces behind various animals. Eagle dances were employed by many groups of people. The eagle is a powerful totem because it soars out of sight. It is believed to have a close relationship with the sun and its power is often sought in healing. Including feathers in the costume, along with mimicking the movements of flight, help manifest its energy. Different feathers are symbols of different qualities of energies of the eagle. Flight feathers are for strength and fluff feathers symbolize the breath of life.

Shamanic dance should be performed as a way of reaching another level of consciousness or being. It should be a way of releasing spiritual meaning into our lives. Dance ritual is not meant to be performed for audiences, which profanes it in many ways. We must participate in and become the priests, priestesses, shamans and medicine people of the ritual. Participation in shamanic dance requires us to remember that energies are not created by the dance but simply invoked, challenged and directed by it. We must remember that the energies function less through our talent for dancing than through our participation. Thus anyone who can move any part of his or her body can create and participate in a shamanic or magickal dance – even if only through the flickering of the eyes or the rhythm of the breath.

Shamanic and magickal dance can be performed by anyone. No formal training is required to utilize the powerful effects of dance. Dances for higher states of consciousness are simple, individual and passionate. They do not require great space, for when a dance pattern is created for special effects, it will create an illusion of great space. Dances to attune to animals require little more than imitating their movements and postures. It is simply a matter of imbuing movement with greater significance and focus. It is not the talent that invokes the energy but the participation. With just a little effort, you will find yourself dancing between worlds. Your spiritual journey will become empowered and more sacred than you ever imagined

The process of pursuing our sacred journey and unfolding our innate powers through shapeshifting involves overcoming preconceived notions and limitations. There is always as much unlearning to do as there is learning. The most difficult part of this step is seeing through the illusions of our lives. We are often taught that we should belong to something, but becoming a shamanic practitioner develops a strong sense of not truly belonging to reality. Many people spend their whole lives attempting to belong, and many times it leads to disappointment. Shapeshifting helps us develop an individuality that is strong. Through the animals we connect with, we learn that we are able to be alone without being lonely.

Another important step in shapeshifting, of course, is building a bridge between our world and the more subtle realms of life. This involves unfolding our intuition, creativity, and creative imagination. We learn to visit the heavens and the underworld by means of an axis. The axis may be the image of climbing a tree, being carried or led by an animal, following a cave through a labyrinth or in our case by becoming a bird or animal.

We must now move beyond the orthodox treatment of sacred journeys so often found in modern religion. They have grown stale. They have lost their ability to touch each of us uniquely. We must restore the experiential aspect to the sacred journey of life and transform our usual perceptions through an epiphany with Nature. Now with practice and a little bit of imagination, we can begin to choreograph our own sacred journeys.

With just the little we have learned so far, we can create sacred shapeshifting dance meditations and rites that become empowering sacred pantomimes. In many ways, this is similar to the mystery plays of more ancient times. The ritual enactment of specific energies and scenes releases corresponding energies to the participants, linking the participants to the spiritual essences more effectively. These kinds of enactments can be a part of shapeshifting rites – performed by an individual or a group.

The Theater of Magickal Dance

There must be messages and focus hidden within our movements. The shapeshifting dance itself is to become our teacher, and we allow the movements to communicate with us on deeper levels. Our higher levels of consciousness communicate to us through symbols, and if we wish to strengthen that communication, we must make it two-way. That is where shapeshifting comes in. This is why role-playing and pantomime are beneficial to magickal dance and shapeshifting. Role-playing activates physical energy to give impetus to what we are trying to set in motion. We use the movement and the role (in our case, the animal) to trigger other levels of consciousness more strongly.

In shapeshifting pantomime, we use sacred space that we create to act out a situation with movement and gesture. We all play-acted when we were children, now we are going to do it in specifically controlled ways to release an archetypal force of Nature into our life.

It may feel silly at first, but that will pass. We are simply breaking down the barriers that block the flow of creative energy into our lives. When we were children, we could act out anything. We could make-believe, and we got caught up in the reality of that play. We are learning to use that same process again, only we are infusing it with symbols and movements that will trigger specific manifestations. We are using this in a controlled, concentrated manner to create new conditions, perceptions, and opportunities for newer conditions in our physical life.

Creating Your Shapeshifting Ritual

Your journal will be beneficial in creating your shapeshifting journeys. If will help you to organize your rites and record what unfolds as a result of them so that in the future, you can make them more effective or eliminate what did not work. In time, it will give you a number of animal rituals that can be done for various areas of your life.

It begins with choosing a subject for your shapeshifting dance. This can be based upon something you hope to accomplish – from overcoming an obstacle to creating a job opportunity. At the end of this chapter, I have provided several examples of ways in which this can be done.

Choose the animal that you wish to help you with this task. Study how that animal accomplishes such activities in its life. How does that animal overcome obstacles? How does that animal deal with threats? How does that animal capture its prize – be it a mate, a home a meal?

Now meditate upon your goal. How would that goal be represented in the animal's life? As food or territory? As a mate or home? As something to play with and enjoy? Create an adventure that reflects that animal accomplishing its goal. For example, if the goal is to overcome certain problems in your life, the problems or obstacles can be depicted as an actual confrontation between this animal and possibly another animal it must compete with – possibly through a fight. It could also be depicted by this animal, quietly stalking and leaping upon its opportunity.

This means you must also symbolize other people involved as an animal as well. How does their animal relate to yours? Are the naturally competitive? Do they tolerate each other in Nature? Are they antagonistic toward each other in Nature? Do they cooperate with each other? For example, you can visualize getting a new job as a treasure. You could do a crow shapeshifting rite and create a scenario where the new job is represented by something bright and shiny, which always fascinates and attracts crows. Crows, being very intelligent, can problem solve to get the shiny object out of some entanglement or the possession of someone else.

Once you have figures out the basic scenario, construct several movements that you can pantomime that reflect this activity. Be as simple or intricate as you wish. *But have fun with it. The more fun you have with it the more powerfully it works.* A shapeshifting, magickal pantomime for overcoming an obstacle can be depicted in three postures, once you have "become the animal". The first could be one that reflects preparedness, standing strong and alert – confident. The second can reflect confrontation and the third could be a pantomime of the reward that you will receive by overcoming an obstacle.

Practice the movements a few times. Don't worry what they may look like to an outsider. Focus on what you believe they look like. See and feel yourself as the animal you have chosen. Have fun. This is a creative process. Think of it as a powerful play time that you have denied yourself for years. And remember, there is really no right or wrong way of doing this. Then just follow the procedures, as described in the exercises at the end of this chapter. Once you have done this a few times, feel free to adapt them to your own style – that is when the power begins to manifest.

The Art of Shapeshifting

Remember that what you do on one level affects you on others. This type of exercise will release energy into your outer life. It may create opportunities to achieve a goal, so look for them. It may bring a reckoning of obstacles. But also remember that the animal's energy is now strong in you, or the situations would not have manifested. You now have the power to claim your rewards and to resolve your problems.

<u>Shapeshifting Journal Entry</u>

Shapeshifting Ritual # _____

Describe the Goal:

Animal for Shapeshifting:

Characteristics of the animal:

How would this animal accomplish the goal in its life?

Animals and symbols for others involved in what you wish to achieve:

Describe basic movements, postures and gestures that might reflect your accomplishing the goal:

Follow-Up notes (the first week following the shapeshifting ritual)

Tools for Shapeshifting

Every shamanic tradition has its own rituals, music, myths and sacred dances. Each tradition had its own means of awakening practitioners to the powerful forces and magic of Nature. Nature teaches us that all life is change. Everything is in a state of transition. All change, all crises, all sacrifice, all death and all birth reflect the archetypal power in Nature. The shamanic practitioner uses rituals and tools to align with these energies and manifest them within his or her life. The most common tools to help with this are specific musical instruments.

Musical Instruments

Three instruments in particular are powerful tools for the shamanic practitioner. They do not require any previous musical knowledge and they can be used for a wide variety of magical and meditative practices. Those on spiritual and shamanic journeys will find them powerful tools.

Drums

Rhythm is the pulse of life and it affects all physical energies. It is the heartbeat and drums enable connection to the heartbeat of animals and the heartbeat of Mother Earth. Rhythms quicken, slow and change heart rates and organs of the body associated with it. Many shamanic practices involve riding the drumbeat to alter states of consciousness and to induce trance conditions. It is used to slow the heart rhythm or to stimulate a change in the heart rhythm to be more resonant with a particular animal. It was almost unthinkable for an ancient shaman, medicine person or healer not to have a drum or a rhythm instrument.

Depending upon the syncopation, or the pauses within the rhythms, specific physiological affects could be generated. In shamanic storytelling, the drum is used to bring the audience into resonance with each other and with the energies of the story. It can be used to align with the rhythms and energies of specific animals. Voudoun., a Haitian religion, does not attempt to disguise the use of the drum for stimulating specific kinds ofd energies. The drum is used to block out the rational mind, activate sexual energies and to induce trance. The incessant rhythmic drumming triggers a forced resonance in the participant, altering normal heart rhythms to elicit contact with primal forces.

Rattle

The rattle is also a rhythmic instrument and like its mate the drum, it is one of the oldest healing instruments. The rattle and its rhythms have a capacity for linking the waking consciousness to the energies of the cosmos or to levels of consciousness deep within. This serves to release energy and power for healing and cleansing.

Its use as a shamanic healing instrument is widespread. The rhythmic sounds of the rattle loosen rigid energy patterns around the body, promoting healing and balance. It has been used in a variety of ways, but in most traditions, it was used while encircling the body of person. Then the rattle is shaken up and down the front and back of the body.

Many rattles of the past were made from dried gourds with seeds placed in them. Some were made from dried bones. And even those who believe they have no sense of rhythm have the ability to use a rattle without any musical knowledge. We can begin to experiment with the rattle and our own energies.

Flute

The flute and whistle is an old shamanic tool. It has existed in various forms in different societies and traditions. It is considered one of the first instruments to enable humanity to connect with the beings of Nature – the faeries, elves, devas and others. It is powerfully effective when used in shamanic and magical storytelling. And it was commonly used as a way of calling specific spirits – including those of the animal kingdom.

The flute is considered an extension of the body. It is played with the breath of life, a true creative force. It can be used to connect with the consciousness of Nature. There are many types that are easy to play, whether you are familiar with music or not. It can be used to create your own musical calls to the spirit world.

The journey to join with the spirit
of an animal
is
one of the most sacred
that we can experience in life.

Shapeshifting
Exercise
(experiential & synthesizing)

Shapeshifting & Psychic Protection

Skills & Benefits:

- **attunement to Nature**
- **increased skill at handling opposition**
- **specific benefits will vary according to the individual animal**

Every animal in Nature has behaviors that it uses to protect itself and to defend its territory. Sometimes it's part of its adaptation. Some animals have physical adaptations, and some animals have behavioral adaptations. Physical adaptations are like the bright colors found on some insects as a warning to predators that if they try and eat them it will leave a bad taste in their mouth. Some caterpillars have white spots or blotches on their backs that resemble the splatter of bird poop. Since their most common predator is a bird, this is a physical adaptation that will help prevent birds from eating them. A bird will never eat something that has been pooped on. Some animals in Nature have behavioral adaptations. Some, such as rabbits, have a wonderful ability to remain still if they feel danger is close by. Most predators recognize prey by movement, so a rabbit's ability to freeze is an adaptive behavior for avoiding becoming someone's meal.

We do need to remember that *every* animal, from a tiny mouse to an eagle, has ways of defending itself and protecting its home. They all have their own unique abilities for defense and protection. Do not assume that a large predator is what you should work with in psychic protection; you will probably find yourself in for an interesting educational lesson. Most people would think that a hawk would have no trouble with a rabbit, and yet jackrabbits have been known to drag hawks, which have sunk their talons into the rabbits back, into their holes and then kick them to death.

A great horned owl is one of the most powerful and aggressive birds of prey. A single crow may not be able to handle it, but a flock of crows will mob an owl to drive it away. If we are working with crows to defend and protect ourselves, we will be ineffective if we do it by ourselves. The crow teaches us to join with others.

If we learn how our spirit animal or totem defends itself, we can then apply it to our own life. That animal has shown up to be a part of our life, to tell us," These behaviors I have are what will work for you right now. Use them!" When we do, we find everything coming together and falling into place. We find it easier to accomplish our goals with less trouble.

Prepare for this exercise a few days before, just as we described earlier. Review what you have written in your journal concerning it. Review the movements.

1. Begin by choosing an animal to help with your protection.

We have spoken about how to determine your own spirit animals and totems. Choose one of these, If you are not sure, choose and animal that you always felt drawn to. Or choose an animal that is appearing in your life right now.

If you do not know your spirit animal, meditate on the problem and then take a walk in nature for about an hour. It can be a park or some other natural environment where there is wildlife. Usually by the end of that walk, some animal has gotten our attention, several times. If unsure, wait 24 hours. Within 24 hours that animal will have shown itself 3-4 times around you. You may see it outside, or on a TV program, but there will be three to four encounters.

2. Study the animal.

Go to the library and learn as much about that animal as possible. Jot down who its predators are and whom it preys upon. Most animals in the wild fall within the middle, being both predators and prey.

Study how it defends its home. This is the most important part. Does it do it alone? Does it have help? Does it hide? Does it camouflage itself? How does it defend and protect itself? This animal has gotten your attention to teach you how to apply these same tactics to your life.

If you have someone or something troubling you, this animal's natural tactics will help. If it is an opossum, you might have to develop some play acting skills around certain individuals so they do not know your business or what is truly going on. Some animals put on an intense show of strength and power as a warning to intruders. If we have people or even spirits that are aggravating us, we may have to put on a stronger display and assert greater control. Find a way of applying the animal's natural defense tactics to our individual situation.

3.   Examine where you are having difficulty.
Make a list of situations that may be troubling you, or about which you may have suspicions. Are there certain phenomena that are unsettling? Are you feeling unbalanced? Write down the ideas. As you are doing this, focus on the animal and its behavior. Ask yourself how this animal would handle such a situation? Would it hide until the trouble goes away and passes? Would it camouflage itself? Would it confront with a display of ferocity? Would it join with others of its kind to handle the situation? The animal is the solution.

4.   Create a scenario on how this animal deals with problems.
Once you have figures out the basic scenario, construct several movements that you can pantomime that reflect this activity. Be as simple or intricate as you wish. *But have fun with it*. The more fun you have with it the more powerfully it works. Remember that a shapeshifting, magickal pantomime for overcoming an obstacle can be depicted in three postures once you have "become the animal". The first could be one that reflects preparedness, standing strong and alert – confident. The second can reflect confrontation and the third could be a pantomime of the reward that you will receive by overcoming an obstacle.

5.   Make preliminary preparations.
Make sure you will be undisturbed. And if you can, plan to perform this exercise outdoors if possible. Set the mood and perform a general relaxation. Then perform the balancing postures.

5.   Perform the movements and postures for the animal that you have chosen.
Perform them slowly and deliberately. Visualize yourself as that animal, making those movements. Repeat them three times. And then take a seat.

6. Relax and imagine yourself growing lighter.
Imagine that with each breath the heaviness of the physical world begins to fade. The more relaxed you are the better the exercise works. Allow your eyes to close and breathe deeply. Take your time with this. See and feel your aura extending out from you, expanding throughout the room, making your body density less. As you do, imagine the veils separating the physical from the spiritual becoming thinner and thinner.

7. Invite the animals to make itself known.

Mentally invite the spirit of the animal to guide you and bless you with this shapeshifting. Visualize the animal appearing before you, its eyes looking into your eyes. As it does, you realize that this creature has your eyes – that it is your eyes looking out of it at you. See and feel yourself resonating with it. Your breathing becomes similar to it. Your hearts synchronize. As you realize this, the animal melts into you. With each breath that you take, its essence grows stronger inside of you. You feel as it feels. Your senses are alive. Try to see and feel it in as much detail as with the owl exercise of chapter 9. You are becoming this animal.

8. Now pantomime the movements for this animal overcoming its obstacle.

This is the time to dance the scenario of the animal overcoming its obstacle or problem, which is just a symbol for your own. Play acts it. Be animated and passionate. As you do, see yourself handling all of the problems in the same way this animal would and with great ease and success. Allow your imagination to run with it.

Although it may seem as if it's a fanciful past time, the effects will be very real over the next three days. Opportunities to correct situations that are out of balance will arise. The tactics that this animal would use are what will work for you.

At the end, just sit and be still for a few moments, Stretch a little, allowing your hands and feet to move. Breathe deeply. As you sit there, you may feel a soft brush of air. You may see shadows shift around you. There may be colored, flickering lights, you may see forms and shapes appear and fade. In the beginning it will probably be subtle things that you may wish to attribute to your imagination. Remember though that most animals see and hear much better than we do. They can detect the subtlest things. Do not respond to them; simply note them and the sensations. Do this for only a few moments. They are after effects of the exercise. As the veils close entirely, they will fade.

Then slowly stand and repeat the animals movements, again giving thanks for this sharing. Follow this with the grounding postures. Stretch and begin to move. And know that in the next few days your senses will be a bit more acute. Opportunities to move past obstacles will manifest. Opposition to you and your efforts will be lessened. There will be a strong sense of guidance and protection.

*Shapeshifting
Exercise
(experiential)*

The Power of Predator and Prey

Skills &Benefits:

- **assertiveness with problems**
- **control over energies**
- **resolution of problems**
- **strong protection**
- **patience**
- **sharpened senses in cases of psychic attack.**

Predators and prey are found everywhere in nature. A predator is defined as one who has the ability to take live prey. There has always been a contest between predator and prey in the natural world, and life is always the prize. The grasshopper eats the grass and the frog eats the grasshopper. The snake eats the frog and the hawk eats the snake.

Predation takes time, patience and skill. It sharpens the senses. The strongest, most alert and knowledgeable will survive. Animals grow stronger and wiser trying to avoid being caught.

This simple meditation/visualization is a powerful tool for protection. It may seem simple, but in its simplicity, it has even greater effectiveness. For this exercise though you will need to choose a predator animal. This may be an animal that you know is already one of your totems. It may be an animal that you have always had an affinity for. It may be an animal that you have dreamt of. It may be an animal that you choose out of the blue.

Only spend 15-20 minutes a day on this exercise, but put a lot of passion into it. Within a week, you will begin to notice a difference. Problems and stresses will begin to ease up. Psychic imbalances will settle. Make sure that you see yourself stronger, healthier and more empowered as a result of this exercise.

1.   Choose your predator and study it.
Again, go to the library and learn something about the animal. How does it attack and defend? What kind of natural weapons and skills does it have? When hunting, what skills does it rely upon?

What is its most common prey? In other words, what animal does it eat? What tactics will its prey most likely use to avoid being caught? (This is most important. By understanding how the prey is more likely to respond, by understanding how it naturally behaves, we can use that to our advantage.)

Now visualize a bad habit, an uncomfortable situation or something negative around you as the natural prey.

2.   Prepare for the meditation.
Make sure that you will be undisturbed. The phone should be off the hook. You might want to use a candle or fragrance to enhance the meditation. Perform a progressive relaxation and your balancing postures. Do a progressive relaxation. The more relaxed you are the more effective it will be.

3.   Visualize yourself as the predator.
See yourself sitting out in Nature and this predator stepping out in front of you. It fixes you with its eyes, and you realize that it has your eyes. Your eyes are looking out of it at you! As you realize this, it melts into you, and with each breath you see and feel yourself as this predator. It does not just live within you and you in it. You are the predator. See, feel and imagine yourself becoming this animal as you learned to do in chapter 9. Perform its movements to reinforce the connection.

5.   Hunt, capture and eat your prey.
Visualize the prey before you, and with the hunting tactics of the predator you are, you attack. Pantomime it. Dance it. You are the predator. See and feel yourself capturing, killing and eating the bad habit, negative attitude, the unbalanced psychic energy, etc. – eliminating it from your life. You become stronger as a result.

Some people have difficulty with the idea of hunting and eating another animal. But this is common in Nature. Most shamanic traditions recognized that the eating of one animal by another was a way of taking in the prey animals medicine. Its medicine then becomes part of the medicine of its predator.

Use the predator's natural hunt cycle and tactics in this meditation. If it hunts primarily at night and by stalking, perform the exercise at night. If it hunts during the day, perform it during the day.

At the end, just sit and be still for a few moments, Stretch a little, allowing your hands and feet to move. Breathe deeply. As you sit there, you may feel a soft brush of air. You may see shadows shift around you. There may be colored, flickering lights, you may see forms and shapes appear and fade. In the beginning, it will probably be subtle things that you may wish to attribute to your imagination. Remember though that most animals see and hear much better than we do. They can detect the subtlest things. Do not respond to them; simply note them and the sensations. Do this for only a few moments. They are after effects of the exercise. As the veils close entirely, they will fade.

Then slowly stand and repeat the animal movements, again giving thanks for this sharing. Follow this with the grounding postures. Stretch and begin to move. And know that in the next few days your senses will be a bit more acute. You may see and hear things more clearly. You will find opportunities to resolve problems or find them being resolved on their own. There will be a strong sense of guidance and protection.

Chapter Twelve

Shapeshifting
and the
Alchemical
Mysteries

D ance and movement are ways to actualize energy. Even simple physical movements and postures can create changes in consciousness. Magickal dance is a way of using physical behavior to release and activate very real energies. Focused movement aligns the hemispheres of the brain. It stimulates the intuitive faculty and creates electrical changes in the body and mind. This in turn helps us to transcend normal perceptions.

Different postures and movements will activate different energies and forces. Physical movement combined with creative imagination opens the ability to touch all worlds through the movement. It helps place you at the gateway of all dimensions. The right movements, combined with the proper creative visualization, allow us to enter and exit through that gateway. This is the art of shapeshifting.

Many societies had movements and postures associated with mythic animals. These postures, when used in conjunction with other animal meditations, empowered them. This is especially true in the case of the four sacred beasts in the Chinese tradition – the unicorn, the dragon, the phoenix and the turtle.

As I have mentioned, when I do workshops on magickal dance, I frequently teach the group simple dance rituals that elicit quick and definite effects. In this way the group experiences and confirms for themselves how much more quickly results are achieved when the proper movement is used in conjunction with meditation alone. The group, magickal dances that I teach most frequently are connected to the fantastic creatures who are the archetypal guardians of the natural world.

The Four Sacred Beasts

Before the Earth had form, a great being by the name of P'an Ku decided to give form to the universe. Even for a being as great as he, the task would be tremendous, so he first created four helpers - the dragon, the phoenix, the unicorn and the turtle. These were the four sacred beasts.

Together they shaped the Earth and univers out of the chaos. When it was done, the dragon went to the oceans to serve as a guardian force in the world of Nature. The unicorn went to the woodlands, and the phoenix took to the sky. The turtle went to the marshlands and deserts. In these realms they serve as guardian forces in the world of Nature. Learning to tap these four great archetypes will empoower all work with shapeshifting, animals and Nature.

1. The Dragon   -   sleeps within the sea but can fly to the heavens; goodness and power flow to all nearby; it can change one's fate; and it controls the climate - of the earth or of one's life.

2. The Phoenix   -   the dragon's wife; helps the dragon right wrongs; considerate of all living things; always attended to by a small train of birds; most beautiful and virtuous; waits for peace to return to the earth.

3. The Tortoise   -   gives power and strength to humans enduring difficulties; strong, wise and kind; always considered a female and can only mate with snakes; assists those going through changes and transitions.

4. The Unicorn   - Always gaily colored; symbol of luck; long life and joy are born from its appearance; brings and awakens justice and law; a sign of illustrious off spring.

Earlier, we spoke of the unicorn as an archetype of the natural world but the unicorn is only one of the guardians of Nature. Its role as guardian is shared. In Chinese lore, the unicorn was one of four sacred beasts who aided in the creation of the universe. The unicorn shared this task with the dragon, the phoenix and the tortoise. When it was completed, they each went to their respective realms. The dragon took to the seas, the phoenix to the sky, the tortoise to the desert and wetlands and the unicorn to the forests. Although they each went to their individual realms, the connection between them and all creatures of the natural world remains strong.

Although relegated to the realm of fiction, these fantastic creatures – these archetypes of the natural world – can be powerful aids in the ancient art of shapeshifting. Throughout the world there are a myriad of tales and myths associated with these four sacred beasts. When examined, we find that these fantastic creatures have many things in common:

1. They embody and stimulate creative power.
2. They are composites of many animals.
3. Because of their great sensitivities, they awaken such in us.
4. They stimulate the creative imagination.
5. Encounters amplify our instinctive intuition.
6. They all appear in a variety of sizes, forms and colors.
7. Encounters are rare for they are all reclusive.
8. Preconceptions are always shattered - pleasantly.
9. All serve as guardians to Nature and the Realm of Faerie.
10. Through them, we open more fully to the hidden wonders of nature and connect more powerfully with all animals of Nature..

The Sacred Beasts

The more aware we are of these fantastic creatures, their characteristics and how to connect with them, the more powerful our own work with animals will be - especially our work with shapeshifting. Using the postures and movements of the four sacred beasts will open you to understanding the language of animals and empower all of your shapeshifting activities. In chapter nine, we discussed the unicorn and postures to align with its energies.

The following contains information for connecting with the other three sacred beasts. There are fragrances which will empower your meditations and postures that will help you align with the sacred beasts. Performing their movements always invites greater animal contact in your outer life.

Dragon

Identifying Fragrance: basil
Common Animal Forms: **snake, dragonfly, firefly, salamander, lizard, hawk**

The dragon is one of the most multi-faceted creatures. Its significance is quite complex. Though Christianity and the western world have made the dragon out to be an evil reflection of the devil, it is truly the epitome of great primal power. Unlike in the West, this great power was honored and revered in the East. The dragon has been depicted as a composite of other animals. As with all of the four sacred beasts, it has been known to take various animal forms. It has been the source of many creation myths around the world. If nothing else, these tales reflect the tremendous power and universality of the dragon.

The dragon embodies the forces of wisdom, strength and spiritual power, the primal power of creation. It is also the guardian, and when a dragon is encountered, you will begin having greater strength and guardianship in your life. Dragons are truly wondrous creatures, and one of the great rewards of working with shapeshifting with animals on any level is encountering a dragon.

The dragon came to be the explanation for much of the unexplained phenomena of nature, and it has always been linked to the powers and doings of the earliest gods and goddesses. Like the early gods and goddesses, dragons were powerful, changeable and contradictory.

Dragons are found throughout the natural world if we know what to look for. They come in a variety of shapes and sizes, and they have been called by a myriad of names. To the Chinese, the dragons were the ultimate power. They could be as tiny as a silkworm or grow to fill the space between Earth and the heavens at will. They control the climate and weather - of Nature or of one's life. Occasionally, when I teach seminars on magical dance, the class is taught and then performs a variation of an ancient dragon dance ritual. Usually within three hours (if not sooner), there is a change in the weather. If it's been sunny, it rains or snows. If it has been raining or snowing, then it clears and becomes sunny. It's an outer cinfirmation of the dragon energy that has been accessed. The dance has succeeded.

Dragons, by nature, are a paradox, and like unicorns, they are very reclusive. They require large amounts of wilderness (land or sea) to live, and with the increasing disappearance of natural lands, their presence upon land has become even more remote. Their sightings are more obscure.

There are still ways to recognize their presence - if we know what to look for. Beloware some of the traditional signs to look for. Their presence is often indicated by the sudden wisp of basil fragrance within the air and in areas where basil is found to be growing wild. (This is especially true for the basilisk form of the dragon.) Dragons are also more likely found where caves exist and in natural circular areas - woods, meadows, lakes, etc. They are more likely to be found in environments that are still a little wild and free.

Traditional Signs of the Presence of Dragons

1. Fjords, rapids and waterfalls are "Dragon Gates".
2. Thunder and lightning are the realm of the dragon. Heat lightning in the summer is often an indicator of a dragon's presence.
3. Areas with caves are frequent homes of dragons.
4. Volcanic areas often reflect the presence (past or present) of dragons. If the volcano has activity, a dragon is likely present.
5. Whirlwinds, especially those that carry heavy objects aloft, reveals the presence of dragons.
6. Waterspouts at sea are signals of a water dragon.
7. Smoking holes in the ground, steam rising, reveal where they emerge or their flights.
8. We cannot usually see a dragon, especially when it rises to the sky, but wind and rain help dragons achieve height. When wind and rain rise suddenly and unexpectedly, it is often the result of dragons.
9. Dragons often appear in the sky as clouds. In fact many clouds are formed by the breath of the dragon. Areas of heavy mist and fog are areas that are frequented or lived in by dragons. Fog and mist are called dragon's breath.
10. Sudden tempests and thunderstorms often reveal their presence.

The Dragon Pose

The flying dragon pose will instill the characteristics of the dragon into the mind and body. It is good to see oneself flying while holding this position. In healing it brings equilibrium to the heart. It should be performed to the right and to the left. Repeat three times (right, left, right, left, right, left). Keep the movements slow and steady.

Phoenix

Identifying Fragrance: myrrh
Common Animal Forms: pheasant, peacock

The phoenix is the great bird of rebirth. Like its companions the unicorn, dragon and tortoise, the phoenix is a mixture of different animals and its significance is quite complex. In China, the phoenix was married to the dragon. The phoenix was female and represented the empress, while the dragon was male and represented the emperor. It is the sacred animal that rules all of the creatures that are feathered.

In the western world, the phoenix is the bird that sacrificed itself to fire and then rose from its own ashes. It is found often within western myth and lore. In Egypt, it was linked to the worship of the sun god Ra who died every night and was born again the next morning. In Christianity, it is a symbol of the death and resurrection of Jesus. Many legends and myths contain common threads that link heroes to this creature. The hero lives a long life, and then the phoenix appears either just before or just after the hero's death. The hero is thus born again.

The phoenix is the symbol of the sun and resurrection, of life after death. It is a symbol of the immortal soul, love and eternal youth. In its form as the peacock, it is a guardian of the forest for the unicorn.

For many people, the phoenix is one of the easiest to encounter. Myrrh is a fragrance that is drawing to it, as well as signaling its presence. When the early morning sun is at its peak or at that time when the last of the evening sun can be seen are also great times to seek it out. This is the time to perform the postures and align with it. Coincidentally, these are times when the pheasant is more active and about, and the pheasant is one of the animal forms that the phoenix will take upon occasion.

Aligning with the phoenix encounter always stimulates and heralds a time of new beginning, of new life. A phoenix shapeshifting can trigger your readiness to begin your own Holy Quest.

The Phoenix Pose

Raise the arms sideways to shoulder level, palms down. The right knee is raised at the same time, while the left heel is lifted off the floor. Then lower the arms and legs back down. Repeat. Raise the arms up, but this time, the left knee is lifted and the right heel is off the ground. Repeat the entire cycle three times (right, left, right, left, right, left). Keep your movements slow and smooth. Imagine yourself as the phoenix rising from the ashes and taking flight through infinite space. See your life moving forward.

Tortoise

Identifying Fragrance: earthy, musky
Common Animal Forms: turtle

The tortoise has had an amazing history in the world of symbology. While the other three sacred beasts are often considered mythical creatures that have come to embody real aspects, the tortoise is a real animal that has achieved mythical proportions. It has been the hero of many legends and has been a guide into the Faerie Realm. Living in border areas, it is a creature with the ability to move solidly and firmly between worlds and dimensions. It is the teacher of how we can learn to do so as well.

The markings of the tortoise have great mythical symbology associated with them. The Chinese emperor Fu Hsi is said to have derived the hexagrams of the I Ching from the markings on the back of the turtle and some patterns of stars he saw in the sky. It is an animal that can help awaken us to psychic forecasts - particularly in the realm of time.

The tortoise is the symbol of immutability and steadfastness. When encountered during a spiritual quest, it is a reminder not to become distracted. It reminds us to stay steadily upon our path and we will succeed.

The tortoise was also known as the "horse dragon" and the "dark warrior". As a group, the turtle and tortoise family group is more ancient than any other vertebrate animal. While tortoises are technically more land bound, in mythology and folklore the words tortoises and turtles were often interchangeable. For our purposes here, we will use tortoise, but it also applies to the turtle.

The tortoise shell was a symbol of heaven and the underside a symbol of earth. Because of this, the tortoise is an animal whose presence would indicate a uniting of two - heaven and earth, spiritual and physical, the faerie and mundane.

The tortoise is also an animal with varying sexual implications. In Nigeria it was a symbol of the female sex organs and sexuality. To the Native Americans it has ties to the lunar cycle - again very feminine. And yet, the manner in which its head pops in and out of the shell was often considered very phallic.

The tortoise also shows up at the time in our life when we need to remember that we are not separate from Mother Nature and all of her aspects - including those that are relegated to the realm of fiction. Just as the tortoise and turtle cannot separate itself from its shell, neither can we truly separate us from the wonders of Nature. In fact, the tortoise or turtle frequently shows up when we begin to doubt that we will ever connect. It strengthens our desire and reminds us to be patient.

The Tortoise Pose

This may be performed sitting or standing. Bring your chin down to your chest. At the same time stretch the top of your head. The back of the neck will feel an upward pull and the shoulders will relax downward. Inhale as you perform this part. Slowly bring the back of the skull down as if to touch the back of the neck. Your chin is pulled upward and your throat is slightly stretched. Exhale as you perform this. Perform this slowly. See and feel yourself as the tortoise, extending the head from its shell and then drawing it back in.

Dance of the Sacred Beasts

The four sacred beasts - the dragon, the phoenix, the tortoise and the unicorn - have a unique relationship. All serve as guardians and protectors to the Earth's animals and to Nature in general. They are also the guardians to the hidden realms to which we have access while upon this planet. In the East, they are steeped in great mysticism, magic and power. They are companions to each other. Because of this, when you develop a relationship with one, you are establishing connections and relationships with the others as well. Such connections are subtle, but they are real.

As mentioned previously, most animals in Nature have had dances associated with them. It was a way of aligning with and invoking the energy and essence of the animal. This had many healing and magical applications. It also involved the creatures that most think of as mythical or fantastic. The movements and postures of creatures, real and fantastic, became a source of great power in the East. They were incorporated into the martial arts, spiritual dances and celebrations, sexual activities and a variety of mystical healing practices.

In chapter 9, I provided guidelines for the unicorn posture. It can be used with the postures of the other three sacred beasts with the powerful results. They will strengthen relationships, open doors to inner realms, stimulate great healing and strengthen your communication and relationship with all animals. Performing all four together becomes a dance of spiritual relationships. They will strengthen healing of the entire body. They will help eliminate blockages and free up energy. They help open all aspects of the natural world. They can assist you in any work with animals, especially in understanding their communications.They strengthen the union of your spirit with all aspects of Nature.

Perform the movements outside whenever possible. Remember to visualize yourself as the sacred creature as you perform its movements. Know and feel its energy and essence coming alive within you and your life.

Begin by standing straight. Relax, closing your eyes and breathing regularly. Open your eyes and perform the unicorn postures, moving from the horse stance to the unicorn pose as described in the chapter 9. See and feel yourself becoming the unicorn. Hold this pose, envisioning everything it means to you and for you. See the energy of the unicorn becoming more alive for you within your day to day life.

Pause. Rise from this pose, and move into the dragon posture depicted upon the previous pages. See and feel yourself becoming the dragon. See and feel its energy coming alive for you and within you. See and feel it touching your life. Perform it to the right and to the left.

Pause. Rise from this pose and move into that of the phoenix, depicted on the previous pages. See and feel yourself becoming the phoenix. See and feel its energies of rebirth awakening within you and your life. Imagine all that is manifesting for you as a result of this exercise. Hold and visualize all that it represents for you.

Pause again. And move from the posture of the phoenix to that of the tortoise. See and feel the strength and power of the tortoise coming alive within you and your life. See and feel its energy manifesting. See and feel yourself as the tortoise. Hold and visualize all that it represents for you.

Now move from this to the posture back to that of the unicorn again. See and feel the unicorn's energy alive within you and your life. See and feel all that it represents for you manifesting. Hold and visualize yourself as the living unicorn. From the unicorn posture, move back into the horse stance. This will ground the energy you have activated. It will also serve to anchor its manifestation into the physical world in which you operate daily

Then stand straight, and relax. Breathe deeply and evenly. Feel your feet solid and parallel upon the ground. You are connected to the earth more strongly than ever before. Take a moment and visualize everything about your life and all of your relationships strengthened. See and feel the energy of all the sacred creatures strong within you - all in great harmony with each other. Know that this harmony extends to all of your relationships with animals - making them stronger and more harmonious.

*The tortoise, unicorn,
phoenix and dragon
are all creatures with subtle
connections to the sexual energies and
thus were loved greatly by women:*

*The tortoise enjoys the Earth without
haste, and as a result, lasts
for a very long time.*

*Born of the Earth, the unicorn is much
loved by women, for though rarely
found, his horn is always hard.*

*The phoenix is born from the ashes of
Earth and rises constantly.*

*The dragon, though originally resting
in the bowels of the Earth,
can always fill the Heavens.*

*When we work
with animals and shapeshifting,
it will stir & awaken
our most primal, creative life forces.
And one expression of that creative force is
our sexuality.*

Alchemy and Shapeshifting

When people think of alchemy, they usually think of medieval scientists working on secret and exotic formulas in their archaic laboratories in an effort to either turn lead into gold or to create an elixir of life. While many of the early alchemists may have actually been doing so, the process had more to do with spiritual initiation. Alchemy is the study and application of the process of transmutation. In medieval times, it did involve chemical science (as it was at that time) and metallurgy, combined with astrology, religion, mysticism and experimentation. Most of the early alchemists focused upon the transmutation of common base metals, such as lead, into silver or gold. On another level though, it hinted of the transmutation of the soul - turning the lead of our physical life into spiritual gold.

Alchemy has within it many symbols of birth and initiation and it has been described in many ways. It is the joining of the crown and scepter, the marriage of the male and female, the uniting of the sun and moon. This uniting of opposites is frequently found within esoteric tales, lore and art. Tales such as "The Quest for the Holy Grail" is but one of the more familiar examples. This alchemical marriage of opposites is also found within the lore of the sacred beasts. In fact, the sacred marriage has been depicted in occult art as the uniting and marriage of the unicorn and the dragon.

This sacred marriage is necessary to give birth - whether of something in the physical or in the spiritual. The problem is that most alchemical images have multiple meaning, and unfortunately, many of the early alchemists created and used their own language and their own associations in describing this alchemical process.

When we work with shapeshifting, we will open ourselves to the alchemical mysteries of sexuality. Shapeshifting is a tremendously creative act and it invokes, activates and releases great energy into our life. It has a sexual aspect that can not be denied. When you work with shapeshifting, you will experience an increase in your sexual drive. Remember that one aspect of our creative energy is sexuality. That increase in the sexual drive though is always a wonderful physical confirmation that the energies we are tapping to shapeshift our life are working. And so it is good to know something about the hidden mysteries of sexuality.

Shapeshifting and Sexuality

In many ways, the West has much to learn in regards to sexuality. In the Western world, sexuality is riddled with guilt and separated from that which is spiritual. The Christian ethic has placed the sexual act in the arena for creating children not pleasure. Western religious traditions separate the flesh from the spirit. They encourage suppression and denial of sexual energies, but there is still an unconscious recognition of its inherent power. It continually seeps into the Western culture in spite of its frequent censorship.

There is tremendous hidden and mystical significance to the sexual act. The linking of the male and female is an act of creating wholeness. The linking of the male and the female always brings new birth. When performed within oneself, it gives birth to the Holy Child within. This sacred marriage, when performed with another, can become an earthly expression of the uniting of gods and goddesses, the sun and moon, heaven and earth, the mortal realm with the Faerie Realm, the physical with the spiritual.

To understand the alchemical significance, we must remember that the sexual energies are physical manifestations of more dynamic spiritual forces at play. These forces are the creative impulses and they are also the key to the true alchemical process. An ancient pagan ritual involves placing a knife into a cup, symbolizing the union of the Father with the Mother. This pagan ritual is symbolic of the act of creation - of giving birth to a new expression of energy. In shapeshifting, we are also giving birth to a new expression of energy and so it does release sexual energies for creativity and healing in our life.

In daily life, the male and female often are out of balance. Ritual and ceremonial sex transmute ordinary space and time, imbuing the sexual act with great sacredness and power. It creates harmony. It becomes an intersection in which male and female, day and night, positive and negative, physical and spiritual are no longer separate. It creates a time and space where all possibilities exist. This transmuting of the ordinary to create extraordinary possibilities is the alchemical process. This transmutation or shapeshifting of energy is greatly determined by the focus of one's thought at the time of the sacred marriage - the time of creation.

With shapeshifting, there occurs a heightened, blending of sexuality and spirit within the individual. This can manifest and reveal itself in a wide variety of ways. The sexual drive becomes stronger, more intense. Sexual responses to others grow stronger. Sexual responses of others toward us intensify. Healing is stimulated. Artistic and creative inspirations are heightened. All are tied to the stimulation of the sexual energy, the creative life force, by the art of shapeshifting.

This spiritual power of sexuality is ingrained in the East. In many Eastern traditions the sexual energy is honored for what it is - an expression and manifestation of the life force. It is directly linked to what is termed the kundalini, the serpent energy. It is the creative life force, the force that we use and draw upon for everything in the physical and the spiritual. In more modern scientific realms, it can be aligned with the energy inherent within the DNA molecule. It is the energy of life -the spiral of creative life force.

Ancient traditions recognized the inherent transforming power (physically and spiritually) of sexuality. Tantrism and Taoism are two of the more commonly known Eastern traditions that incorporate the sexual energy in ways that can easily heal and transform. These traditions recognize that there is more involved to the sex act than mere procreation and genital orgasm. Sexual energy is a powerful and sacred force that can be used to transmute everyday conditions, attitudes, health imbalances and more. And it will be awakened through shapeshifting.

When we work with shapeshifting, we feel our sexual power. What we feel is what in the East is associated with the activation of the kundalini - the great power inherent within the human organism. We feel an inner thrill, titillation. Our breath is taken away. There is a sense of electricity, a feeling of lightness and liberation. We experience flashes, alternating flushes of heat and cold. Sensuality and even erotic visualization are stimulated. These are some of the tangible signals of our creative life force being triggered through shapeshifting.

It then becomes our task to circulate it. We must direct it and express it appropriately. We must tame it. Only then does it stay alive and become a force that we can use to transmute and shapeshift the conditions of our lives. And that is why dance and movement is so important to shapeshifting.

In this position there occurs a balancing and controlling of the masculine sexual energy and force. Balancing upon one leg for overall balance and poise is combined with the mystic Tantric gesture, which symbolizes the lingam - the male organ and masculine force.

Shapeshifting
Exercise
(experiential)

Sex and the Sacred Beasts

Skills & Benefits:

- **harmony and healing**
- **passion**
- **transcendence and new birth**
- **sacred union of heaven & earth, human and Nature**
- **strengthening of relationships**

Imitating the lovemaking of animals has had many mystical and magical aspects to it. In the Orient, it was done to harmonize the elements between heaven and earth and to open to the power of animals. Often eroticism was used to represent and activate various divine forces found in Nature and give expressions of those forces. Most often, it was considered one of the most powerful ways of opening to the healing power of animals and Nature.

Sexual arousal is considered the raw emotion of love, used to stimulate passions and to awaken the life force more fully. That awakened life force then can be directed and focused for a variety of tasks. These tasks can be healing of the individuals involved or for harmonizing and healing the environment. In the latter case, the participants represent divine forces so that their union - their sacred marriage - releases dynamic energies into the living environment. That energy can be focused and used for inspiration and enlightenment. It all depends upon the specific sacred ceremony.

In Taoist and Tantric traditions, various sexual positions will awaken and direct the creative energy along specific avenues. Often these positions are based upon the way specific animals perform the sexual act. The four sacred beasts - dragon, the phoenix, the tortoise and the unicorn - have their own sexual positions as well. These can be performed solely or alternating, from one to the next with great effects.

This is most effective when performed in a ritual and sacred manner. Sacred does not mean somber and serious. Lovemaking is pleasurable and should be enjoyed. The sacredness occurs naturally when each participant is honored and respected, and both participants recognize that the sexual act will entwine their energies powerfully. It becomes sacred when both recognize that the intimacy will awaken physical and spiritual energies.

It is not the function of this book to teach the multitude of aspects associated with ritual and ceremonial lovemaking. For now, it is enough to know that the energy generated can be and should be directed toward a goal that both participants have agreed upon. This shapeshifts the sexual act to a level beyond the mundane, opening and linking the spiritual with the physical, the infinite with the finite.

There are, in fact, many kinds and forms of sex rites and ceremonies. For our purposes, we will focus upon the postures and positions of the four sacred creatures to balance, harmonize and heal - to shift and give birth to our relationship on new levels.

Sexual Positions of the Sacred Beasts

The Turning Dragon
Benefits: **Overall healing position for both, particularly so for the man if the semen is retained**

In this position the woman lies back, and the man lies between her legs, his knees on the bed. The woman guides the not quite erect penis into her vagina. While she does this, the male caresses and strokes her upper body. The male then intersperses two deep strokes between eight shallow strokes. The rhythm is slow and smooth. The man must refrain from orgasm, but the woman may experience satisfaction.

Variation: The typical "missionary" position

The Phoenix
Benefits: **Believed to cure one hundred ailments; one of the nine Taoist healing positions**.

In this position the woman lies on her back. She raises her legs, placing her feet upon his chest. The male kneels between her legs and penetrates her as deeply as possible. He alternates three deep strokes with eight shallow. The movements should be as vigorous as possible, with the male pressing firmly against her buttocks. The mail should refrain from orgasm and bring the woman to climax.

Variations:
(a) Instead of kneeling, the man sits, pressing his buttocks against hers and with his legs extended along the sides of her body. Movement is less rapid.

(b) Male kneels between her legs. Instead of her feet resting upon his chest, he holds her feet and legs straight up.

The Tortoise

Benefits: **Builds longevity in both; stamina; strengthens the nervous system**

The woman lies on her back and raises her knees, with the help of the man, till pressed against her chest. The man is on his knees and penetrates from the front. The male alternates deep and shallow strokes, refraining from orgasm. The male should cease moving entirely when the woman climaxes.

Variations: The man sits with the woman on his lap, her legs extended over his, on either side. Mouth, arms, and body parts touch the corresponding parts of the partner.

The Unicorn

Benefits: **Mutual pleasure and orgasm; pregnancy; balancing of the elements**

The woman lies on her back and lifts her right leg, placing it on the left shoulder of the male. He kneels as close to her as possible, and guides himself into her. The rhythm should be whatever is most enjoyable to each other. The female should reach orgasm first; then the male.

Variations:
(a) Both legs of the female are placed over the shoulders of the male.

(b) The woman faces away from the male on elbows and knees, or with the legs straight. The male enters her from behind.

(c) The woman lies down with face, breasts and stomach against the bed. From behind, the man works under, extending himself flat on top of her. The woman should raise the lower part of her body to assist his movements.

The Sacred Rite

1. Make appropriate preparations.
Take the phone off the hook. Make sure you will be undisturbed.

2. Prepare the space where the ritual will be performed.
For most people, it may be the bedroom, but it can be any space where both will feel safe and undisturbed. It should be clean and fresh, and appropriate incense and candles can help enhance the mood. Have soft music available. No heavy drums or percussion. The music should be soft, low volume. It is background only.

3. Food and drink can be a wonderful additive.
The food should be light, nothing heavy. The participants may want to feed each other as foreplay. Some fruit, crackers, cheeses, etc. will help stimulate without weighing heavily upon the body and mind. After the ceremony, it can be used to help ground the energy of the participants.

4. Prepare the body.
Bathe and cleanse. The participants may wish to bathe together. Something as simple as this builds harmony. It is also arousing and can be wonderful foreplay. Take turns drying each other. A soft massage with a fragrant oil for each other can be arousing and heighten the energy.

5. Stand facing each other, and perform the dances to the sacred creatures.
Perform them slowly, mirroring each other. This, in itself, builds harmony and aligns your individual energies.

6. Begin to slowly caress each other, and gently move into and through all of the positions.
Use the same order that you use for the dance. Make the unicorn the last sexual position. Take your time with all of these positions. You may wish to cycle through them several times before the final climax.

7. Don't be afraid to adapt or change.
Do what is comfortable for both. Relax and allow yourself to truly enjoy the feelings. Try to maintain as much focus as possible throughout.

*Shapeshifting
Exercise
(experiential)*

The Unicorn and the Wood Nymph

Skills & Benefits:

- **strengthen shapeshifting abilities**
- **clear perspectives on relationships**
- **triggers transformation through love**
- **stimulates healing of the past**
- **breaks down outworn patterns**

There is an old tale in which a mortal man falls in love with a wood nymph by the name of Nephele. In time he wins her heart as well. The goddess Diane hears of this romance, and since it is forbidden for a mortal to love a wood nymph, she decides to punish the man. She splashes water in his face, and he begins to change. He turns into a unicorn, and he begins to hear and understand the voices of animals. He is filled with more life of the forest than ever before, but he doesn't realize that he has become a unicorn. He soon spies Nephele, and he runs toward her. She does not recognize her lover in his new form, and she draws an arrow from her quiver and shoots him.

This exercise is based somewhat upon this tale. I have changed aspects of the tale to make it more beneficial. It is a good idea to perform this exercise at least two days in a row. On one day visualize yourself in the role of the individual who falls in love with the beautiful woodland being, and on the following day as the woodland being.

I have tried to make the exercise as non-sexist as possible. The wood nymph in the original story is now a woodland being, so that you can visualize it as male or female - however you desire. When you switch the role, and you see yourself as the woodland being, the mortal (the person of the outer world) can be male or female as you desire.

Performing this exercise in each of the roles will elicit different effects. As the mortal who falls in love with the woodland being, you will find in the weeks that follow how other people perceive you and the changes you are going through. You will find that opportunities to break from outworn patterns will surface within your life. The choice is always yours, but the opportunities will surface. If you are not ready for them, you may wish to avoid this exercise.

When you perform this exercise as the woodland creature, you will begin to see how your life is affecting others around you. Choices will also arise as to whether it is time to commit to that which is new or to stay with old habits and patterns.

This exercise will stimulate the sexual energies in you. You will probably find that others will become more strongly attracted to you, and you will find yourself responding with stronger sexual energies to others as well. In the week or two that follows, you will find yourself encountering others who are of more like mind to you. New horizons will open.

This exercise also stimulates heightened perception and empathy. You will feel what others are feeling. You will be more aware of how others see and feel you. This exercise can also stimulate greater passion for and empathic communication with all of nature, but particularly animals. Remember that nature spirits and woodland beings - not to mention the unicorn - can help open our senses more fully to the wonders of nature.

As in the other exercises, make your preparations. If possible, at some point, perform this exercise in the woods. Perform the dances for the sacred creatures. As you complete the movements for the unicorn, make yourself comfortable, breathe deeply and relax. Allow our opening scenario to unfold. Allow yourself to see and feel the wonders of love about to open for you:

The Unicorn and the Wood Nymph

A scene begins to unfold for you. You find yourself standing within that beautiful meadow that has now become so familiar to you. The sunlight sparkles off the water, and the sound of the waterfall is soothing.

Today you decide to enjoy the green woods at the edge of the meadow. There is a sense of quiet anticipation, as if the woods themselves are waiting for you. You cross the edge of the meadow and step into the woods, and a soft quiet settles around you.

You spot what looks to be a deer path through the thick underbrush, and you follow it. As you walk along, you feel yourself coming more alive. Your can smell the wood and greenery about you. The ground is cushioning, and then you hear something in the distance. You pause, tilting your head, listening more closely.

At first there is nothing, but then...yes...a soft voice, faint and indistinct, but there is no doubt it is a voice. You step further into the woods, pausing every few feet to listen. You realize someone is singing, and it draws you further in into the woods. The song rises and falls in a haunting, enticing manner.

Soon you are standing behind a large tree at the edge of the clearing. In the center of this clearing a small bubbling spring rises out of the heart of the earth itself. In the trees and at the edges of this clearing are a myriad of forest animals, drawn to this spot by the haunting song, just as you were.

In the center of the clearing you see a figure dancing around that spring, singing that haunting song. This figure has wreathes of wild flowers and greenery upon the wrists and in the hair. The sunlight shimmers off this figure, casting a soft glow.

The figure turns to some of the animals, and walks toward them. You are surprised when they do not scatter. Then each is softly and lovingly touched by this figure. As the figure turns from the animals to face in your direction, your heart jumps and you catch your breath. Never have you seen anyone so beautiful! And in that moment you realize that this is a being of the woods.

There is such a youthful vitality to this being, and yet the eyes tell you that this being is much older than the appearance would indicate. It is a primitive wildness that you can feel, although it is masked. And you feel twinges of sexual arousal. A part of you would love nothing better than to spend the rest of your life just watching this being dance and listening to that song.

Then you realize that this being has seen you. The eyes only hold yours for a moment, and goose bumps rise all over your body. Then the figure turns and darts into the shadows of the woods on the other side of the clearing, disappearing from your sight. Your heart sinks, and you step from behind the tree into the clearing.

Sadness comes over you. In just those brief minutes, that being had filled your heart. It was like meeting one of your favorite dreams. You look down at the small pool of water. There in the grass beside it is a small flute. You pick it up, and you realize that it must be the flute of that magnificent being.

You bring it up to your lips and tentatively blow on it, making a soft sound. A breeze brushes over you and there is a soft tinkling of invisible bells within it. You smile. Sitting softly in the grass, you begin to play the flute. You are surprised that you are able to do so, and you immediately decide that the flute must be enchanted.

With each note you feel yourself growing more tired, and in just a few minutes you are drifting off into a soft sleep. The sleep is filled with images of people and situations within your life. You see the pattern of your life, and you feel the boredom pressing in upon you. You see the activities and duties you perform daily, not out of love or responsibility, but out of habit. You see the dreams you have had and did not act upon.

Then you begin to see those things you loved as a child and that gave you great joy. You see how your own joy affected those around you, lightening and making their days a little better. You see the people who have encouraged you to follow your heart and your dreams, who have tried to show you that anything is possible.

Then you see yourself getting older and forgetting your dreams. You see yourself acting more grown up, and you see the dreams trying to surface so that you can capture them once more. Then you see others in your life looking at you funny - as if you've gone a little crazy. You hear voices telling you to grow up, that this is no way for an adult to behave. They tell you to look at what you will be giving up. They tell you this is no time to be chasing rainbows. But there is something strange in their voices. You realize that it is fear and sadness you are hearing beneath their words, and you know that there can be no other choice for you.

It is only then that you wake up, lying in the grass next to that small pool of water in the clearing. You raise your head, and the air smells sweeter and fresher than it has ever been. You seem to be able to distinguish a myriad of smells. The individual flowers, animals nearby, traces of everything within the woods are in the air about you and you recognize them all! You are amazed.

The sounds of the woods are sharper. You hear a mouse moving in the grass 100 yards away. You can even hear the sound of your waterfall beyond the woods. And the colors about you are so much brighter. It's as if the dream has awakened your senses for the first time. Never have you felt so alive, so sensual, so vibrant.

You lower your head to drink from the pool, and your eyes widen. Your heart jumps. You close your eyes, shaking your head. Surely this can't be! It must be the light. You open your eyes and stare at your reflection in the pool. What looks back at you is the face of a magnificent unicorn.

You twist your head to look at your body, and you see the white fur and the four legs. You look to your reflection and the horn in the middle of your head shimmers, casting a soft glow of light about you.

You leap to your feet, and find yourself halfway across the clearing in that single leap. It is almost as if you were flying. You are so light, so airy. Never have you felt so free. You begin to do leaps back and forth across the meadow, and you begin to laugh. The sound of that laughter becomes the sound of soft bells within the breeze.

You walk over to the stream, and leaning over it you gaze at your reflection. This time you see your own face inside that of the unicorn. Then the sound of the flute is heard, and as you turn to look in its direction, you see that magnificent being, that step from the woods into the clearing.

Your heart jumps, and you are filled with great love. As you gaze upon this being, you can see and feel everything this being sees and feels. You realize that your love is returned, and ever so softly, this beautiful woodland being caresses your face with a touch that sends shiver through your body. You lower your head to give this

297

being access to your horn. With a touch as gentle as a breeze and as loving as a mother with her newborn child, the alicorn is stroked from its tip to its base. You shiver and then rear up, filled with joy, your blood hot and pulsing with new life.

Then this beautiful being steps back from you and bringing the flute up, plays a haunting series of tones. It is repeated three times, and then the flute is laid upon the ground. The air around this being begins to shimmer, and you watch as the figure begins to shift and change. Your eyes widen with joy and surprise as this magnificent being becomes an even more magnificent unicorn before your eyes.

Slowly this unicorn steps toward you and caresses your horn with its own. Again you rear. You are filled with a sense of promise. All truly is possible! The other unicorn seems to smile and you both swing around and gallop silently into the shadows of the deep forest to share the wonders of the world together. You leave whispers of bells and the fragrance of apple blossom behind as a promise of hope to others who may follow.

At the end, just sit and be still for a few moments, Stretch a little, allowing your hands and feet to move. Breathe deeply. As you sit there, you may feel a soft brush of air. You may see shadows shift around you. There may be colored, flickering lights, you may see forms and shapes appear and fade. In the beginning it will probably be subtle things that you may wish to attribute to your imagination. Remember that animals see and hear much better than we do. This is heightened ene more through connecting with the fantastic creatures. They can detect the subtlest things.

Do not respond to what you experience; simply note them and the sensations. Do this for only a few moments. They are after effects of the exercise. As the veils close entirely, they will fade.

Then slowly stand and repeat the unicorn movements, giving thanks for this sharing. Follow this with the grounding postures. Stretch and begin to move. And know that in the next few days your senses will be a bit more acute.

Conclusion

The Magic of Shapeshifting

Magic is a word that means "wisdom". It is the wisdom and ability to work with energy to make things happen. Understanding how to make energies work for you takes a lot of time and practice, but when we combine believing with effort and wisdom, magic does happen! The shapeshifting occurs. But believing must be practiced everyday so that it becomes second nature. This is why so many of the exercises in this book are experiential. They strengthen your beliefs.

The magic of shapeshifting is natural. How aspects of it happen may still be somewhat occult. I know that's a trigger word to some people, but it simply means "hidden". It is veiled. The truth is that we just do not yet completely understand how most magic works – including shapeshifting. Think of it like electricity. Most people still do not know how it works, but we do know that it is real. We also know there are tools that help us to control and direct electricity to make our lives much more comfortable.

Magic is the wisdom of directing energy to produce specific effects. It is a skill that involves working with natural forces or energies. True magic is a craft that involves doing something to awaken, strengthen, control and direct the energies of life. Of all the tools that we can use to help ourselves with this, none is more important than our own belief. **No magic - including that of shapeshifting - ever happens without belief on some level.** We must believe in who we truly are and what we truly can do. The art of shapeshifting helps teach us how to believe once more and how to use that belief to weave magic into our life more fully.

Veils of Magic

All of the methods in this book deal with learning to open the doors that are closed. It does not matter who closed them; what is important is that we allowed them to be closed. We each have the ability to open the doors that will shed light into the dark corners of our life and on our greatest potentials.

Much has been written about meditation and its various practices. There are, in fact, as many methods of meditation as there are people. As to which method or combination of methods is best, no one can answer that but the individual. What is important is that the method chosen be an active one.

It is not enough to simply quiet the mind and allow pleasant images to arise. Over time, this can lead to self-deception. We need to act upon what we are stimulating. We operate predominantly within the physical dimension, and thus all energies activated on other levels need to be grounded into the physical. Shapeshifting is an active form of development with applications to our daily life. It develops our innate potentials. It helps us to solve problems, achieve goals, open ourselves to higher capabilities and re-instill color and a joy of life.

It is the destiny of humans to conquer matter. This is the quest for the spirit, a search for our innermost part, the point of our greatest reality. It is not a path up to some divine light from which there is no return. Neither is it a path in which our problems and trials are dissolved in a blinding light of spirituality. It is our destiny to bring out the spirit into matter. That is when "the kingdom of heaven" manifests. Part of our life duty is to spiritualize matter, not to escape from it. The spiritual path is the search for a way to bring the spiritual aspects of life into our daily existence.

All of the ancient teachings and scriptures use similar terms to describe this magickal process. Gateways, doors, the outer court, the inner court, temple, the Holy of Holies, the quest, the pilgrimage and many other such words and terms are part of the ancient mystery language that hinted at and veiled the teachings that could assist the individual in shapeshifting his/her life and manifesting a higher destiny, a more magickal existence.

Every civilization and religion has had its magickal teachings - its spiritual *Mysteries*. The phraseology may have changed and differed, but only to conform to the needs of the time and place. What is extraordinary, however, is that there are more similarities than differences in the methods used by the ancient traditions to change the consciousness and help individuals on their spiritual quests. And ultimately, the form of the quest does not really matter, because the great secret of the spiritual quest is that **all who go forth, in whatever manner, will succeed!** Unfortunately not everyone has the wisdom or patience to see this.

Shapeshifting helps us step out onto our own path, away from the old. It teaches us to trust our inner nature and to act upon it. The most difficult aspect is that initial stepping. It has been compared to walking upon a razor blade. The first step is precarious, but with each step thereafter, the edge widens, becoming a living bridge to new realms that are much more magickal.

The Magical Life

There is no great secret to living a magical life. It is not done through spells or charms or incantations. It is not accomplished by hiding from life or our responsibilities. It is accomplished by involving ourselves in life as creatively as possible.

When we were small children the world was full of possibilities. Each day offered new adventures and new wonders. Everything and everyone was special. Anything we could imagine was real – whether a ghost, a faerie or time travel. We could be anything we wanted. There were no limits or boundaries.

Fear and disbelief closes the door to a magical life. It silences the streams and it stops the wind. The world is no longer enchanted and we can no longer see and feel the wonders around us.

To live a magical life requires practice and watchfulness. We must learn to see ourselves as a walking, breathing, living force. We must feel every touch as a passing of power – to heal or hurt. We must hear every word as a stream of energy – to bless or curse. We must learn to see through the eyes of others – human, plant and animal. Each breath should be a prayer and each step an adventure.

Creativity is natural for us and magic is an expression of our creativity. When we are not using our creativity, when we are not using our magic, we are not being who we should be. We live in a society that has a small view of creativity. It is something that is cute. It can be a hobby, but it is not practical. It is not a way of life. Because of this the focus in schools and in life is often one of seriousness and practicality. It must come first. It's the only way to be responsible. If this is true, why are so many people unhappy in what they are doing?

Why not be creative first? Why not develop our magic first? Then when we develop skills for survival in the outer world, we will bring a greater power to those skills. Yes, we do need both parts. We need to be creative and magical. We also need to be practical. We can be both, but it takes a little more time and effort. The rewards though are well worth it. We can learn to be creative – to be magical - in whatever we do.

There is magic in all things. Whether you are trying to manifest a job or clean up your room. When I am feeling disorganized, when I have a little creative block, when I can't quite get my thoughts together or even when I am having trouble making a decision, I will clean something up that I have been ignoring. I'll take a closet and clean it out. I'll straighten out my office or rearrange it. I'll clean out the attic or reorganize my files.

Within a week (usually sooner) the creative ideas start to flow strongly. I'll know what decision needs to be made. I'll realize how best to accomplish a task. The cleaning and straightening is a magical act. What we do on one level affects us on other levels. As I clean one area of my life up, other areas straighten up as well.

This will work for you also. While you are cleaning up your room or straightening out your clothes, focus on a particular problem or area of your life that you would like to have straightened out. Within a few days time you will see a difference. You begin to shapeshift your life.

Everything we do is magical. The Zen Buddhists have a wonderful 3-line poem:

> *"I chop wood.*
> *I carry water.*
> *This is my magic."*

They recognize that we have already performed the greatest feat of magic – we are spiritual beings that have taken on a physical body. Because of this, everything we do in the physical is a magical act – whether it's chopping wood or solving a math problem. And if we can perform magic as magnificent as taking on a physical body, we should then be able to manifest a little better health, joy, prosperity and love in our life as well.

The best way of shapeshifting our life and keeping our magic strong is to be as creative as possible. Involve yourself in creative activities. But they must be fun. You must enjoy participating in them; otherwise their magic is lost. The following are some of the best activities for awakening the shapeshifting magic and keeping it strong within our life:

- **Take an art class.**
(It doesn't matter whether you are good at it or not, or if anyone ever sees it. Just have fun doing it. It can be used for healing and psychic development.)

- **Learn to play a music instrument**.
(Sound, music and voice are some of the most powerful forms of magic. It can be a wonderful tool for weaving glamour.)

- **Study some form of healing.**
(It develops your psychic ability and it helps keep you balanced as you open more and more to your magical self.)

- **Learn a foreign language**.
(This can be a wonderful magical tool. As you learn the language, see it as learning the ability to more fully understand the language of animals, plants or even spirit.)

- **Spend time in Nature.**
(Nature is not only healing but also inspirational. It can open us to the Faerie Realm and other wonderful spirits in a balanced way.)

- **Read myths, folktales and fairy tales.**
(These stories remind us of possibilities. Remember that the magic spoken of in all of them is true...at least in part.)

Magic happens in the time, manner and means that is best for us, if we allow it to. This doesn't mean we do nothing but wait. Our magical beliefs must be acted upon. We do what we can and then we allow the energy to unfold. Sometimes the effort must be repeated, but each time we act upon our beliefs, successful or not, the power grows. Then when the time and place is right – most beneficial for us - the energy crystallizes. The magic happens.

We can become the shapeshifters of our lives, shifting the shape of them into alignment with our greatest dreams and visions. We can recreate and re-manifest what has been relegated to fiction and myth. Our lives can become like that of all the sages throughout history. We can walk in all environs - visible and invisible. We can bridge the physical to the spiritual and back again. We can weave a fabric of life that becomes a carpet of continually shifting fibers of light and radiance, a carpet upon which we can walk through all doorways, all times and all dreams. And all that we need to do is act upon our beliefs and follow our dreams.

Design Your Own Shapeshifting

Design Your Own Shapeshifting

Bibliography

Shapeshifting, Animals & Myths:

Andrews, Ted. *Animal-Speak.* St. Paul: Llewellyn Publications, 1993.
_____. *Animal-Wise.* Jackson, TN: Dragonhawk Publishing,1999.
_____. *Discover Your Spirit Animal (audiocassette).* Dayton, OH: Life Magic Enterprises, Inc., 1996.
_____ . *Dream Alchemy.* St. Paul: Llwellyn Publications, 1991.
_____ . *Enchantment of the Faerie Realm.* St. Paul: Llewellyn Publications, 1993
_____ . *Faerie Charms.* Jackson, TN: Dragonhawk Publishing, 2005.
_____ . *Magical Dance.* St. Paul: Llewellyn Publications, 1992.
_____ . *The Animal-Speak Workbook.* Jackson, TN: Dragonhawk Publishing, 2002.
_____ . *The Animal-Wise Tarot.* Jackson, TN: Dragonhawk Publishing, 1999.
_____ . *Treasures of the Unicron.* Jackson, TN: Dragonhawk Publishing, 1996

Arnott, Kathleen. *African Myths and Legends.* New York: Oxford University Press, 1989.

Benyus, Janine. *Beastly Behaviors.*New York: Addison-Wesley, 1992.

Caduto, Michael and Bruchac, Joseph. *Keepers of the Animals.* Golden, CO: Fulcrum Publishing, 1991.
_____. *Keepers of the Earth.* Golden, CO: Fulcrum Publishing, 1988.

Campbell, Joseph. *The Way of the Animals,* Vol. I & II. New York: Harper & Row, 1988.
_____. *Mythologies of the Primitive Hunters and Gatherers.* New York: Harper & Row, 1988.
_____. *The Masks of God 4: Creative Mythology.* New York: Viking Press, 1968.

Carrier, Jim and Bekoff, Marc. *Nature's Life Lessons.* Golden: Fulcrum Publishing,1996.

Cornell, Joseph. *Sharing Nature with Children.* Nevada City: Dawn Publications, 1979.

Christa, Anthony. *Chinese Mythology.* New York: Peter Bedrick Books, 1983.

Cirlot, J.E. *Dictionary of Symbols.* New York: Philosophical Library, 1962.

Doore, Gary. *The Shaman's Path.* Boston: Shambhala Press, 1988.

Edroes, Richard and Ortiz, Alfonso. *American Indian Myths and Legends.* New York: Pantheon Books, 1984.

Harlow, Rosie and Morgan, Gareth. *175 Amazing Nature Experiements.* New York: Random House, 1991.

Malin, Edward. *A World of Faces.* Portland: Timber Press,1978.

Palmer, John. *Exploring the Secrets of Nature.* New York: Reader's Digest, 1994.

Rezendes, Paul. *Tracking and the Art of Seeing.* Charlotte, VT: Camden House Pub., 1992.

Smith. Penelope. *Animal Talk.*Hillsboro, OR: Beyond Words Publishing, 1999.

Tanner, Ogden. *Urban Wilds.* Alexandria: Time-Life Books, 1975.

Sacred Dance and Mask Making:

_____. *Costumes of the Ancient World (Series).* New York: Chelsea House Publications, 1987.

Adams, Doug and Apostolos-Cappodona, Diane. *Dance as Religious Study.* New York: Crossroads Press, 1990.

Alkema, Chester Jay. *Monster Masks.* New York: Sterling Publications, 1973.

Ashcroft-Nowicki, Dolores. *First Steps in Ritual* Northamptonshire: Aquarian Press, 1982.
_____.*Ritual Magic Workbook.* Northamptonshire: Aquarian Press, 1986.

Beck, Lilla and Wilson, Annie. *What Colour Are You?* Great Britain: Turnstone Press, 1981.

Bellamak, Lu. *Dancing Prayers.* Ariwna: Cybury Graphics, 1982.

Brain, Roben. *The Decorated Body.* New York: Harper and Row, 1979.

Buckland, Raymond. *The Complete Book of Witchcraft.* St. Paul: Llewellyn Publications, 1988.

Cohen, Roben. *The Dance Workshop.* New York: Simon and Schuster, 1986.

Copeland, Roger and Cohen, Marsha. *What Is Dance?* New York: Oxford University Press, 1983.

Davies, Sir John. "Penelope Full of Dance," *Orchestra,* 1596.

Douglas, Nik and Slinger, Penny. *Sexual Secrets.* New York: Destiny Books, 1979.

Fonteyn, Margot. *The Magic of Dance.* New York: Alfred A. Knopf, 1979.

Grater, Michael. *Complete Book of Mask Making.* New York: Dover Publications, 1967.

Haberland, Wolfgang. *The Art of North America.* New York: Crown Publishers, 1964.

Highwater, Jamake. *Dance-Ritual of Experience.* New York: Alfred Van Der Marck Editions, 1978.

Hittleman, Richard. *Guide for the Seeker.* New York: Bantam Books, 1978.
_____. *Introduction to Yoga.* New York: Bantam Books, 1975.

Humphrey, Doris. *The Art of Making Dances.* New York: Grove Press Inc., 1980.

Joyce, Mary. *Dance Techniques for Children.* California: Mayfield Publication Company, 1984.

Kalinin, Beverly. *Power to the Dancers!* Ponland: Metamorphous Press, 1988.

Kraus, Richard. *History of Dance.* Englewood Cliffs: Prentice-Hall, Inc., 1969.

Laws, Kenneth. *The Physics of Dance*. New York: Schirmer Books, 1984.

Lawson, Joan. *Teaching Young Dancers*. New York: Theatre Arts Books, 1975.

Mattlage, Louise. *Dances of Faith*. Pennsylvania: County Press.

Novack, Cynthia J. *Sharing the Dance*. Madison: University of Wisconsin Press, 1990.

Peters, Joan and Sutcliffe, Anna. Boston: *Creative Masks for Stage and School Plays Inc.*, 1975.

Seitering, Carolyn. *The Liturgy As Dance*. New York: Crossroads Publishing, 1984.

Sherbon, Elizabeth. *On the Count of One*. Chicago: Chicago Review Press, 1990.

Snook, Barbara. *Making Masks for School Plays*. Boston: Plays Inc., 1972.

Sorell, Walter. *Dance Has Many Faces*. New York: Columbia University Press, 1966.

Tegner, Bruce. *Kung Fu and Tai Chi*. California: Thor Publishing, 1973.

Thevoz, Michel. *The Painted Body*. New York: Rizwli Publishing, 1984.

Wilson, Chaz. *Martial Dance*. Nonhamptonshire: Aquarian Press, 1988.

Zarina, Xenia. *Classic Dances of the Orient*. New York: Crown Publishing, 1967.

Index

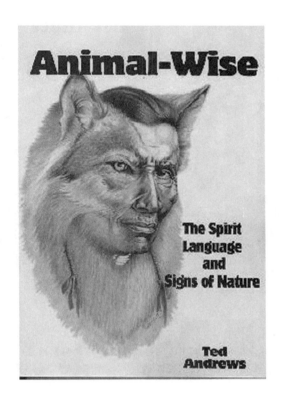

Also by Ted Andrews

The Animal-Speak Workbook

COVR
2002
Visionary Award Winner!

Best Non-Fiction Book

Best General Interest Book

$1795
ISBN 1-888767-48-0

Explore The Wonders of the Animal World!

From the author of the best selling and award winning books, *Animal-Speak* and *Animal-Wise* comes a companion manual to connect you more fully to your animal guides and guardians and to help you understand animal messages.

- Use pets to bridge to wild totems.
- Explore hawk and owl medicine.
- Develop animal communication and telepathy.
- Make and use medicine shields and sacred journey staffs.

Available from Dragonhawk Publishing and all major distributors.

Also by Ted Andrews

The Animal-Wise Tarot

Also by Ted Andrews

Nature-Speak
~ Signs, Omens & Messages in Nature ~

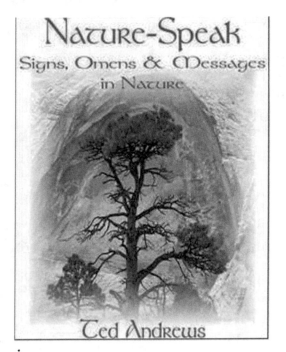

2005 COVR Visionary Award Winner!
Best Spirituality Book
Best Non-Fiction Book

**Nature-Speak is to the plant kingdom what
Animal-Speak and Animal-Wise
are to the animal kingdom!**

- Learn to read signs and omens in Nature.
- Interpret the meaning of landscapes.
- Explore the meaning and lessons of the plant kingdom through extensive dictionaries of landscapes, trees, flowers, herbs and more.

ISBN 1-888767-37-5, softbound, 7x10, 448 pages, $22.95

About the Author

Ted Andrews is an internationally recognized author, storyteller, teacher and mystic. A leader in the human potential, metaphysical and psychic field, he has written more than 30 books, which have been translated into twenty-six foreign languages. He is a popular teacher throughout North America, Europe and parts of Asia.

Ted has been involved in the serious study of the esoteric and the occult for more than 35 years. He has been a certified spiritualist medium for 20 years. He brings to the field an extensive formal and informal education.

A former school teacher and counselor, his innovative reading programs and his creation of fun, readable and skill-oriented classroom materials received both state and local recognition. Ted is schooled in music and he has been a student of sacred dance, ballet and kung fu.

Ted holds state and federal permits to work with birds of prey and he conducts animal education and storytelling programs with his hawks and owls and other animals in classrooms throughout the year. In his spare time, he hangs out with his menagerie of animals and enjoys horseback riding and ballroom dance.

Visit Dragonhawk Publishing online at:
www.dragonhawkpublishing.com

Dragonhawk Publishing   PO Box 10637   Jackson, TN 38308